150 GREAT
SCIENCE
EXPERIMENTS

150 GREAT SCIENCE EXPERIMENTS

Ingenious, easy-to-do projects explore and explain the wonders of science and technology

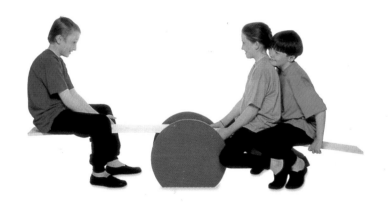

General Editor: Rasha Elsaeed

Consultant: Chris Oxlade

HERMES HOUSE

CONTENTS

Science at Home   6

Our Restless Earth

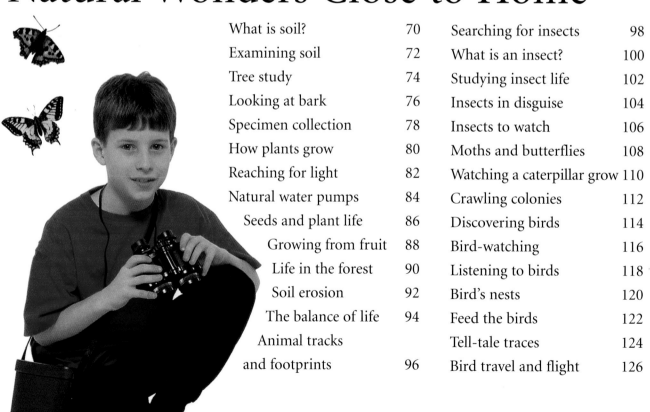

Natural Wonders Close to Home

Physical and Material Marvels

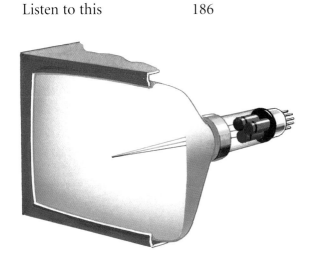

Travel and Transport

Science at  Home

Science is the search for truth and knowledge. It is the process of finding information about the world around us. It tries to answer questions about how it works. Scientists are people who gather this knowledge of the world. They develop techniques for investigating how things work. They work in controlled environments, such as laboratories, so that they can study results. We call this experimentation.

Why experiment?

Experiments help you discover and understand how things work and why things happen. When you try ideas out, concepts that seem hard to grasp become easier to understand. This is why scientists experiment – to test their ideas. By experimenting, people invent and perfect machines and processes that make our lives easier. Today, the quality of our lives depends on science for everyday comfort, health and entertainment, transport and communication.

Innovation and change

This book of experiments demonstrates many of the breakthroughs and discoveries that have had an impact on our lives. The technique of asking questions and trying to answer them through observation and experiment is important to science. The continuous process of discovery and experiment mean that scientists come up with different answers. This is why science is always changing. Innovations and inventions change the way we look at the world, so we see it differently. Imagine, for example, what people must have thought the stars were before the telescope was invented to help them see the sky more clearly.

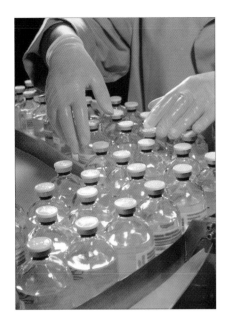

Finding your way around this book

This book is divided into four sections of experiments. Each section explores various specialized areas of science within an everyday theme:

Our Restless Earth looks at the Earth's formation. You will see how weather and geological activities, such as volcanoes and earthquakes, affect the shape of the land.

Natural Wonders Close to Home explores nature and the environment by discovering the habitats in your own garden or in nearby woods and parks.

Physical and Material Marvels investigates the basic principles of physics and chemistry, from how machines work to construction and building. This section focuses on power and energy, chemical change, light and cameras, electricity and magnets.

Finally, *Travel and Transport* explores how trains, cars, airplanes and rockets, and ships have developed from the beginning of time to the present day. This section will also explain how each of these machines work.

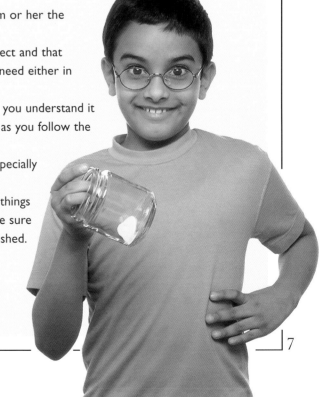

EXPERIMENTING HINTS

• Before you start, tell an adult what you are going to do. Show him or her the experiment and explain where and how you intend to do it.
• Make sure you have all the necessary items required for the project and that materials and equipment are clean. You should find everything you need either in your home or from a local shop.
• Read the whole project first. Then read each step and make sure you understand it before you begin. All the experiments in this book are safe as long as you follow the instructions exactly, and ask for adult help when advised to do so.
• When you have finished a project, clear everything away safely, especially breakable items, such as glass. Remember to wash your hands!
• Take extra care with experiments that involve electricity, heating things up, handling chemicals, soil and glass. If you are using any food, make sure you have permission to use it and throw it away after you have finished. If a project advises using gloves, be sure to do so.
• Do not worry if an experiment doesn't work or you miss what happens. Try to work out why it has gone wrong and do the experiment again. It's all part of the fun!

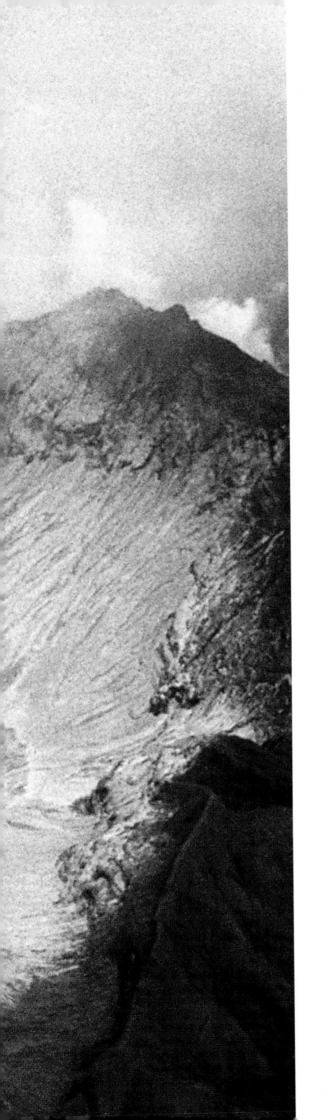

Our Restless Earth

Earthquakes and volcanoes are a reminder that the Earth's surface is constantly and dramatically changing. Fossils reveal how many kinds of plants and animals that were once alive have now disappeared. Scientists realize that it is part of the Earth's nature to undergo violent changes caused by natural processes that act over billions of years. In the following pages, you can discover how some of these natural processes, such as wind erosion, rivers and mountain formation, affect the Earth.

Spinning planet

The Earth is like a giant ball spinning in the darkness of Space. The only light falling on it is the light of the Sun glowing 150 million kilometres away. The Earth turns once a day, and it orbits the Sun once a year. The experiments on these pages investigate the two ways of moving, and explain why night and day, and the seasons, occur. The ball represents the Earth and the torch the Sun. In the final project, you can make a simple thermometer using water to record changes in temperature from night to day and from season to season.

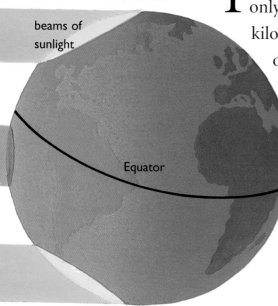

North Pole

beams of sunlight

Equator

South Pole

▲ Variable sunlight

The Sun's light does not fall evenly over the Earth because our planet is round. Imagine three identical beams of sunlight falling on the Earth. One falls on the Equator and the others on the North and South Poles. The beam falling on the Equator covers a much smaller area, so its energy is more concentrated and the temperature is higher.

YOU WILL NEED

Night and day: felt-tipped pen, plastic ball, piece of thin string, non-hardening modelling material, torch.

The seasons: felt-tipped pen, plastic ball, bowl just big enough for the ball to sit on, torch, books or a box to set the torch on.

Make a thermometer: water, bottle, food colouring, clear straw, reusable adhesive, card, scissors, felt-tipped pen.

Night and day

1 Draw or stick a shape on the ball to represent your country. Stick the string to the ball with modelling material. Tie the string to a rail, such as a towel rail, so that the ball hangs freely.

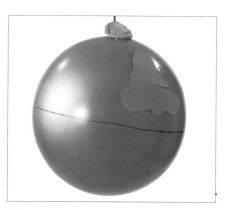

2 Shine the torch on the ball. If the country you live in is on the half of the ball in shadow on the far side, then it is night because it is facing away from the Sun.

3 Your home country may be on the half of the ball lit by the torch instead. If so, it must be daytime here because it is facing the Sun. Keep the torch level, aimed at the middle.

4 Turn the ball from left to right. As you turn the ball, your country will move from the light half to the dark half. You can see how the Sun comes up and goes down as the Earth turns.

The seasons

1 Use the felt-tipped pen to draw a line around the middle of the ball. This represents the Equator. Sit the ball on top of the bowl so that the Equator line is sloping gently.

2 Put the torch on the books so it shines just above the Equator. It is summer on the half of the ball above the Equator where the torch is shining, and winter on the other half of the world.

3 Shine the torch on the Equator. It sheds equal light in each hemisphere. This is the equivalent of spring and autumn, when days and nights are of similar length throughout the world.

Solar power ▶

The Sun pours energy on to the Earth as heat and light. The amount of energy received in any one place on the Earth changes with the seasons. This is because the Earth's axis is tilted. In summer, one half of the Earth tilts towards the Sun, and is warmer. In the winter, it tilts away from the Sun and is colder.

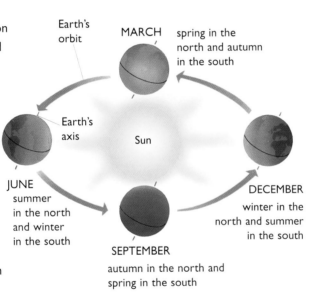

Earth's orbit

MARCH — spring in the north and autumn in the south

Earth's axis

Sun

JUNE summer in the north and winter in the south

DECEMBER winter in the north and summer in the south

SEPTEMBER autumn in the north and spring in the south

Make a thermometer

1 Pour cold water into the bottle until it is about two-thirds full. Add some food colouring. Dip the straw into the water and seal the neck tightly with reusable adhesive.

4 On a hot day, the Sun's heat will make the air and water expand, forcing the water level in the straw above the room temperature mark. Cool the thermometer in the fridge. Mark the different levels.

2 Blow down the straw to force some extra air into the bottle. After a few seconds, the extra air pressure inside will force the water level to rise up the straw.

3 Cut the card and slot it over the straw. Let the bottle stand for a while. Make a mark on the card by the water level to show room temperature. Take your thermometer outside.

Phases of the Moon

The Moon is Earth's closest neighbour in space. We know more about the Moon than about any other heavenly body because astronauts have landed on it and explored the surface. The Moon is Earth's only satellite. It measures 3,476km across, about a quarter of the size of the Earth. It circles around the Earth at a distance of about 385,000km, and makes the journey about once a month. The Moon does not give out any light of its own. We see it because it reflects light from the Sun. The sunlight illuminates different parts of the Moon as the month goes by. This makes the Moon seem to change shape. The Moon spins around slowly as it circles the Earth, so the same side is always turned towards the Earth.

We only see the Moon lit up completely once a month, but you do not have to wait a month to see the changes in its shape or phases. The project here will show you in just a few minutes how the Moon goes through its phases!

▲ Face of the Moon
This picture shows a view of the Moon from the Earth. When the whole of the Moon is lit up like this, we call it a full Moon. The darker regions on the surface are great dusty plains called seas, or maria. The lighter areas are highlands. These are pitted with craters that are sometimes hundreds of kilometres across. Mountains on the Moon rise to more than 6,000m.

Make your own Moon

YOU WILL NEED

football or beach ball, glue, glue brush, glass, silver paper or foil, scissors, reusable adhesive, torch.

1 Make sure that you have washed and dried your ball thoroughly before using! Paint glue all over the ball. Rest it on a glass or something similar to keep it still.

2 Carefully cut the silver paper or foil into large square sheets. Wrap up the ball in the silver paper. Try to ensure that the wrapping is as smooth as possible. You now have your Moon!

3 Place your Moon on a table. Wedge a small ball of reusable adhesive under the ball. This will hold it firm and stop it from rolling off the table.

4 Get your friend to stand at one side of the table to shine a torch with a strong beam on your Moon. Go to the opposite side of the table. Look at your Moon with the main lights out.

5 Gradually move round the table, still looking at your Moon, which is lit up one side by the torch. You will see the different shapes it takes. These shapes are the Moon's phases.

Going through the phases ▶

When you are opposite your friend in the project, the side of the ball facing you is dark. This is what happens once a month in the night sky. We can only see a thin sliver of light, which we call a new or crescent Moon. As you move around the table, more of the ball is lit by the torch. All of it will be lit when you are behind your friend. When this happens to the real Moon, we describe it as full. As you move around, the ball gradually fades into darkness. When you are opposite your friend again you will see a new Moon again.

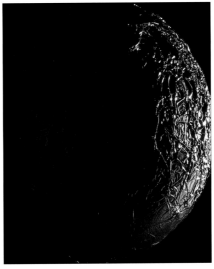

crescent Moon

first quarter phase

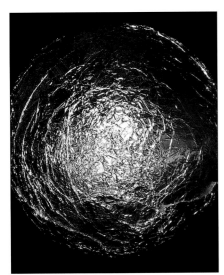

full Moon

last quarter phase

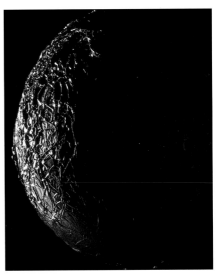

crescent Moon

The rise and fall of tides

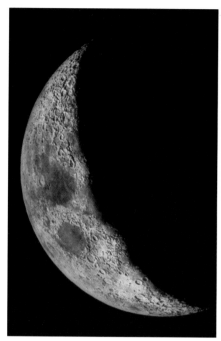

▲ **Close neighbour**

The Moon is a lifeless desert of rock. It has no atmosphere to protect it from the Sun's dangerous rays, and no water to sustain life. The shape of the Moon appears to change during the month. We call these changes in shape the Moon's phases. It takes the Moon 29½ days to change from a slim crescent to a full circle and back again.

The Earth appears blue from the darkness of Space. This is because more than 70 per cent of its surface is covered with oceans. The seas make up more than one million million million tonnes of seawater.

Every 12 hours or so, the seawater rises then falls back again. These rises and falls are called the tides. When the water is rising, we say the tide is flowing. When it is falling, we say the tide is ebbing. The movement of the ocean waters is caused by the Moon and by the Earth spinning. Gravity pulls the Moon and Earth together. As the Earth turns, the Moon pulls at the ocean water directly beneath it, causing the water to rise. A similar rise in sea level occurs on the opposite side of the Earth, where the water bulges out as a result of the Earth spinning. At these places, there is a high tide. Some six hours later, the Earth has turned 90°. The sea then falls to its lowest point and there is a low tide.

The two experiments opposite explain how the oceans rise and fall without any change in the amount of seawater, and how the tidal bulges of water stay in the same place below the Moon, as the Earth spins beneath it.

How tides occur

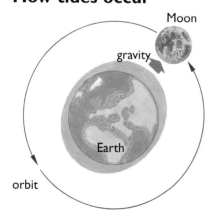

Tides rise beneath the Moon as the Earth turns. The gravity of the Moon tugs at the oceans, pulling the water around with it.

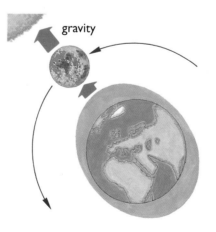

Once every two weeks, the Sun and the Moon line up with the Earth. Their combined pull creates a spring tide, where the tides are higher than usual.

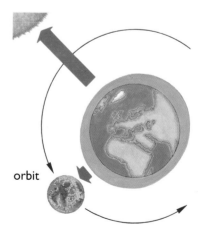

One week later, the Sun and the Moon are at right angles to each other. Pulling in different directions, they create a lower tide than usual, called a neap tide.

High and low tide

1 Place the bowl on a firm, flat surface, then half fill it with water. Place the ball gently in the water so that it floats in the middle of the bowl, as shown in the picture.

2 Place both hands on top of the ball, and push it down into the water gently but firmly. Look what happens to the level of the water. It rises in a 'high tide'.

3 Let the ball gently rise again. Now you can see the water in the bowl dropping again. So the tide has risen and fallen, even though the amount of water is unchanged.

The tidal bulge

YOU WILL NEED

High and low tide: plastic bowl, water, plastic ball to represent the world.

The tidal bulge: strong glue, one 20cm length and two 40cm lengths of thin string, plastic ball to represent the world, plastic bowl, hand drill, water.

1 Glue the 20cm length of the string very firmly to the ball and leave it to dry. Meanwhile, ask an adult to drill two holes in the rim of the bowl, one on each side.

2 Thread a 40cm length of string through each hole and knot the string around the rim. Half fill the plastic bowl with water and float the ball in the water.

3 Ask a friend to pull the string on the ball towards him or her. There is now more water on one side of the ball than the other. This is called a tidal bulge.

4 The Moon pulls on the water as well as the Earth. So now ask the friend to hold the ball in place while both of you pull out the strings attached to the bowl until it distorts.

5 There is now a tidal bulge on each side of the world. One of you slowly turn the ball. Now you can see how, in effect, the tidal bulges move round the world as the world turns.

15

Ocean waves and currents

▲ Powerful seas

In stormy weather, giant waves rear up and crash down, turning the sea into a raging turmoil.

The sea is rarely still. Even on a calm day, you will see ripples on the surface. Waves move over the ocean's surface. They are driven mainly by the wind. The stronger the winds, and the longer the fetch (the distance they have travelled), the bigger and higher the waves are. Waves usually only affect the surface of the water. As they travel, the water itself does not move. It just moves up and down as the wave passes through it. At a very deep level in some oceans, the water does move in giant streams called ocean currents. These can be hot or cold and can affect the world's climate. Ocean currents are usually caused by differences in the water's saltiness or temperature, rather than by the wind.

The first project shows how waves are made, and the second, how currents are set up by the wind blowing. Currents such as the ones in the third project happen on a much larger scale in the world's major oceans.

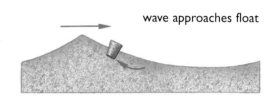
wave approaches float

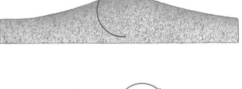
float maintains position

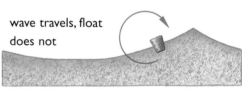
wave travels, float does not

▲ Wave goodbye

The diagrams above show how waves travel across the water surface, while objects floating on the water hardly move at all.

Making waves

1 Place the bowl on the floor or on a table. Choose a place where it does not matter if a little water spills out. Fill the bowl with water until it almost reaches the brim.

2 Blow very gently over the surface of the water. You will see that the water begins to ripple where you blow on it. This is how ocean waves are formed by air movement.

3 Fill the bath or pool with water. Blow gently along the length of the bath or pool. Blow at the same strength as in step 2, and from the same height above the water.

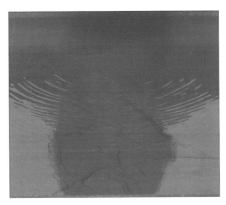

4 Keep blowing for a minute or so. Notice that the waves are bigger in the bath or pool, even though you are not blowing harder. This is because they reach farther across the water.

5 Now drop a small piece of modelling material into the water. Watch how it sets up waves. Ripples travel out in circles from where the modelling material entered the water.

Ocean currents

YOU WILL NEED

rectangular plastic bowl, jug,

water, talcum powder.

1 Place the bowl on the floor or on a table. Choose a place where it does not matter if a little water spills out. Fill the bowl with water until it almost reaches the rim.

2 Scatter a small amount of talcum powder over the water. Use just enough powder to make a very fine film over the water's surface. The less you use, the better.

3 Blow very gently across the water from the centre of one side of the bowl to the other. You will see how the water starts to move. Ocean currents begin to move in the same way.

4 Keep blowing and the powder swirls in two circles as it hits the far side. This is what happens when currents hit continents. One current turns clockwise, the other turns anticlockwise.

Changing coastlines

Of all the natural forces that erode (wear away) the land, the sea is the most powerful. It carries sand particles that act like a grindstone on the shore. Waves are forced into cracks in the rocks. They widen the cracks, eventually breaking up the rock face. Huge cliffs are carved out of mountains, broad platforms are sliced back through rocks and houses are left dangling over the edges of the land.

New land can also be created at the ocean's edge. Where headland cliffs are being eroded by waves, the bays between may fill with sand. On coasts where the sea is shallow, waves build beaches of shingle, sand and mud. The first experiment demonstrates the destructive effect of the sea when it hits the shore. The second project shows how waves make ripples on sandy beaches.

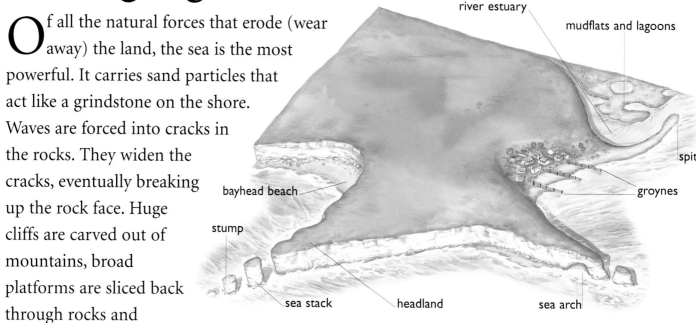

river estuary

mudflats and lagoons

spit

bayhead beach

groynes

stump

sea stack   headland   sea arch

▲ Everchanging landscape

The sea's power to build and destroy a coastline can be seen in this picture. Coastal areas that are exposed to the full force of the waves are eroded into steep cliffs. Headlands are worn back, leaving behind stacks, stumps and arches. In more sheltered places, the sand piles up to form beaches, or waves may carry material along the coast to build spits and mudflats.

▲ Relentless assault

The sea is at its most spectacular at the edges of big oceans, where the waves are big and powerful. Their continuous assault on the land will, in time, break up the toughest rocks into tiny pieces.

Attacking the shore

1 Mix a little water with the sand in a bucket until it is quite wet and sticks firmly together. Then pack the sand into a wedge shape at one end of the tank.

2 Carefully pour water into the empty end of the tank so as not to disturb the sand too much. Fill the tank until the water level comes about two-thirds of the way up the sloping sand.

3 Make gentle waves in the water on the side opposite the sand. Notice how the waves gradually wear away the sloping sand. This is what happens on a sandy seashore.

How ripples are formed in sand

YOU WILL NEED

Making waves: sand, plastic bucket, water tank, water, jug.

How ripples are formed in sand: heavy filled round tin, round plastic bowl, jug, water, fine clean sand, spoon.

1 Place a heavy tin in the centre of the plastic bowl, then fill the bowl with water to at least half way. The water should not cover more than two-thirds of the tin.

2 Sprinkle a little sand into the bowl to create a thin layer about ½cm deep. Spread the sand until it is even, then let it settle into a flat layer at the bottom of the bowl.

3 Stir the water gently with the spoon. Drag the spoon in a circle around the tin. As the water begins to swirl, stir faster with the spoon, but keep the movement smooth.

4 As you stir faster, lift the spoon out and let the water swirl around by itself. The sand will start to develop ripples. As you stir faster, the ripples become more defined.

Water on the move

Rivers start high in the hills and wind their way down towards the sea, or sometimes, a lake. At its start, a river is a tiny stream tumbling down the slopes. It is formed by rain running off a mountainside or by water bubbling up from a spring. As the water flows downhill, it is joined by other streams and grows bigger.

The first project shows how water shapes the landscape by physically eroding (wearing away) the rock. The second experiment demonstrates how in some places, erosion can be a chemical process, in which water dissolves the rock and carries it away.

Over millions of years, a river can carve a gorge deep through solid rock, or deposit (lay down) a vast plain of fine mud called silt. The great rivers of the world take millions of tonnes of mud, rock and sand from the land every day and carry them into the sea. If the river meets a low-lying shoreline, the sediment is dropped. It may spread out into a fan-shaped muddy plain called a delta. When this happens, the river is forced to branch out into smaller streams as it flows into the sea. You can see how this happens in the third experiment.

upper reaches

middle reaches

lower reaches

◄ The course of a river

As it moves across the land, a river changes character. In the upper reaches, it is a fast-flowing, tumbling stream cutting down through steep, narrow valleys. Lower down, it broadens and deepens into a river. Eventually it moves across a broad floodplain before reaching the sea.

The destructive power of water

1 Put one end of a baking tray on a brick. Put the other end of the baking tray on a lower tray or bowl, so that it slopes downwards. Make a sandcastle on the baking tray.

2 Slowly drip water over the sandcastle. Watch the sand crumble and form a new shape. This happens because the sand erodes away where the water hits it.

3 Make sure that the water flows down the centre of the baking tray. This way, the water hits the middle of the sand castle, eroding the centre to form a natural stack.

Chemical erosion

1 Build a pile of brown sugar on a
tray. Imagine that it is a mountain
made of a soluble rock (that dissolves
in water). Press the sugar down firmly
and shape it to a point.

2 Drip water on your sugar
mountain. It will erode as the
water dissolves the sugar. The water
running off should be brown, because
it contains dissolved brown sugar.

Making a delta

1 Use scissors to trim the top of
the cardboard container so that it
is about 10–15cm deep. Now take
the two plastic bin liners to make the
box waterproof.

2 Cover the inside of the box with
the bin liners and tape them
securely at each end of the box.
Make sure that the seal between the
bin liners is secure.

3 Using the trowel, carefully spread
a layer of sand over the bottom of
the tray until the sand is about 4–5cm
deep. Flatten the sand with the trowel
until it is smooth.

4 Rest one end of the container on
a block of wood or something
similar, to make a slope. Pour water
from the jug on to the sand in the
middle of the higher end.

5 If you continue pouring, you will
find that the water gradually
washes away a path through the sand.
It deposits sand it has washed away at
the lower end in a delta region.

Cloud and rain

Water moves around the Earth and its atmosphere in a continuous process called the water cycle. Heat from the Sun causes water from oceans, lakes and rivers to evaporate into water vapour. Water is also released into the atmosphere from plants in a process called transpiration Flowers and trees take up water from their roots. They use some and release the rest back out through their leaves - water vapour rises into the atmosphere. It cools as it rises, and changes back into tiny droplets of liquid water. This is called condensation. The droplets gather together and form clouds. When the water in the atmosphere becomes too heavy to be held in the air, it returns to the Earth's surface as precipitation (dew, rain, sleet and snow). The land has a fresh supply of water and so the water cycle continues.

The first experiment shows you how water changes to vapour and back again, when a cold surface makes the water vapour condense into water droplets. In the second project you can make a simple rain gauge to measure the amount of rain you get where you live. If you live in a desert region, you may have to wait a long time!

cloud of ice crystals

cloud of water droplets

water vapour rises

▲ Forming clouds

Clouds form when warm air containing water vapour rises into the air and cools. The vapour turns into droplets of water, forming clouds. If the air is very cold, the vapour turns into a cloud of tiny ice crystals.

YOU WILL NEED

heat-proof jug, water, saucepan, oven gloves, plate.

Water vapour

1 Fill up the jug with water from the hot tap. Pour the water into the saucepan. Switch on one of the hotplates or light a gas ring on the cooker and place the saucepan on it.

2 Heat the water until it is boiling hard and steam is rising. Lift the plate with the oven gloves. Hold it upside-down above the saucepan. After a few minutes, turn off the heat.

3 Take the plate away, using the oven gloves. You will see that the plate is covered with drops of water. This is water vapour that has cooled and turned back into liquid.

Measuring rainfall

YOU WILL NEED

scissors, sticky paper, large jar (such as a sweet jar), ruler, ballpoint pen, large plastic funnel, notebook, tall narrow jar or bottle.

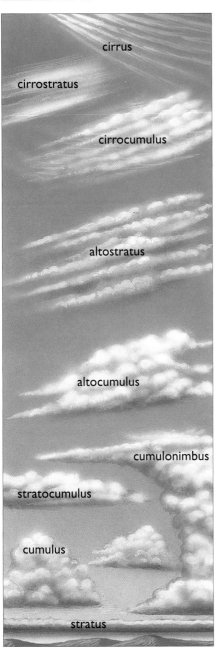

cirrus

cirrostratus

cirrocumulus

altostratus

altocumulus

cumulonimbus

stratocumulus

cumulus

stratus

▲ Cloud spotter

The main kinds of clouds we see in the sky can be grouped according to how far they are above the Earth's surface. High clouds include cirrus clouds. Altostratus and altocumulus are middle clouds. Stratus and cumulus clouds are examples of low clouds.

1 Cut a strip of sticky paper the same height as the jar. Stick it on the outsideof the jar. Use a ruler and pencil to mark 1cm intervals on the paper strip.

2 Place the funnel in the jar. Put the gauge outside in an open space away from any trees. Look at the gauge at the same time each day. Has it rained in the last 24 hours?

3 If it has rained, use the scale to see how much water is in the jar. This is the rainfall for the past 24 hours. Make a note of the reading. Empty the jar before you return it to its place.

4 You can measure rainfall more accurately if you use a separate, narrower measuring jar. Stick another strip of sticky paper along the side of this jar. Pour water into the large collecting jar up to the 1cm mark. Then pour the water into the narrow jar. Mark 1cm where the water level reaches. Divide the length from the bottom of the jar to the 1cm mark into 10 equal parts. Each will be equivalent to 1mm of rainfall. You can now extend the scale past the 1cm mark to the top of the narrow jar. Use this jar to measure the rainfall you collect to the nearest millimetre, just as professional meteorologists do.

What is humidity?

The temperature of a place is mainly controlled by the amount of heat it absorbs from the Sun. Another factor is altitude (how high the land is). Areas at very high altitudes are colder than areas at sea level. Distance from the sea also affects temperature. The sea has a moderating effect. You can see how this works in the first project. Water takes more time to heat up than the land, but holds its heat for much longer. Therefore on the coast, summers are cooler and winters milder than inland.

A temperature of 21°C in the Caribbean feels much hotter than 21°C in Egypt. This is due to humidity – the amount of water vapour in the air. When there is high humidity, the air feels moist and sticky. The perspiration on our skin cannot evaporate as there is too much water in the air already. When there is little water vapour in the air, the air feels dry. The perspiration on our skin escapes more easily and cools us down. The second experiment shows you how to measure humidity using a simple device called a hygrometer. When air is very humid, there is more chance that it will rain.

▲ Water from plants

Plants play a vital role in creating humidity. A plant's leaves give off water vapour in a process called transpiration. Cover a pot plant with a clear plastic bag. Seal the plastic around the pot with sticky tape. Put the plant in direct sunlight for two hours. Notice that the bag starts to mist up and droplets of water form on the inside. They form when the water vapour given off by the plant turns back to a liquid.

Measuring temperature changes

YOU WILL NEED

Measuring temperature changes: two bowls, jug of water, sand, watch, thermometer, notebook, pen.

Measuring humidity: two sheets of coloured card, scissors, ruler, pen, glue, toothpick, used matchstick, straw, reusable adhesive, blotting paper, hole punch.

1 Pour water into one bowl and sand into the other bowl. You do not need to measure the exact quantities of sand and water – just use roughly equal amounts.

2 Place the bowls side by side in a cool place. Leave them for a few hours. Then note the temperature of the sand and water. The temperature of each should be about the same.

3 Place the bowls side by side in the sunlight. Leave the bowls for an hour or two. Then measure and record the temperatures of the sand and water in each bowl.

4 Put each bowl in a cool place indoors. Measure and record the temperature of the sand and water every 15 minutes. The sand cools down faster than the water.

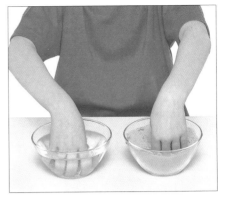

5 In this experiment, the sand acts like land and the water acts like the ocean. The sand gets hot quicker, but the water holds its heat longer. Dip your hands in to feel the difference.

Measuring humidity

1 Cut out a card rectangle. Mark regular intervals along one side for a scale. Cut a 2cm slit in one short side. Split the parts out as shown above and glue them to a card base.

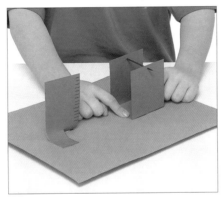

2 Cut another long rectangle from the card. Fold it and stick it to the card base as shown above. Pierce the top carefully with a toothpick to form a pivot.

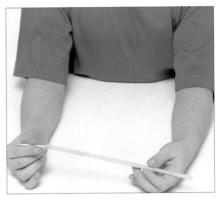

3 Fix the used matchstick to one end of the straw using some reusable adhesive, to make a pointer. Both the matchstick and the adhesive give the pointer some weight.

4 Carefully cut out several squares of blotting paper. Use the hole punch to make a hole in the middle of each square. Slide the squares over the flat end of the pointer.

5 Now carefully pierce the pointer with the toothpick pivot. Position the pointer as shown above. Make sure that the pointer can swing freely up and down.

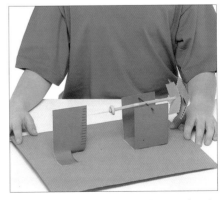

6 Adjust the position of the toothpick so that it stays level. Take the hygrometer into the bathroom and run a bath. The humidity makes the blotting paper damp. The pointer tips upwards.

The way the wind blows

The wind is moving air. Wind can move dust, sand and other small items. The first experiment shows how the weight of a particle affects how far it travels. The wind also brings about changes in the weather. Meteorologists study the wind to help them predict these changes. They use a weather vane to find out its direction. The second project shows how to make a simple weather vane. Wind speed is measured using an anemometer. This device consists of a circle of cups that spin when the wind blows, like a windmill. The faster the wind blows the faster the anemometer spins.

YOU WILL NEED

YOU WILL NEED

How wind sorts sand: two empty ice cube trays, piece of card large enough to fit over an ice cube tray, spoon, mix of fine and coarse sand, hairdryer.

Make a weather vane: reusable adhesive, plastic pot and its lid, scissors, garden stick, two plastic straws, coloured card, pen, sticky tape, pin, plywood, compass.

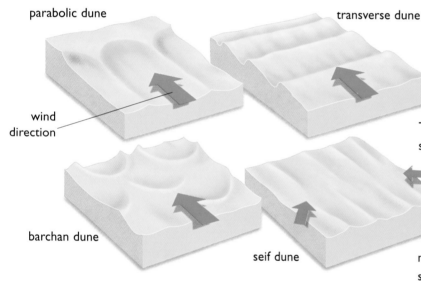

parabolic dune

transverse dune

wind direction

barchan dune

seif dune

◀ Name that dune

Some deserts contain vast seas of sand, called ergs, where the wind piles sand up into dunes. The shape of the dune depends on the amount of sand and changeability of the wind direction. Crescent-shaped dunes called parabolic dunes are common on coasts. Ones with narrow points facing away from the wind are called barchans. These dunes creep slowly forward. Transverse dunes form at right angles to the main wind direction. Seifs occur where there is little sand, and wind comes from different directions.

How wind sorts sand

1 Turn one ice cube tray over, and lay it down end to end with another ice cube tray. Place the card over the upturned tray and spoon the sand over it to make a sand dune.

2 Hold a hairdryer close to the upturned tray, pointing it towards the other tray. Turn the hairdryer on so that it blows sand into the open ice cube tray.

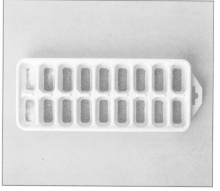

3 Look at the grains in each box. The distance a grain travels depends on its weight. Heavy grains fall in the end of the tray nearest to you. Light grains are blown to the farthest end.

Make a weather vane

1 Stick a ball of reusable adhesive to the middle of the lid of the pot. Ask an adult to pierce a hole in the bottom of the pot with the scissors. Place the pot on top of the lid.

2 Slide the stick into one of the straws. Trim the end of the stick so that it is a little shorter than the straw. Push the straw and stick through the hole in the pot and into the adhesive.

3 Cut out a square of card. Mark each corner with a point of the compass – N, E, S, W. Fold in half and snip a hole in the middle. Carefully slip the card over the straw.

4 Cut out two card triangles. Stick them to each end of the second straw to form an arrow head and tail. Put a ball of reusable adhesive in the top of the first straw in the pot.

5 Push a pin through the middle of the arrow. Stick the pin into the reusable adhesive in the first straw. Be careful not to prick your finger when you handle the pin.

6 Secure your weather vane to a plywood base using a piece of reusable adhesive. Test it for use – the arrow should spin round freely when you blow on it.

7 Take your weather vane outside and use a compass to point it in the right direction. You can now discover the direction the wind is blowing.

Turning the sails ▶

The miniature windmills on this toy spin faster the harder you blow on them. The sails of real windmills also spin faster as the speed of the wind increases. As a result, windmills need a 'governor'. This device regulates the speed of the sails' rotation so they are not damaged in very windy weather.

Recording weather

Meteorologists gather information about the weather from satellites, balloons and other instruments. Powerful computers help them to analyze the data. Using this information, meteorologists draw weather maps. These can show the state of the weather at any one time, or they can be a forecast of weather in the future. The maps use symbols to represent conditions such as rainfall and wind direction.

You can set up your own weather station to record daily conditions with a few simple devices. You will be able to use some of the instruments you have made in other projects, such as the weather vane, hygrometer and rain gauge. You will also need to buy a thermometer to measure the temperature. Take measurements with your weather instruments every day. Write them down in a special weather book. Also, make a note of what the weather is like generally – fine, cloudy, drizzly, frosty and so on. Don't forget to make a note of the date!

Meteorologists look at records from the past to discover changes in climate. The project opposite shows you how to make your own discoveries about climate changes by looking at the record of tree growth.

▲ Forecasting rain

A hygrometer will gauge the amount of moisture in the air. When the pointer tilts up on the scale, the air is moist and rain may be on the way.

▲ Measuring rainfall

A rain gauge will tell you how much rain has fallen. Rainfall is collected over a set period in a jar or measuring bottle, and the amount is recorded.

▲ Wind direction

A windmill shows how hard the wind is blowing. A weather vane will tell you the wind's direction. The arrow points in the direction that the wind is blowing from. So if the arrow points west, the wind is a west wind.

The wooden weather record

YOU WILL NEED

newly cut log, decorator's
paintbrush, ruler with millimetre
measurements, metric graph
paper, pen or pencil.

1 Ask a tree surgeon, the local council or a sawmill for a newly cut slice of log. Use the paintbrush to brush away the dust and dirt from the slice of wood.

2 When the log slice is clean, examine it closely. Look at the pattern of rings. They are small in the centre and get bigger and bigger towards the outer edge of the log.

3 Each ring is a year's growth. So count the rings out from the centre carefully. This tells you how old the tree is. If there are 105 rings, for instance, the tree is 105 years old.

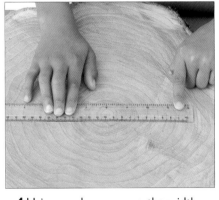

4 Using a ruler, measure the width of each ring. Start from the centre and work outwards. Ask a friend to write down the widths as you call them out.

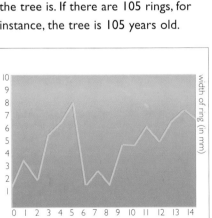

5 On graph paper, mark five squares for each year along the bottom. Mark widths for the rings up the side, five squares for each millimetre. Plot your measurements as dots for each year.

6 Join the dots with a line. This line shows how the weather has changed with each year. If the line is going up, the weather was warmer so the tree grew a lot. If the line falls, the weather was colder so the tree grew less.

Broken Earth

The surface of the Earth is not one piece but cracked, like a broken eggshell, into giant slabs. There are about 20 of these huge pieces of rock which are called tectonic plates. Tectonic plates are not fixed in one place, but slide around the Earth. They move very slowly – at about the pace of a fingernail growing. But tectonic plates are so gigantic that their movement has dramatic effects on the Earth's surface. Earthquakes and volcanoes happen where plates slide apart or past each other, or collide. Colliding plates also push up mountain ranges.

The continents drift around the world on tectonic plates. Once, they were all joined together in one huge continent called Pangaea. Around 200 million years ago, the tectonic plates beneath Pangaea began to move apart, carrying fragments of the continent with them. These fragments slowly drifted to the positions they are in now. The experiment opposite demonstrates how the continents may have once been, and how they move.

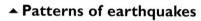

▲ Patterns of earthquakes

The Earth's rigid shell is called the lithosphere, from the Greek word lithos (stone). It is broken into the huge fragments shown on this map. The African plate is gigantic, underlying not only Africa, but half of the Atlantic Ocean too. The Cocos plate under the West Indies is much smaller. Black dots mark the origins of major earthquakes over a year. See how they coincide with the plate margins.

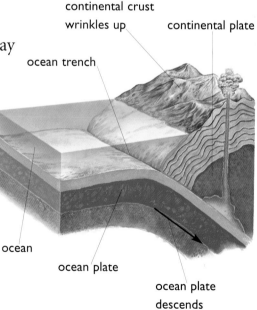

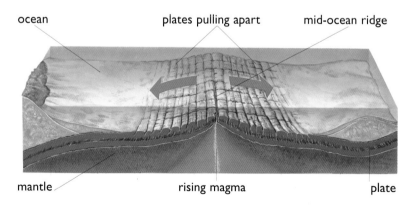

▲ Pulling apart

Right down the middle of the sea bed in the Atlantic Ocean, there is a giant crack where the tectonic plates are pulling apart. Molten (melted) rock from the Earth's interior wells up into the crack. As it cools it solidifies (becomes solid) to form the mid-ocean ridge.

▲ Pushing together

In many places tectonic plates slowly crunch together with enormous force. As they collide, one plate may be forced under the other. Earthquakes and volcanoes are often the result.

A continental jigsaw

YOU WILL NEED

atlas, pencil, sheets of tracing paper, sticky tape, sheets of coloured card, scissors, paper clips, two boxes.

1 Find the continents of North and South America, Europe and Africa in an atlas. Trace the outlines of the shape of these continents on to tracing paper.

2 Stick the tracing paper on to different coloured sheets of card. Then carefully cut around the outlines of the continents you have drawn from the atlas.

3 Move the eastern (right-hand) coasts of North and South America up to the western (left-hand) coasts of Europe and Africa to see how well they fit together.

4 You will find that the coastlines of the Americas, Europe and Africa fit together quite well. Scientists believe that these continents were once joined together in this way.

5 The continents of the Americas, Europe and Africa sit on plates that are moving in opposite directions. Use the continent cards you have made in the above project to see how they drift apart. Fold a large sheet of card in half and attach paper clips along the fold. Drape it over two boxes. Stick the Americas on one sheet and Europe and Africa on the other. Push upwards on the fold and see the continents move apart.

Restless Earth

The movement of rocks that causes earthquakes usually occurs deep inside the Earth's crust. The exact point at which the rocks start to break or fracture is known as the focus. This can lie as deep as hundreds of kilometres or as close as a few tens of kilometres down. The most violent disturbance on the surface occurs at a point directly above

▲ **Earthquake alert**
Most earthquakes originate in rock many kilometres below the surface, at the focus. The most intense vibrations on the surface are felt immediately above the focus, at the epicentre.

the focus, called the epicentre. The closer the focus, the more destructive is the earthquake. San Francisco, in California, sits near a line of weakness in the Earth's crust known as the San Andreas Fault. The fault marks the boundary of the eastern Pacific plate and the North American plate. As they try to slide past each other, they make the ground shake violently. Earthquakes and volcanoes occur around the boundaries of all the plates on the Earth's surface.

YOU WILL NEED

Tremors: set of dominoes, card.

Quakes: scissors, strong elastic band, ruler, plastic seed tray (without holes), piece of card, salt.

Tremors

I This project investigates how the energy in earthquake waves (tremors) varies with distance. Near the end of a table, build a simple house out of dominoes. Stand them up on edge.

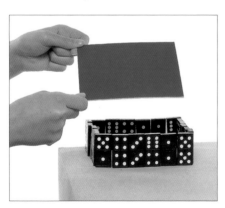

2 Place the card on the dominoes to make the roof of your house. Many people in earthquake zones live in the simplest of houses, built not too differently from this one.

3 Go to the opposite end of the table and hit it with your hand, but not too hard. Your domino house probably shakes, but still stays standing. Now hit the table at the other end.

4 The waves you create when you hit the table are strong enough to knock down the house. When you hit the other end of the table, the waves are too weak to knock it down.

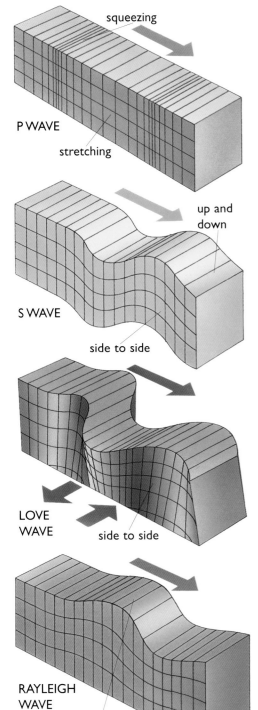

P WAVE

squeezing

stretching

S WAVE

up and down

side to side

LOVE WAVE

side to side

RAYLEIGH WAVE

rippling up and down

▲ How earthquakes move

The enormous energy released by an earthquake travels through the ground in the form of waves. The P (primary) wave compresses, then stretches rocks it passes through. The S (secondary) wave produces a side-to-side and up-and-down action. Love waves travel on the surface, making the ground move from side to side. Rayleigh waves are surface waves that move up and down.

Quakes

1 With the scissors, cut the elastic band at one end to make a long strip. This represents a layer of rock inside the Earth before it is affected by an earthquake.

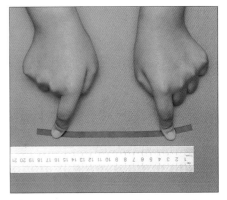

2 Measure the strip of elastic with a ruler. This represents the original length of the rock in the ground. Make a note of how long the elastic is at this stage.

3 Stretch the elastic band and hold it tightly above the tray. In the same way, rocks get stretched by pulling forces inside the Earth during an earthquake.

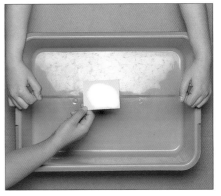

4 Ask a friend to hold the card on top of the elastic and sprinkle some salt on it. The salt layer on the card represents the surface of the ground above the stretched rock layer.

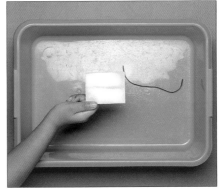

5 Now let go of the ends of the elastic. Notice how the salt grains on the card are thrown about. This was caused by the energy released when the elastic shrunk.

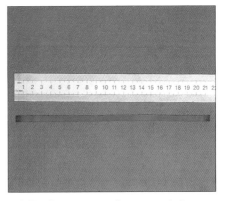

6 Finally, measure the strip of elastic again. You will find that it is slightly longer than it was at the start. Rocks are often permanently stretched a little after an earthquake.

Measuring earthquakes

Scientists who study earthquakes are called seismologists. They have a variety of instruments to gather data. The Newton's cradle experiment below explains how waves (tremors) work. The other projects show two ways in which seismologists detect how ground moves at the beginning of an earthquake. A gravimeter measures small changes in gravity. The tiltmeter detects whether rock layers are tilting.

Newton's cradle

1 Tie the beads to the ends of the wool threads. Tape the other ends to the cane. Make sure the threads are all the same lengths, and that the beads just touch when they hang down.

2 Prop up the cane at both ends on a pair of blocks supported by more blocks underneath. Secure the ends of the cane with tape. Lift up the bead at one end of the row and let go.

3 The bead at the other end flies up. The energy of the falling bead at one end travels as a pressure wave through the middle ones. It reaches the bead at the other end and pushes it away.

Gravimeter

1 Draw a scale on a strip of sticky paper using a ruler and pen. Stick the scale on the jar. In a real instrument this would measure slight changes in gravity.

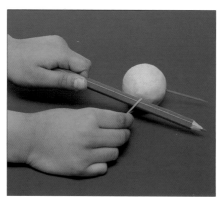

2 Bury one end of an elastic band in a ball of modelling material. Stick in a toothpick at right angles to the band to act as a pointer. Pass the pencil through the loop of the band.

3 Lower the ball into the jar, so the tip of the pointer is close to the scale. Fix the pencil on top with modelling material. Move the jar up or down and the pointer moves down or up the scale.

Tiltmeter

1 Use the bradawl to make a hole in the side of each plastic cup, just about half-way down. Be careful not to prick your fingers. Ask an adult to help you if you prefer.

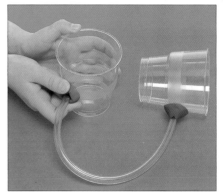

2 Push one end of the tubing into the hole in one of the cups. Seal it tight with modelling material. Put the other end in the hole in the other cup and seal it as well.

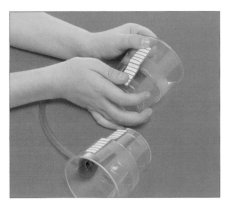

3 Using the pen, draw identical scales on two strips of the sticky paper. Use a ruler and mark regular spaces. Stick the scales at the same height on the side of the cups.

4 Stick the cups to the wooden baseboard with adhesive. Position them so that the tube between is pulled straight, but make sure it doesn't pull out.

6 Your tiltmeter is now ready for use. When it is level, the water levels in the cups are the same. When it tilts, the water levels change as water runs through the tube from one cup to the other. Scientists use tiltometers to detect whether rock layers are moving by comparing the water levels in two connected containers.

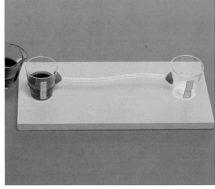

5 Add food colouring to water in the jug, and pour it into each of the cups. Make sure to fill the cups so that the water level reaches over the openings to the tubes.

Do-it–yourself seismograph

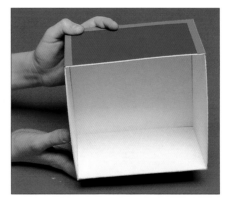

There are hundreds of seismic (from the Greek word *seismos*, meaning earthquake) centres around the world. Within minutes of a quake, scientists begin analyzing data from their seismographs. They then compare notes with scientists in other countries. The Italian scientist Luigi Palmieri built the first seismograph in 1856. All seismographs work on the same principle. They have a light frame attached to the ground and a heavy weight attached to the frame by a spring. The heavy weight has a high inertia, which means it is more difficult to get moving than a light object. When an earthquake happens, the frame shakes with the ground but the heavy weight stays in the same place because of inertia. The movement of the frame around the steady weight is recorded by a pen on a roll of paper, which draws a wavy line. The same principle of the inertia of a heavy weight is used to detect tremors in the seismograph shown here.

▲ Catching the tremors

The Chinese invented a type of seismograph in AD 132. When there was an earthquake, a ball was released from one of the dragons and fell into a frog's mouth. This showed the direction of the vibrations. The instrument detected a earth tremor 500km away.

Building a seismograph

YOU WILL NEED
cardboard box, bradawl, sticky tape, non-hardening modelling material, pencil, felt-tipped pen, string, piece of card.

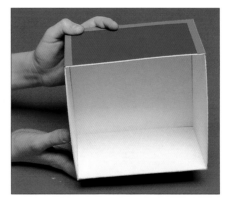

1 The cardboard box will become the frame of your seismograph. It needs to be made of quite stiff card. The open part of the box will be the front of your instrument.

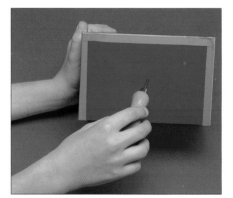

2 Make a hole in what will be the top of the frame with the bradawl. If the box feels flimsy, strengthen it by taping round the corners as shown in the picture.

3 Roll a piece of modelling material into a ball and make a hole in it with the pencil. Push the felt-tipped pen through the modelling material to extend a little way beyond the hole.

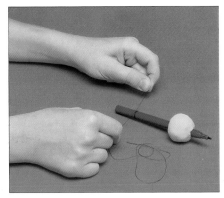

4 This will be the pointer of your seismograph and make a record of earthquake vibrations. Tie one end of the piece of string to the top of the pen.

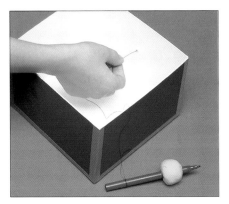

5 Thread the other end of the string through the hole in the top of the box. Now stand the box upright and pull the string through until the pen hangs free.

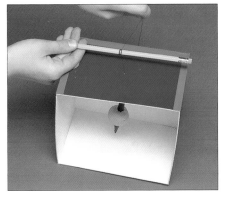

6 Tie the top end of the string to the pencil and roll the pencil to take up the slack. When the pen is at the right height (just touching the bottom), tape the pencil into position.

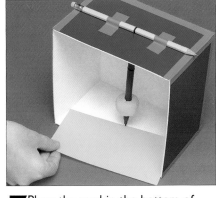

7 Place the card in the bottom of the box underneath the pen. If you have adjusted it properly, the tip of the pen should just touch the card to mark it.

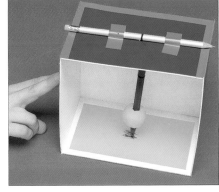

8 Your seismograph is now ready for use. It uses the same principle as a proper seismograph. The heavy bob, or pendulum, will be less affected by shaking motions than the frame.

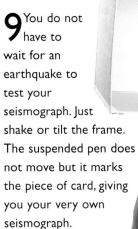

9 You do not have to wait for an earthquake to test your seismograph. Just shake or tilt the frame. The suspended pen does not move but it marks the piece of card, giving you your very own seismograph.

Slips and faults

Every earthquake, from the slightest tremor to the violent shaking that destroys buildings, has the same basic cause. Two plates of rock grind past each other along a fault line where the Earth's crust has fractured. Friction between the plates means they do not slide past each other smoothly, but jam and then jump. The first experiment on the page opposite shows how friction at fault lines causes great destructive energy.

Crustal plates float on top of the mantle beneath. The oceanic crust is heavier and denser than the continental crust so it sits lower down. The experiment below demonstrates this.

There are several kinds of fault. When blocks slide past each other horizontally, it is called a transform, or strike-slip fault. In a normal fault, the rocks are pulling apart and one block slides down the other. In a thrust fault, the blocks are pressing together, causing one to ride up above the other. The second project on the opposite page shows how these movements create landforms, such as mountains and valleys.

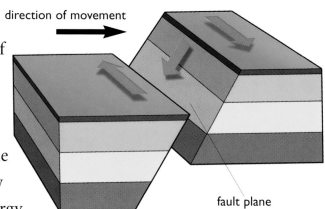
direction of movement

fault plane

▲ **Making mountains**

Fault mountains form by the slow, unstoppable movement of tectonic plates. This puts rocks under such huge stress that they sometimes crack. Such cracks are called faults. Where they occur, huge blocks of rock slip up and down past each other, creating cliffs. In places a whole series of giant blocks may be thrown up together, creating a new mountain range. The Black Mountains in Germany are an example of block mountains formed in this way.

Floating plates

YOU WILL NEED
wooden block, polystyrene block, bowl of water

1 The two blocks should be roughly the same size and shape. Polystyrene represents the continental crust, wood the oceanic crust and water the fluid mantle.

2 Place the blocks in the water. The polystyrene floats higher, because it is less dense, just as the continental crust floats higher on the mantle. Which of the two blocks weighs more?

Fault movements

I Hold a block in each hand so that the sides of the blocks are touching. Pushing gently, try to make the blocks slide past each other. You will find this quite easy.

2 Wet the sides of the blocks with the oil, and try to slide them again. You should find that it is easier because the oil has lessened the friction between the blocks.

3 Pin sheets of sandpaper on the sides of the blocks and try to make them slide now. You will find it much harder. The sandpaper is rough and increases friction between the blocks.

Building mountains

YOU WILL NEED

Fault movements: two wooden blocks, baby oil, drawing pins, sheets of sandpaper.

Building mountains: 20cm square sheet of paper, non-hardening modelling material in various colours, rolling pin, modelling tool.

I On the sheet of paper, roll out several flat sheets of modelling material, each one a different colour. The sheets should be about the same size as the sheet of paper.

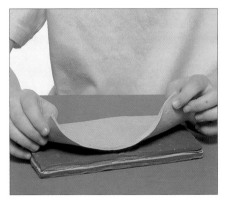

2 Place the square, flat sheets of modelling material on top of each other to make a layered block. The differently coloured layers are like the layers of rock strata in the Earth's crust.

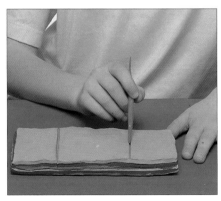

3 Lay the layered block flat on the table. With a modelling tool, carefully make two cuts in the clay – one towards the left and the other towards the right, as shown above.

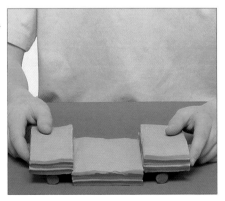

4 Make two small balls. Lift each of the outside pieces that you have cut on to a ball, as shown above. This forms a block mountain separated by a rift valley.

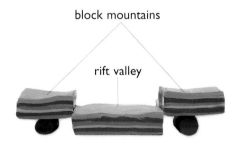

block mountains

rift valley

The crust breaks away at a rift zone where the plates are moving apart. Uplifted rock strata form block mountains, while a descending mass of rock creates the valley.

Building fold mountains

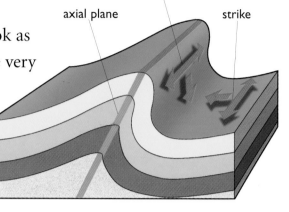

ost high mountains are part of great ranges that stretch for hundreds of kilometres. They may look as if they have been there forever, but geologically they are very young. They have all been thrown up in the last few hundred million years.

The biggest – and youngest – mountain ranges in the world, such as the Himalayas and the Andes, are fold mountains. They started life as flat layers of rock called strata. Layers of rock are laid down over millennia. Some strata form as successive layers of sediments such as sand, mud and seashells settle on the ocean floor. Other strata may be made up of molten rock thrown up from the heart of the Earth by volcanoes.

Fold mountains are layers of rock which have been crunched up by pressure – in a similar way to the pressure you will be exerting in these two projects. In real mountain formation, two of the tectonic plates that make up the Earth's surface push against each other, forcing the rock layers along their edges into massive folds. As the layers of rock are squeezed the folds become more exaggerated.

▲ Anatomy of a fold
Geologists describe an upfold as an anticline and a downfold as a syncline. The dip is the direction the fold is sloping. The angle of dip is how steep the slope is. The strike is the line along the fold. The axial plane is an imaginary line through the centre of the fold – this may be vertical, horizontal or at any angle in between.

YOU WILL NEED

thin rug

Simple folds

1 Find an uncarpeted floor and lay the rug down with one short, straight edge up against a wall. Make sure the long edge of the rug is at a right angle to the wall.

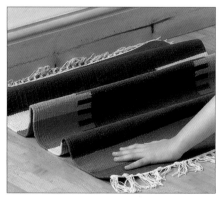

2 Now push the outer edge of the rug towards the wall. See how the rug crumples. This is how rock layers buckle to form mountains, as tectonic plates push against each other.

3 Push the rug up against the wall even more and you will see some of the folds turn right over on top of each other. These are like folded-over strata or layers, called nappes.

Complex folds

YOU WILL NEED

rolling pin, non-hardening modelling
material in various colours,
modelling tool, two blocks of
5cm square wood, two bars
of 10 x 5cm wood.

1 Roll out the modelling material into flat sheets in different colours, each about 0.5cm thick. Cut into strips about the same width as the blocks of wood. Square off the ends.

2 Lay the strips carefully one on top of the other, in alternating colours or in a series of colours. These strips represent the layers or strata of rock.

3 Place the blocks of wood at either end of the strips. Lay the bars of wood down on either side of the strips to prevent them from twisting sideways.

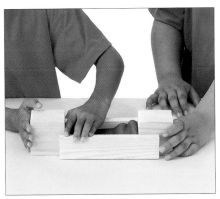

4 Ask a friend to hold on to one block, while you push the other towards it. As you push, the effect is similar to two tectonic plates slowly pushing together.

5 From time to time, stop and pull away the bars of wood so that you can have a look at what is happening. As you push harder, see how the layers crumple increasingly and start to turn over themselves. Overlapping folds like this are called nappes.

Fire down below

Volcanoes begin many kilometres beneath the Earth's surface. The landscape that makes up the surface of our planet is only a thin 'crust' of hard rock compared with what lies beneath. First, there is a thick layer of semi-liquid rock called the mantle. Then comes an intensely hot core of iron and nickel. This reaches temperatures of 3,700°C, but the surrounding pressure is so great that it cannot melt.

Heat moves out from the core to the mantle. Here, rocks are semi-liquid and move like treacle. They cannot melt completely because of pressure.

In some parts of the upper mantle, though, rocks do melt and are known as magma. This collects in chambers, and may bubble up through gaps in the crust via a volcano. You can watch how solids such as magma react to heat – become soft, then melt, and finally flow – in this project.

Most of the world's volcanoes lie along fault lines, where plates (sections of the Earth's crust) meet. A few, however, such as those in Hawaii, lie over hot spots beneath the Earth's crust. A hot spot is an area on a plate where hot rock from the mantle bubbles up underneath. The plate above moves but the hot spot stays in the same place in the mantle. The hot spot keeps burning through the plate to make a volcano in a new place. A string of inactive (dead) volcanoes is left behind as the plate moves over the hot spot. Some form islands above the ocean surface. Others, called sea mounts, remain submerged.

inner core

outer core

mantle

crust

continent

ocean

▲ Inside the Earth

Our planet is made up of different layers. The top layer is the hard crust. It is thinnest under the oceans, where it is only about 5–10km thick. Underneath the crust is a thick layer of semi-liquid rock known as the mantle. Beneath the mantle is a layer of liquid metal, mainly iron and nickel, that makes up the Earth's outer core. The inner core at the centre is solid, made up of iron and other metals.

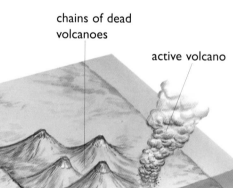

chains of dead volcanoes

active volcano

ocean plate

hot spot

Volcano chain ▶

Magma breaks through the surface plate. As the plate moves, a new part moves over the hot spot. A new volcano forms and the old one dies.

Magma temperature

1 Scoop out some margarine and drop it on to the bottom of the jar. For the best results, use hard cooking margarine, rather than a soft margarine spread.

2 Pick up the jar and tilt it slightly. See what happens to the margarine. The answer is, not a lot. It sticks to the bottom of the jar and does not slide down.

3 Fill the jug with hot water and pour some into the bowl. Shake it around to heat the bowl, then pour it away. Now pour the rest of the hot water into the bowl.

4 Pick up the jar and tilt it again. The margarine still will not move. Now place the jar on the bottom of the bowl. Keep your fingers clear of the hot water.

5 Start the stopwatch and after one minute, take out the jar. Tilt it and see if the margarine moves. Return it to the bowl and after another minute, look at it again.

6 Continue checking the jar for a few more minutes. After even a minute, the margarine will slide along the bottom as it warms and starts to melt. After several minutes, it is quite fluid. Rocks in the upper mantle of the Earth react to heat in a similar way as the margerine.

Moving magma

The temperature of the rocks in the Earth's mantle can be as high as 1,500°C. At this temperature the rocks would normally melt, but they are under such pressure from the rocks above them that they cannot melt completely. They are, however, able to flow slowly. This is rather like the solid piece of modelling material in the experiment below that flows slightly when you put enough pressure on it. This kind of flow is called plastic flow. In places, the rocks in the upper part of the mantle do melt completely. This melted rock, called

▲ Surprise eruption

Mount St Helens, in the north-east USA, lies in a mountain range that includes many volcanoes. Until 1980, Mount St Helens had not erupted in 130 years.

magma, collects in huge pockets called magma chambers. The magma rises because it is hotter and lighter than the semi-liquid rocks. Volcanoes form above magma chambers when the hot magma can rise to the surface. The second project demonstrates this principle using hot and cold water.

◀ Flowing like rock

Underneath the Earth's hard crust, the rock is semi-liquid and moves slowly. It flows in currents. Hot rock moves upwards and cooler rock sinks down.

YOU WILL NEED

non-hardening modelling material,

wooden board.

Plastic flow

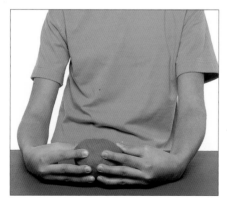

1 Make sure that the table is protected by a sheet. Knead the lump of modelling material in your hands until it is quite flexible. Make it into a ball and place on the table.

2 Place the board on top and press down. The modelling material flattens and squeezes out. It is just like semi-liquid rock flowing under pressure. Make it into a ball again.

3 Press it with the board. Push the board forwards at the same time. The modelling material will flow and allow the board to move forwards like the plates in the Earth's crust.

Rising magma

YOU WILL NEED

dark food colouring, small jar, small jug, transparent plastic food wrapping, scissors strong elastic band, sharpened pencil, large jar, oven gloves, large jug.

1 Pour some of the food colouring into the small jar. You may need to add more later to give your solution a deep colour. This will make the last stage easier to see.

2 Fill the small jug with water from the hot tap. Pour it into the small jar. Fill it right to the brim, but not to overflowing. Wipe off any that spills down the sides.

3 Cut a circular patch from the plastic food wrapping a few centimetres bigger than the top of the small jar. Place it over the top and secure it with the elastic band.

4 With the sharp end of the pencil, carefully make two small holes in the plastic covering the top of the jar. If any coloured water splashes out, wipe it off.

Watch what happens. The coloured hot water begins rising from the holes. This happens because the hot water is lighter, or less dense, than the cold water around it. Magma also rises because it is less dense than the semi-liquid rock surrounding it.

5 Now place the small jar inside the larger one. Use oven gloves because it is hot. Fill the large jug with cold water and pour it into the large jar, not into the small one.

Erupting volcanoes

Volcanoes are places where molten (liquid) rock pushes up from below through splits in the Earth's crust. The word volcano comes from Vulcan, the name of the ancient Roman god of fire. Vulcanology is the term given to the study of volcanoes and the scientists who study them are known as vulcanologists.

People usually think of volcanoes as producing molten rock. But volcanoes emit much more than just lava. The hot rock inside volcanoes produces many kinds of gases, such as steam and carbon dioxide. Some of these gases go into the air outside the volcano and some are mixed with the lava that flows from it. The project opposite shows you how to make a volcano that gives out lava mixed with carbon dioxide. As you will see, the red floury lava from your volcano comes out frothing, full of bubbles of this gas. In a real volcano, it is the gas that is mixed with the lava that makes the volcano suddenly explode.

▲ **Spectacular explosion**
This gigantic volcano has erupted with explosive violence. Huge clouds of rock and ash have been blasted into the air and rivers of red-hot lava cascade down its slopes. Explosive volcanoes have magma inside them that is full of gas. Gas bubbles swell inside the volcano to push out a mixture of lava and gas violently.

◄ **Forming a cone**
When an explosive volcano erupts, magma (red-hot molten rock) forces its way to the Earth's surface. It shoots into the air along with clouds of ash and gas, and runs out over the sides of the volcano. In time, layers of ash and lava build up to form a huge cone shape. Quiet volcanoes (those which do not explode because their magma contains very little gas) form a different shape.

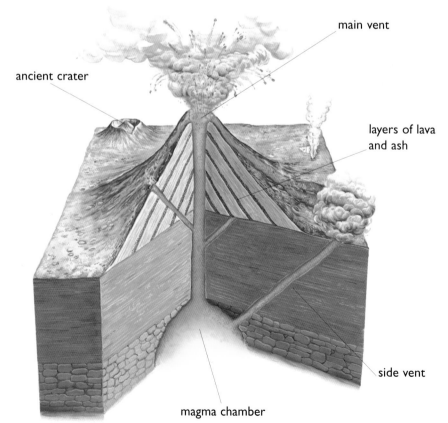

ancient crater

main vent

layers of lava and ash

side vent

magma chamber

Eruption

1 Make sure the jug is dry, or the mixture will stick to the sides. Empty the baking soda into the jug and add the flour. Thoroughly mix the two using the stirrer.

2 Place the funnel in the neck of the plastic bottle. Again, make sure that the funnel is perfectly dry first. Now pour in the mixture of soda and flour from the jug.

3 Empty sand into the tray until it is half-full. Fill the jug with water and pour it into the tray to make the sand sticky but not too wet. Mix together with the stirring rod.

4 Stand the bottle containing the flour and soda mixture in the centre of the plastic lid. Then start packing the wet sand around it. Make the sand into a cone shape.

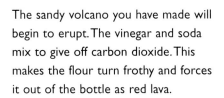

The sandy volcano you have made will begin to erupt. The vinegar and soda mix to give off carbon dioxide. This makes the flour turn frothy and forces it out of the bottle as red lava.

5 Pour the vinegar into the jug. Then add enough food colouring to make the vinegar a rich red colour. White wine vinegar will make a richer colour than malt vinegar.

6 Place the funnel in the mouth of the plastic bottle and quickly pour into it the red-coloured vinegar in the jug. Now remove the funnel from the bottle.

47

Volcanic shapes

Some parts of the world have ancient lava (molten rock) flows that are hundreds of kilometres long. Flows such as these have come from fissures (cracks) in the crust, which have poured out runny lava. This lava is much thinner than the lava produced by explosive volcanoes, which is sometimes called pasty lava. Scientists use the term viscosity to talk about how easily a liquid flows. Thin, runny liquids have a low viscosity, and thick liquids a high viscosity. The project shows the viscosities of two liquids and how quickly they flow.

Heating solids to a sufficiently high temperature makes them melt and flow. Rock is no exception to this rule. Deep inside a volcano, hot rock becomes liquid and flows out on to the surface as lava. Its temperature can be as high as 1,200°C. Volcanoes grow in various shapes depending on how runny or thick the lava is.

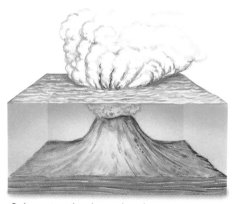

Submarine (undersea) volcanoes may grow in size until they rise above the surface of the sea.

Fissure volcanoes are giant cracks in the ground from which lava flows.

Shield volcanoes have runny lava and gentle slopes.

Plinian volcanoes produce thick, gassy lava and shoot columns of ash high into the air.

Vulcanian volcanoes produce thick, sticky lava and erupt with violent explosions.

Strombolian volcanoes spit out lava bombs in small explosions.

Lava viscosity

YOU WILL NEED

two paper plates, pen, saucer, jar of
liquid honey, tablespoon, stopwatch,
jug of ordinary washing-up liquid.

1 Mark a large circle on each plate by drawing around the edge of a saucer. Pour a tablespoon of honey from the jar into the middle of one of the circles. Start the stopwatch.

2 After 30 seconds, mark with the pen how far the honey has run. After another 30 seconds mark again. Stop the watch when the honey has reached the circle.

3 Part-fill the jug with washing-up liquid and pour some into the centre of the other plate. Use the same amount as the honey you poured. Start the stopwatch.

After 30 seconds, note how far the liquid has run. You will probably find that it has already reached the circle. It flows faster because it has a much lower viscosity than honey.

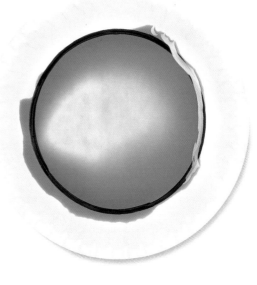

◄ Fast-flowing river

A river of molten lava flows down the slopes of the volcano Kilauea on the main island of Hawaii. Like the other volcanoes on the island, Kilauea is a shield volcano. It pours out very runny lava that flows for long distances, usually at speeds up to about 100m an hour. The fastest lava flows are called by their Hawaiian name of pahoehoe.

Vicious gases

The experiments here look at two effects that the gases given out by volcanoes can have. In the first project you can see how the build up of gas pressure can inflate a balloon. If you have put too much gas-making mixture in the bottle, the balloon may explode. Be careful! When the gas pressure builds up inside a volcano, an enormous explosion takes place, often releasing a deadly hot gas cloud.

Volcanoes often give out the gas carbon dioxide. This is heavier than air, so a cloud of carbon dioxide descends, pushing air out of the way. Carbon dioxide can kill people and animals. They suffocate because the cloud of carbon dioxide has replaced the air, so oxygen cannot reach their lungs. The second project shows the effect of carbon dioxide. The candle needs oxygen to burn, just as we need it to breathe. Carbon dioxide replaces the air, so the candle goes out.

▲ **Blast off**
An enormous cloud of thick ash billows from the top of Mount St Helens, in the USA. The volcano erupted on 18 May 1980. The ash cloud rose to a height of more than 20km.

> ### YOU WILL NEED
> funnel, drinks bottle, baking soda, vinegar, jug, balloon.

The balloon starts to blow up because of the pressure, or force, of the gas in the bottle. The more gas given out, the more the balloon fills. Don't burst the balloon!

Gas pressure

1 Place the funnel in the top of the bottle and pour in some baking soda. Make sure the funnel is dry or the baking soda will stick to it. Pour the vinegar into the bottle using the funnel.

2 Remove the funnel. Quickly fit the neck of the balloon over the top of the bottle. Notice that the vinegar and soda are fizzing and giving off bubbles of gas.

Suffocating gas

1 Place the funnel in the bottle and add the baking soda. Pour in the vinegar from the jug. This bottle is your gas generator. The gas produced is carbon dioxide.

2 Knead a piece of modelling material until it is soft, then push it into the mouth of the bottle. Make sure it fits tightly. This will keep the gas from escaping.

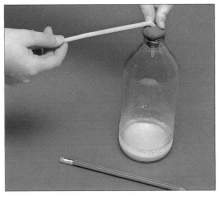

3 Make a hole in the clay stopper with the pencil. Carefully push the straw through the hole, so that it hangs down into the bottle. Press the modelling material around the straw.

4 Stand both candles in the bottom of the large jar. Ask an adult to light them. Light the short one first to avoid the danger of being burned if the tall candle were lit first.

5 Direct the straw of your gas generator into the bottom of the jar. Keep your arms well away from the candle flames. Soon you will find that the short candle goes out. The carbon dioxide gas has covered it and blocked out the oxygen that would let it burn.

▲ **A record of the past**
Gas killed many of the victims at the Roman town of Pompeii. In AD79 Pompeii was buried by avalanches of hot ash and rock from the erupting Vesuvius. Archaeologists have recreated the shapes of people and animals who died there. They filled hollows left by the bodies with wet plaster of Paris and let it harden. Then they removed the cast from the lava that had covered the bodies.

Steaming hot

In some places in the world, often near plate boundaries, there is magma (hot molten rock) quite near the Earth's surface. This causes other volcanic features such as geysers and hot springs, called geothermal features. The word comes from geo meaning the Earth and thermal meaning heat.

Water from the Earth's surface trickles down through holes and cracks in the land. Geothermal features are almost always caused by magma affecting underground water.

The most spectacular geothermal feature is the geyser. This is a fountain of steam and water that erupts from holes in the ground. Vents (holes) called fumaroles, where steam escapes gently, are more common. Geysers and fumaroles may also give out carbon dioxide and sulphurous fumes.

Hot water can also mix with cooler water to create a hot spring, or with mud to form a bubbling mud hole. Water becomes heated in underground rocks to a temperature above body heat (about 37°C). Some hot springs can be twice this hot. Many are rich in minerals. For centuries, people have believed that bathing in these mineral-rich springs is good for health.

The first experiment on the opposite page shows you how to make a geyser using air pressure to force out water. Blowing into the top of the bottle increases the air pressure there. This forces the coloured water out of the bottle through the long straw. In the second project, you can create a mud hole and discover the sort of bubbles that form in them.

> ### YOU WILL NEED
>
> **Geyser eruption:** non-hardening modelling material, 3 bendy straws, jug, food colouring, large plastic bottle, large jar.
>
> **Mudbaths:** cornflour, chocolate powder, mixing bowl, wooden spoon, measuring jug, milk, saucepan, oven glove.

◀ **Regular show**

One of the most famous geysers in the world is Old Faithful, in Yellowstone National Park in Wyoming, USA. This geyser erupts regularly about once every 45 minutes. Yellowstone is the most significant geothermal region in the USA. The National Park boasts the world's tallest geyser, known as Steamboat. Its spouting column has been known to reach more than 115m.

Geyser eruption

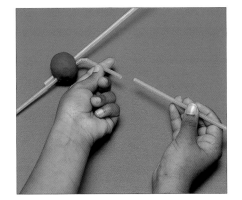

1 Make two holes in a little ball of modelling material and push two bendy straws through it, as shown. Push another straw through the end of one of the first two straws.

2 Pour water into the jug and add the colouring. Then pour it into the bottle. Push the clay stopper into the neck so that the lengthened straw dips into the coloured water.

3 Place the jar under the other end of the lengthened straw and blow into the other straw. Water spurts into the jar. If the long straw was upright, the water would spout upward like a geyser.

Mudbaths

1 Mix together two tablespoons of cornflour and two of chocolate powder in the bowl, using the wooden spoon. Stir the mixture thoroughly until it is an even colour.

2 Pour about 300ml of milk into the saucepan, and heat it slowly on a hotplate. Keep the hotplate on a low setting to make sure the milk does not boil. Do not leave it unattended.

3 Add some cold milk, little by little, to the mixture of cornflour and chocolate in the bowl. Stir vigorously until the mixture has become a thick smooth cream.

4 Pour the creamy mixture into the hot milk in the saucepan. Hold the handle of the saucepan with the oven mitt and stir to stop the liquid sticking to the bottom of the saucepan.

5 If you have prepared your flour and chocolate mixture well, you will now have a smooth, hot liquid looking something like liquid mud. Soon it will start sending up thick bubbles.

The thick bubbles in the mixture will burst with gentle plopping sounds. This is exactly what happens in hot mud pools in volcanic areas.

Volcanic rocks

The lava that flows out of volcanoes eventually cools, hardens and becomes solid rock. Different sorts of lava form different kinds of rocks.

In the first project we see how keeping a liquid under pressure stops gas from escaping. The magma (molten rock) in volcanoes usually has a lot of gas dissolved in it. As it rises through the volcano, the gases start to expand. They help push the magma up and out if the vent is clear. If the vent is blocked, the gas pressure builds up and eventually causes the volcano to explode. The lava that comes from volcanoes with gassy magma forms rock riddled with holes. In some explosive volcanoes, the lava contains so much gas that it forms pumice. This rock is so frothy and light that it floats on water.

When rising magma becomes trapped underground, it forces its way into gaps in the rocks and between the rock layers. This process is known as intrusion and is demonstrated by the second project. The rocks that form when the magma cools and solidifies are called intrusive rocks. Granite is the most common intrusive rock. Often the heat of the intruding magma changes the surrounding rocks. They turn into what are called metamorphic (changed form) rocks.

YOU WILL NEED
Dissolved gas: small jar with tight-fitting lid, bowl, jug, antacid tablets.
Igneous intrusions: plastic jar, bradawl, pieces of broken tiles, non-hardening modelling material, tube of coloured toothpaste.

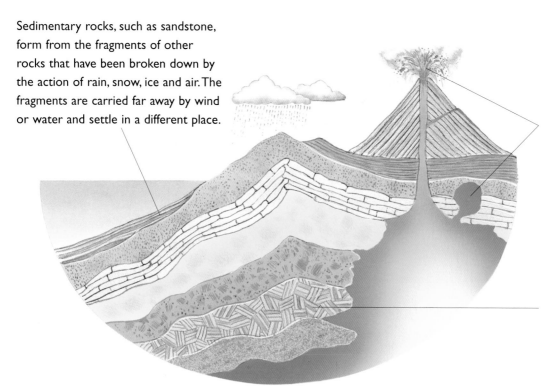

Sedimentary rocks, such as sandstone, form from the fragments of other rocks that have been broken down by the action of rain, snow, ice and air. The fragments are carried far away by wind or water and settle in a different place.

At some hot parts of the Earth beneath the crust, huge pockets of liquid rock (magma) form. The magma rises, cools and solidifies to form igneous rocks such as granite. If magma reaches the surface of the Earth, it erupts as lava.

Within the Earth, the heat and pressure sometimes become so great that the surrounding rocks are changed. The new rocks are called metamorphic rocks. Marble is formed this way. It comes from limestone rock.

Dissolved gas

1 Stand the jar in the bowl. Pour cold water into the jar from the jug until the jar is nearly full to the top. Break up two antacid tablets and drop them into the jar.

2 Quickly screw the lid on the jar. Little bubbles will start to rise from the tablets but will soon stop. Pressure has built up in the jar and prevents any more gas escaping.

3 Now quickly unscrew the lid from the jar and see what happens. The whole jar starts fizzing. Removing the lid releases the pressure, and the gas in the liquid bubbles out.

Igneous intrusions

1 Make a hole in the bottom of the plastic jar with a bradawl, enough to fit the neck of the toothpaste tube in. Keep your steadying hand away from the sharp end of the bradawl.

2 Place the pieces of broken tiles on the bottom of the jar. Keep them as flat as possible. They are meant to represent the layers of rocks that are found in the Earth's crust.

3 Flatten out the modelling material into a disc as wide as the inside of the jar. Put the disc of modelling material inside the jar. Push it down firmly on top of the tiles.

4 Unscrew the top of the toothpaste tube and force the neck into the hole you have made in the bottom of the bottle. You may have to widen it a little to get the neck in.

5 Squeeze the toothpaste tube. You will see the toothpaste pushing, or intruding, into the tile layers and making the disc on top rise. Molten magma often behaves in the same way. It intrudes into rock layers and makes the Earth's surface bulge.

Making crystals

Everything around you is made up of tiny particles called atoms. Crystals consist of atoms that are arranged in a regular repeating pattern. This gives the crystal its fixed outer shape. Most solid substances, including metals and minerals found in rocks, are in crystal form.

Igneous rocks are usually made of crystals that form as hot magma (molten rock) cools and solidifies. Crystals may also grow when a water solution containing minerals on the surface of the Earth evaporates. These two ways are demonstrated in the first two experiments.

The type of crystals that form depend on the substances that are dissolved in the liquid. Each mineral forms crystals with a characteristic shape. You can compare the crystals from the first two projects, which use two different solutions. The final experiment demonstrates how atoms are arranged in a crystal. In a liquid, the atoms are loosely joined together and can move about, which is why a liquid flows. As a liquid solidifies, the atoms join together in a regular pattern, like a pyramid, to form a crystal. When atoms are arranged in a disorderly way, they produce a gas.

▲ **Making crystals**
Place a drop of water on a small, dry mirror and then put it in the freezer. The water will freeze into crystals which can be seen with a hand lens.

> ### YOU WILL NEED
> water, measuring jug, saucepan, sugar, tablespoon, wooden spoon, glass jar.

Growing crystals from sugar solution

1 Ask an adult to heat half a litre of water in a saucepan until it is hot, but not boiling. Using a tablespoon, add sugar to the hot water until no more sugar will dissolve in the solution.

2 Stir the solution well, then allow it to cool. When it is quite cold, pour the solution from the pan into a glass jar and put it somewhere where it will not be disturbed.

After a few days or weeks, the sugar in the solution will gradually begin to form crystals. The longer you leave it undisturbed, the larger your crystals will grow.

Growing crystals from washing soda

1 Get an adult to pour about 250ml of very hot water into a jug. Add a spoonful of washing soda. Stir until it all dissolves. Add more soda until no more will dissolve.

2 Dissolving a solid in a liquid makes a solution. Your solution is said to be saturated because no more solid will dissolve. Pour the solution into a bowl, leaving any undissolved solids in the jug.

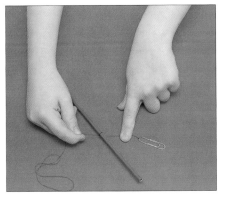

3 A crystal needs somewhere to start growing. Use a piece of cotton to attach the paper clip to the straw. The distance from straw to clip should be about two-thirds the depth of the bowl.

4 Balance the straw on top of the bowl to let the paper clip dangle in the water. As time goes by, water evaporates leaving crystals on the paper clip.

5 After several days, remove the clip and crystals from the solution and wash them under the cold tap. Look at the crystals through a hand lens. The shapes of your crystals are all the same.

Make a model crystal

1 Fit a layer of blue marbles into the tray in a square pattern. Each central atom is surrounded by eight others. (In some substances, atoms are arranged in a hexagon – a six-sided shape.)

2 Add a second layer. Each marble sits in a dip between four marbles in the layer below. Add a third layer. Each marble is directly above a marble in the first layer.

3 Add two more layers of marbles to make up a complete model crystal. The model crystal you have made is the shape of a square pyramid because you used a square tray.

Glass and bubbles

Igneous rocks start off deep within the Earth as magma (molten rock). The word igneous means 'of fire'. Magma rises towards the surface where it may erupt as lava from a volcano, or cool and solidify within the Earth's crust as igneous rock. Rocks formed in this way are a mass of interlocking crystals, which makes them very strong and ideal as building stones.

The size of the crystals in an igneous rock depends on how quickly the magma cooled. Lavas that cool quickly contain very small crystals. Basalt and andesite are two common kinds of fine-grained igneous rocks, with small crystals. Other rocks, such as granite, cooled more slowly because they solidified inside the Earth's crust. These have a grainy texture because the crystals had time to grow.

The experiments opposite show how igneous rocks can be grainy, or smooth and glassy. They use sugar to represent magma. Sugar melts at a low enough temperature for you to experiment with, but it will still be very hot , so ask an adult to help you carry out these projects. To make real magma, you would need to heat rock up to around 1,000°C until it melted! You can also make the sugar mixture into bubbly honeycomb, a form similar to pumice stone.

▲ Basalt
Dark, heavy basalt is one of the most common volcanic rocks. It is formed from the thin, runny lava that pours out of some volcanoes. This sample is known as vesicular basalt because it is riddled with vesicles (holes).

▲ Andesite
Lava from explosive volcanoes is thicker and less runny. It can form andesite, which is a lighter-coloured rock than basalt. Andesite is so-called because it is the typical rock found in the Andes Mountains in Peru.

honeycomb (pumice)   toffee (obsidian)

fudge (granite)

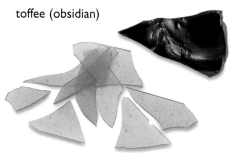

▲ Pumice
The bubbles in honeycomb are like those in pumice. Pumice is a very light rock that is full of holes. It forms when lava containing a lot of gas pours out of underwater volcanoes.

▲ Obsidian
Glassy toffee cools too rapidly to form crystals. Obsidian is a volcanic rock that is formed when lava cools very quickly. It looks like black glass and is often called volcanic glass.

▲ Granite
Fudge's grainy texture is similar to granite. The crystals are large because they grew slowly as the magma cooled slowly. Rhyolite is a kind of granite with smaller crystals and sharp edges.

Crystalline rock

1 Ask an adult to heat 500g of sugar with a little water in a pan. Continue heating until the mixture turns brown, but not black, then add a dash of milk. Leave the mixture to cool.

2 After an hour, you should see tiny crystal grains in the fudge mixture. Once it is completely cool, feel its grainy texture in your hands. The texture is similar to granite.

Glass and bubbles

1 Use greaseproof paper to spread the butter over a metal baking tray. Put in the freezer for at least an hour to get cold. Use oven gloves to take the tray from the freezer.

2 Ask an adult to heat about 500g of sugar with a little water in a saucepan. The sugar dissolves in the water, but the water soon evaporates, leaving only sugar.

3 Stir the sugar mixture with a wooden spoon while it is heating. Make sure that the sugar does not burn and turn black. It should be golden brown.

4 Pour the mixture on to the cool baking tray. After 10 minutes, the glassy and brittle toffee will be cool enough to pick up. Like obsidian, toffee cools too rapidly to form crystals.

◄ Holey honeycomb
To make honeycomb, stir in a spoonful of bicarbonate of soda in Step 3, just before you pour the sugar on to the tray. This will make tiny bubbles of gas in your 'magma'.

Layers on layers

Many of the most familiar rocks around us are sedimentary rocks. Particles of rock, shells and bones of sea creatures settle in layers, and then harden into rock over thousands of years. Rock particles form when other rocks are eroded (worn down) by the weather and are carried away by wind, rivers and ice sheets. They become sediments when they are dumped and settle. Sediments may collect in river deltas, lakes and the sea. Large particles make conglomerates (large pebbles cemented together), medium-size ones make sandstones, and fine particles make clays.

To understand the processes by which sedimentary rocks are made and how they form distinct layers called strata, you can make your own sedimentary rocks. Different strata of rock are laid down by different types of sediment, so the first project involves making strata using various things found in the kitchen. The powerful forces that move parts of the Earth's crust often cause strata to fold, fault or just tilt and you can see this, too. In the second project, you can make a type of sedimentary rock called a conglomerate, in which sand cements pebbles together.

▲ **Cracks in the rockface**
Once formed, sedimentary rocks may be subject to powerful forces caused by the movement of the Earth's crust. Splits in the ground reveal how this strata has folded and cracked.

YOU WILL NEED

large jar, non-hardening modelling material, spoon, flour, kidney beans, brown sugar, rice, lentils (or a similar variety of ingredients of different colours and textures).

Your own strata

1 Press one edge of a large jar into a piece of modelling material, so that the jar sits at an angle. Slowly and carefully spoon a layer of flour about 2cm thick into the jar.

2 Carefully add layers of kidney beans, brown sugar, rice, lentils and flour, building them up until they nearly reach the top of the jar. Try to keep the side of the jar clean.

3 Remove the jar from the clay and stand it upright. The differently coloured and textured layers are like a section through a sequence of natural sedimentary rocks.

Making conglomerate rock

1 Put on a pair of rubber gloves. In an old plastic tub, make up some plaster of Paris with water, following the instructions on the packet. Stir with a fork or spoon.

2 Before the plaster starts to harden, mix some small pebbles, sand and earth into the plaster of Paris. Stir the mixture thoroughly to make sure it is all evenly distributed.

3 Leave the mixture for 10 minutes, until the plaster begins to harden, then take a small lump of it in your hand and mould it into a ball shape to look like conglomerate rock.

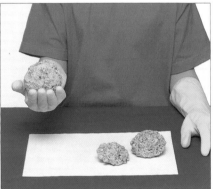

4 Make some more conglomerate rocks in different sizes with different amounts of pebbles in. Place the rocks on a spare piece of paper so that they can harden and dry out completely.

▲ **Natural cement**
Conglomerates in nature can be found in areas that were once underwater. Small pebbles and shells become rounded and cemented together by the water.

◄ **Clues in the cutaway**
The 1.6km deep Grand Canyon, in Arizona, USA, was cut by the Colorado river. The cliff face reveals colourful strata (layers of rock). The strata at the bottom are more than 2,000 million years old. Those at the top are about 60 million years old. Each layer is a different type of rock, suggesting that conditions in this region changed many times in the past. For this reason, sedimentary rock strata can provide valuable clues about the distant history of the Earth.

What's a fossil?

The remains of some plants and animals that died long ago can be seen in rock as fossils. After an animal dies, it may become buried in sediments – rock particles ground down by wind and water. Slowly, over thousands of years, the sediments compact together to form sedimentary rock. The shape or outline of the plant or animal is preserved.

The study of fossils, called palaeontology, tells us much about how life evolved, both in the sea and on the land. Fossils give clues to the type of environment in which an organism lived and can also help to date rocks.

These projects will help you to understand how two types of fossil came to exist. One type forms when sediment settles around a dead animal or plant. It hardens to rock and the plant or animal rots away. This space in the rock is an outline of the dead animal or plant. This is usually how the soft parts of an animal, or a delicate leaf, are preserved. You can make this kind of fossil using a shell. In this case the shell does not decay – you simply remove it from the plaster.

The second project shows you another kind of fossil. Here, the skeleton of a decaying animal is filled with minerals. The minerals gradually become rock. This gives a solid fossil that is a copy of the original body part.

fern

ammonite

▲ Turned to stone

Two common fossils are shown here. Fossils of sea creatures are often found, because their bodies cannot decay completely underwater. Ammonites were hard-shelled sea creatures that lived between 60 million and 400 million years ago. Fern-like fossils are often found in coal.

YOU WILL NEED

Fossil imprint: safety glasses, plastic tub, plaster of Paris, water, fork, strip of paper, paper clip, non-hardening modelling material, shell, wooden board, hammer, chisel.

Solid fossil: spare paper, rolling pin, modelling material, shell, petroleum jelly, paper clip, strip of paper, glass jar, plaster of Paris, water, fork.

How fossils are formed

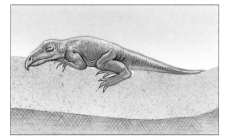

An animal or plant dies. Its body falls on to the sand at the bottom of the ocean or into mud on land. If it is buried quickly, then the body is protected from being eaten.

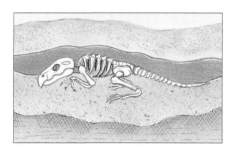

The soft parts of the body rot away, but the bones and teeth remain. After a long time the hard parts are replaced by minerals – usually calcite but sometimes pyrite or quartz.

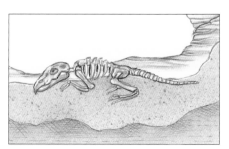

After millions of years the rocks in which the fossils formed are eroded and exposed again. Some fossils look as fresh now as the day when the plant or animal was first buried.

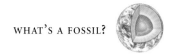

Fossil imprint

1 In a plastic tub, mix up the plaster of Paris with some water. Follow the instructions on the packet. Make sure the mixture is fairly firm and not too runny.

2 Make a collar out of a strip of paper fixed with a paper clip. Use modelling material to make a base to fit under the collar. Press the shell into the clay. Surround the shell with plaster.

3 Leave your plaster rock to dry for at least half an hour. Crack open the rock and remove the shell. You will then see the imprint left behind after the shell has gone.

Solid fossil

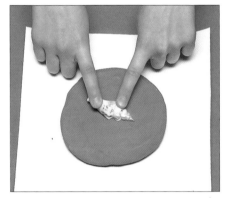

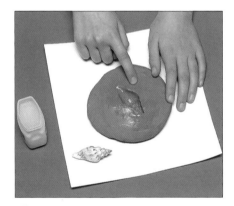

1 Put a spare piece of paper down on your work surface to protect it. Using the rolling pin, roll out some modelling material into a flat circle, roughly 2cm thick.

2 Press your shell, or another object with a distinctive shape, deep into the clay to leave a clear impression. Do not press it all the way to the paper at the bottom.

3 Remove the shell and lightly rub some petroleum jelly over the clay circle, which is now the shell mould. This will help you to remove the plaster fossil later.

4 Use the paper clip to fix the paper strip into a collar for the mould. Mix up some plaster of Paris according to the instructions, pour it in and leave it to set for half an hour.

5 Remove the solid plaster from the mould. In order not to damage them, palaeontologists have to remove fossilized bones or teeth from rock or earth very carefully.

These are the finished results of the two projects. Real fossils are imprints of organisms that lived millions of years ago.

Hard as nails!

The best way to learn about rocks is to look closely at as many different types as you can find. Look at pebbles on the beach and the stones in your garden. You will find that they are not all the same. Collect specimens of different pebbles and compare them. Give each stone an identification number and record where you found it, and its characteristics. A hand lens will help you see more details than can be seen with the naked eye. Look for different colours, shapes and hardness. Ask an adult to take you to a geological museum to compare your stone with the specimens there.

You can try simple versions of tests that geologists use, on the following pages. They will help you identify some samples that you have collected. The first test involves rubbing a rock on to the back of a tile to leave a streak mark. The colour of the streak can give a clue to what minerals are present in the rock. The second test shows you how to discover a rock's hardness by seeing how easily a mineral scratches. Hardness is measured on a scale devised in 1822 by Friedrich Mohs. He made a list of ten common minerals called Mohs' scale, which runs from 1 (the softest) to 10 (the hardest). The hardest natural mineral is diamond, with a hardness of 10. It will scratch all other minerals.

▲ Be a detective
Clean a rock with a stiff brush and water. Stand in plenty of light and experiment to find the correct distance to see the rock's details clearly with a hand lens.

beach pebbles

▲ Wearing away
Look at the different sizes of pebbles on a beach. The constant to-and-fro of the waves grinds the pebbles smaller and smaller. Eventually these particles will form sedimentary rock.

quartz

copper

▲ What is a mineral?
All rocks are made up of one or more minerals. Minerals, such as copper and quartz, are natural, solid, non-living substances. Each mineral has definite characteristics such as shape and colour, that distinguish it from other minerals.

◄ Hidden inside
When mineral-rich water fills a crack or cavity in a rock, veins and geodes form. A geode is a rounded rock with a hollow centre lined with crystals. The beautiful crystal lining is revealed when it is split open. Geodes are highly prized by mineral collectors.

ouside of geode

inside of geode

Streak test

1 Place a tile face down, so that the rough side is facing upwards. Choose one of your samples and rub it against the tile. You should see a streak of colour appear on the tile.

2 Make streaks using the other samples and compare the colours. Rocks made of several minerals may leave several coloured streaks. Try to identify them in your field guide.

Testing for hardness

1 Clean some rock samples with water using a nail brush. Scratch the rocks together. On the Mohs' scale, a mineral is harder than any minerals it can make scratches on.

2 A fingernail has a hardness of just over 2. Scratch each rock with a fingernail – if it scratches the rock, the minerals out of which the rock is made have a hardness of 2 or less.

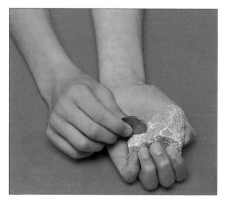

3 Put aside those rocks scratched by a fingernail. Scratch those remaining with a coin. A coin has a hardness of about 3, so minerals it scratches are less than 3.

4 Now scratch the remaining rocks on a glass jar. If any of the rocks make a scratch on the jar, then the minerals they contain must be harder than glass.

5 Put aside any rocks that will not scratch the glass. They are less hard than glass, which measures somewhere between 5 and 6. Try scratching the remainder of the rocks with a steel file (hardness 7) and finally with a sheet of sandpaper (hardness 8).

Testing for minerals

Rocks and minerals are the naturally occurring materials that make up planet Earth. Rocks are used for buildings and many minerals are prized as jewels. Most people think of rocks as hard and heavy, but soft materials, such as sand, chalk and clay, are also considered to be rocks. Different rocks are made up from mixtures of different minerals. The minerals inside a rock form small crystals that are locked together to form a hard solid.

Geologists (scientists who study the Earth and its rocks) use many different methods to identify minerals that make up rocks. These experiments will help you to discover which minerals are in a rock sample. You can also identify rocks with a hand lens or from their hardness.

The acid test demonstrates if a gas is given off by the mineral. The second experiment is used to discover a rock sample's specific gravity. It compares a mineral's density to the density of water. Density measures how compact the particles are that make up a sample. Every mineral has a different density, which means that samples of the same mineral will have the same density.

▲ Weighing up the evidence
These two blocks are the same size and shape, but do not weigh the same. The materials they are made of have different densities.

YOU WILL NEED

vinegar, bowl, spoon, samples of

different stones, hand lens,

reference book.

Acid test

1 Pour some vinegar into a bowl. Drop rock samples into the vinegar. If gas bubbles form, then the rock contains minerals called carbonates (such as calcite).

2 Alternatively you can put a few drops of vinegar on each rock sample. Watch them carefully for clues to what they might be. Chalk, marble and limestone make vinegar fizz.

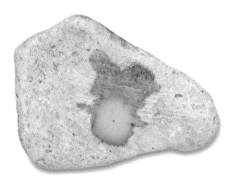

3 Limestone reacts with vinegar. Like chalk and marble, it reacts because it is a type of calcium carbonate. Common rocks such as flint, granite and sandstone are unaffected.

4 Now scratch one sample with another. Harder rocks leave marks on softer ones. Hardness also helps you to identify rocks. Think how difficult it might be to carve the harder ones.

flint   granite

limestone   sandstone

5 Arrange your rocks in order of hardness. Igneous rocks, such as granite, are usually the hardest. Sedimentary rocks, such as sandstone, are usually the softest.

6 Use a lens to examine your rocks. There are sharp crystal minerals in igneous rocks. Metamorphic rocks look smooth and sedimentary rocks have layers and tiny bits in them.

Density or specific gravity test

YOU WILL NEED

mineral or rock samples, accurate weighing scales, notebook, pen or pencil, measuring jug, water.

1 Choose a rock or mineral sample and weigh it as accurately as you can to find its mass. The figure should be in grams. Make a note of the mass in your notebook.

2 Fill a clear measuring jug to the 200ml mark with water. Choose your first rock or mineral sample and carefully place it in the water.

3 Look at the scale on the jug to read off the new water level. Make a note of the level of the water in your notebook. Now subtract 200 from that figure.

4 The new figure is the sample's volume in millilitres. Now divide the mass by the volume. You can use a calculator to do this sum if you wish. This will give you the rock sample's density, or specific gravity.

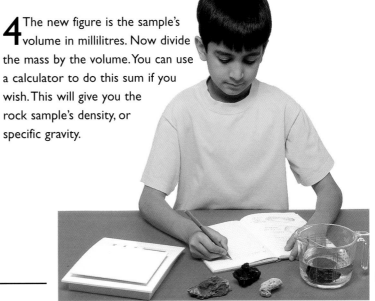

Natural Wonders Close to Home

When forests are cut down, the plants and animal habitats that depend on the trees in those forests are put at risk. This section focuses on the natural habitats near your home to explore the importance of plants, insects and birds in the way nature works on Earth.

What is soil?

Soil is formed from decayed vegetable matter (dead leaves and plants), mineral grains and larger pieces of rock. Creatures, such as earthworms, help the decomposition process by mixing the soil. The process by which rocks are often broken down into smaller pieces is called weathering. Chemical weathering occurs when minerals are dissolved by water. Some minerals break down or dissolve quickly. Others, such as quartz, are not dissolved but stay behind in the soil as stones. The action of burrowing animals, insects and growing plants is called physical weathering. Attrition (grinding down) is another kind of physical weathering and occurs when wind-blown particles rub against each other. This kind of weathering occurs mainly in dry areas, such as deserts. You can see how attrition works simply by shaking some sugar cubes together in a glass jar.

In the first experiment, you can examine what makes up the soil. The second shows you the range of sizes of mineral and rock particles in a soil sample. In the last project, you can find out how sediments form in rivers, lakes and seas. First large and then finer particles of sediment are deposited.

▲ **On the horizon**
Soil occurs in layers, called horizons. There are four main horizons. The top horizon (also known as topsoil) is a layer of fine particles that supports the roots of plants and trees. The next two layers, beneath the topsoil, have larger soil particles. The bottom layer is partly solid rock.

Wormery

1 Cut the top off the large clear plastic bottle, as shown. Place the smaller bottle inside the larger one. Make sure the gap is evenly spaced all the way around the smaller bottle.

2 Fill the gap with layers of soil and sand to within 5cm of the top. Press the soil down lightly. Gently place the worms on top of the soil and cover them with rotting leaves.

3 Cover with black paper. Keep the soil moist. After a few days, remove the paper to see how the worms have tunnelled away from the light and dragged leaves into their burrows.

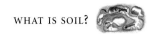

What is in soil?

1 Put on a pair of gardening gloves and place a trowel full of soil into the sieve. Shake the sieve over a piece of paper for about a minute or so.

2 Tap the side of the sieve gently to help separate the different parts of the soil. Are there bits that will not go through the sieve? Can you see if any of the bits are rock?

3 Use a magnifying glass to examine the soil particles that fall on to the paper. Are there any small creatures or mineral grains? Make a note of what you see in your notebook.

Big or small?

YOU WILL NEED

Wormery: large and small plastic bottles, scissors, funnel, gloves, damp soil, sand, six worms, rotting leaves, black paper, sticky tape.

What is in soil?: gloves, trowel, soil, sieve, paper, magnifying glass, notebook, pen.

Big or small?: scissors, large clear plastic bottle, wooden spoon, gravel, earth, sand, water, jug.

1 Use a pair of scissors to cut off the top of a large, clear plastic bottle. Ask an adult to help, if you need to. You can throw away the top part of the bottle.

floating soil and plant fragments

water made cloudy by fine particles of clay

settled mineral particles

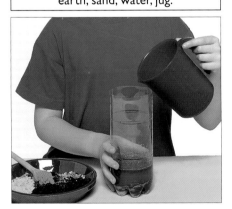

2 Use a spoon to scoop some gravel, earth and sand into the bottom of the bottle. Add water to the mixture until it nearly reaches to the top of the bottle.

3 Stir vigorously to mix the stones, earth and sand with the water. In a river, soil and rock particles are mixed together and carried along by the moving water.

Leave the mixture to settle. You should find that the particles settle into different layers, with the heaviest particles at the bottom and the lightest at the top.

Examining soil

Beneath the ground, the soil teems with life. Worms, slugs, millipedes and beetles live there, feeding on decaying matter. Tiny living creatures, called decomposers, break down everything that remains. Decomposers include microscopic bacteria, fungi, woodlice, mites and small insects. They digest organic material such as dead animals, leaves and plants, and break it down into nutrients. This process, called decomposition, creates a rich fertilizer for plants growing in the soil. As organic material rots, it returns its nutrients or goodness to the soil. The nutrients dissolve in rain water and trickle down to tree and other plant roots below.

The first experiment demonstrates the best conditions for decomposing plants. It shows that plant material decays quickest in warm, moist areas. You can take a closer look at the decomposers themselves in the second project, which shows how to separate creepy-crawlies from the rotting leaves they live in. You could repeat the experiment with leaves from a different area and see if the insects you find are the same.

▲ **Feast for woodlice**

Rotting, in nature, does not happen by itself. Dead leaves are food for decomposers, such as woodlice. They eat the fallen leaves and pass many of the nutrients back into the soil, to be taken up again by the trees' roots.

Watching decay in the soil

YOU WILL NEED

gardening gloves, trowel (optional), two clean plastic containers, soil, dead leaves, water in a watering can, one container lid.

1 Be sure to wear a pair of rubber gloves for this project. Use your hand, or a trowel if you prefer, to fill two plastic containers with plenty of dry soil.

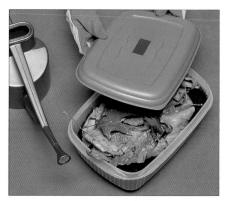

2 Put a layer of dead leaves on top of the soil in one of the containers. Water the leaves and soil thoroughly, then press the lid on to the container to cover it.

3 Place a layer of leaves on the dry soil in the other container. Do not water it and do not cover the container. Store both containers in a dry place.

After a few weeks, the leaves in the wet soil (*above left*) will have begun to rot, while those in the dry soil (*above right*) will have shrivelled.

Studying decomposers

I Rotting leaves are covered in insects and other creepy-crawlies. You can separate them by using a lamp, a funnel and a large jar. Put the funnel inside the jar, as shown.

2 Wearing a pair of gardening gloves, loosely fill the funnel with rotting leaves. Tape a sheet of black paper around the sides of the jar to block out the light.

3 Place the lamp so that it shines on to the leaves. The creatures will move away from the heat and light of the lamp and fall down the slippery funnel into the jar below.

After an hour, there will be several creatures in the jar. Look at them with a magnifying glass and use a field guide to identify them. Then return the creatures to where you found them.

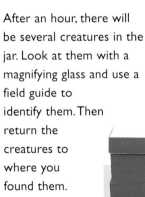

Tree study

There are several kinds of trees. In tropical rainforests, where it is warm and wet all year, most trees are evergreen and keep their leaves all year round. Tropical rainforests are found near the Equator, where there is little difference between the seasons. In countries with a temperate (moderate) climate, deciduous, broad-leaved trees shed their leaves in autumn. Losing leaves reduces evaporation. This helps the tree conserve energy and water when the ground water is frozen, and reduces damage by frost.

Trees can be identified by looking at such characteristics as bark, leaves and flowers, and in autumn by their fruits and nuts, some of which are shown on the right. The size and shape of the trunk and branches can also help to identify a tree, and scientists record the tree's girth by measuring the distance around the trunk at chest height. You can study trees in your garden, a local park or wood following the same checks. Choose an area of mixed woodland with many different trees. Always remember to take an adult with you to keep you safe.

leaf from a plane tree

seedcase from a sycamore tree

hips and leaves from a cockspur thorn tree

a chestnut and its case from a horse chestnut tree

seeds from a lime tree

acorn and its cup from an oak tree

Identifying trees

1 Walk along a path in your chosen area. Try to identify the trees you find there from their general height and shape. Use a field guide to help you.

2 Bark can help you identify some trees. Silver birch bark is smooth and white with dark cracks. Match the bark of different trees with pictures in your guide.

3 Study leaf colours and shapes, and the fruits and seeds of trees. Learn to identify trees with the help of the field guide, and make a record of them in a notebook.

Measuring a tree's height

YOU WILL NEED

Identifying trees: field guide to
local trees, notebook, pen,
coloured pencils.

Measuring a tree's height: metre
ruler, 1m-long stick,
felt-tipped pen.

1 With the metre rule, measure
19m from the tree and push the
stick into the ground. Measure
another metre from the stick and
lie down straight on the ground.

2 Use one eye to line up the top of
the tree with the stick. Get a friend
to mark this point on the stick in the
ground. The height of the tree is 20
times this distance.

Measuring a tree's girth

YOU WILL NEED

sticky tape, string, metre ruler or
tape measure, pen, notebook,
coloured pencils, graph paper,
field guide.

1 Stick a piece of tape on the end
of a piece of string. Wrap the
string around a tree trunk at chest
height. Mark where it meets the tape
with your finger.

2 Lay the string along the ruler to
find the length. This figure is the
girth of the tree. Measure another
tree of the same species. Is its girth
the same? Why might they differ?

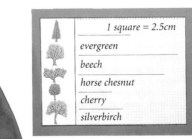

	1 square = 2.5cm
	evergreen
	beech
	horse chesnut
	cherry
	silverbirch

3 Make a chart with
drawings of the
different trees that you
have measured. The
trees with the thickest
trunks are usually older
than those with
slender trunks.

▲ Rings of age

You can clearly see the growth rings
on the trunk of this old oak tree. Each
year the tree grows a new ring of
wood just under the bark.

Looking at bark

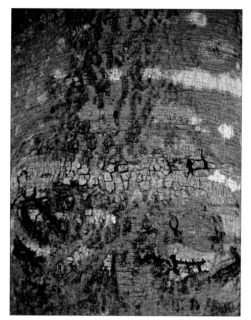

▲ Close-up view

If you look closely at the bark of a tree you can discover many clues about its life. Plants and fungi may be clinging to the surface. There might also be insects and other tiny creatures hiding inside cracks...

YOU WILL NEED

magnifying glass, field guide,

notebook, pencil.

Become a bark detective

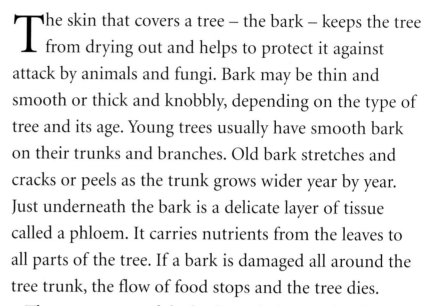

The skin that covers a tree – the bark – keeps the tree from drying out and helps to protect it against attack by animals and fungi. Bark may be thin and smooth or thick and knobbly, depending on the type of tree and its age. Young trees usually have smooth bark on their trunks and branches. Old bark stretches and cracks or peels as the trunk grows wider year by year. Just underneath the bark is a delicate layer of tissue called a phloem. It carries nutrients from the leaves to all parts of the tree. If a bark is damaged all around the tree trunk, the flow of food stops and the tree dies.

The appearance of the bark can help you decide what species (type) a tree is. Different trees have different kinds of bark. A mature beech tree has smooth, thin bark that is about 1cm deep. A redwood tree of the same size has hairy, fibrous bark that is up to 15cm thick. Many conifers, such as pines and spruces, have bark that flakes off. Follow the first two projects and become a bark detective by studying the bark up close and making a collection of your own bark rubbings. The third project will help you estimate the size of a tree.

1 Bark does not stretch, but cracks and peels as a tree grows. Use a magnifying glass to search in the cracks during spring and summer for tiny insects and other creatures.

2 The bark has fallen away from this dead tree revealing the holes chewed by beetle grubs underneath. Some grubs live under the bark for several years.

3 Where the bark is damp, you will often find powdery green patches. These are millions of microscopic plants called algae that live side by side on the bark's surface.

Bark rubbing book

1 Ask a friend to hold a sheet of paper steady against the bark. Rub the side of a crayon over the paper with long, even strokes. Write the name of the tree beside each rubbing.

2 Punch holes into pieces of coloured card and link them with ribbon. Stick your rubbings on to each page. You could include a silhouette of each tree as well.

Measuring the crown

1 Using the compass, walk away from the tree towards north. Ask a friend to call out when you reach the edge of the area covered by the leaves. Place a marker at this point.

2 Repeat for the other seven main compass directions (NE, E, SE, S, SW, W, NW). Measure the distances back to the trunk with a metre ruler and note them down.

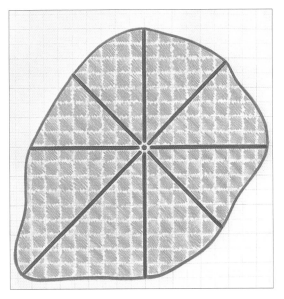

3 Plot your results on a piece of squared paper. Measure 1cm on the paper for each metre on the ground. Draw lines from the centre of the paper, for each compass direction.

What you have sketched and coloured in shows the shape of the area covered by trees leaves and branches (the crown). Count the squares and half squares to find the size of the area of the crown. Do not count part-squares if they are less than a half. Each 1cm square represents 1m. Compare with other trees in the area. Generally, the older the tree, the more likely it will have a larger crown.

Specimen collection

Different kinds of trees grow naturally in different parts of the world. Where they grow depends mainly on climate. Look closely at trees in winter and you will see that even deciduous trees are not completely bare. Each twig has buds along its sides and at the tip. Buds have protective skins with tiny immature leaves and stems curled up inside. When spring sunshine warms the trees, buds begin to grow and swell. Finally they burst open and small leaves emerge. Leaves contain pipes called veins. Water pumps into these veins, making the leaves stiffen and flatten as they grow to full size.

To learn about trees, you can make a collection of dead leaves, cones and bark from each one you study. Do not forget to look for things throughout the year – flowers and buds in spring, seeds and fruit in autumn. Label your collection.

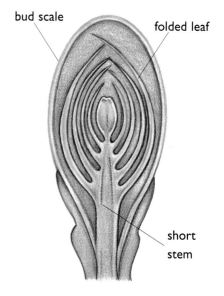

▲ Budding

Buds grow in the centre of a twig between two leaf stems. An unopened bud contains tiny leaves and a shoot that will grow in spring and make the leaf stem longer. The illustration above shows what it looks like inside.

Tree zones

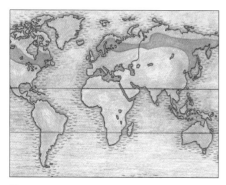

Evergreen conifer trees, such as pine and firs, usually grow where the climate is cold. Long snowy winters are followed by short cool summers, with moderate amounts of rain. Forests of conifers grow in a band across North America, Europe and Asia.

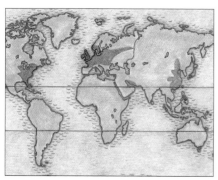

Broad-leaved deciduous trees, such as oak, ash and maple, grow in temperate climates away from hot, dry tropics or the snowy poles. There are more kinds of trees than in a coniferous forest. Temperate forests are found in North America, Europe, Asia and New Zealand.

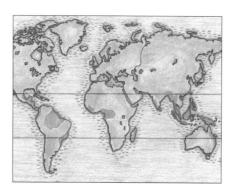

Tropical countries lie close to the Equator. The weather is hot and daylight lasts for 12 hours a day for most of the year. Dense rainforests grow where heavy rain falls almost continuously, such as South America, Africa, Asia and Australasia.

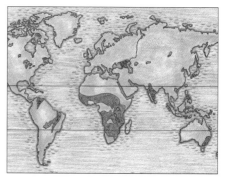

Savanna is a dry, tropical grassland, with some shrubs and bushes. Trees grow alone or in widely spaced small groups. Forests cannot grow because the dry season lasts most of the year. Trees that do grow here are species that can survive for long periods without water.

Collecting specimens

1 How many different leaves and cones can you find? Make sure you note down the name of the tree that each specimen comes from. Start a collection with your friends.

2 To dry and flatten your leaves, place sheets of kitchen paper between the pages of a large and heavy book. Lay your leaves out on the paper on one side only. Close the book.

3 Pile more books on top. Make sure the pile cannot topple over and will not get disturbed. The weight presses the leaves flat while the kitchen paper absorbs moisture.

4 Wait for at least one month until the leaves are flat and dry. Glue them into your notebook or on to sheets of thick paper and make them into a book. Use a field guide to identify each leaf.

5 For bark specimens, only collect bark from dead trees that have fallen over. You can make bark rubbings from living trees. See page 76 for instructions on how to make rubbings.

6 Springtime flowers soon wither and die. These young horse chestnut conkers will last much longer. It is better to take photographs of flowers rather than pick them.

7 You can look at young cones and leaves from the lowest branches of evergreen pines, firs and cedars. Look under these trees for cones that have fallen.

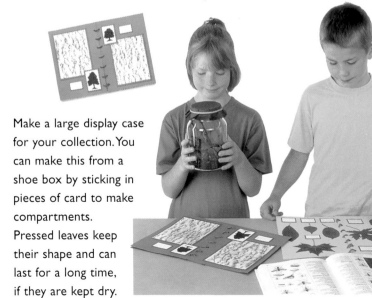

Make a large display case for your collection. You can make this from a shoe box by sticking in pieces of card to make compartments. Pressed leaves keep their shape and can last for a long time, if they are kept dry.

How plants grow

All plants need water to live. They do not take in food as animals do, but make their own using water from the ground and carbon dioxide gas from the air. Water is absorbed through a plant's roots. It travels up through the stem or trunk and on to the leaves, shoots and flowers. The water also carries the nutrients from the soil to all parts of the plant. In the leaves, nutrients and water are used for photosynthesis, the process of making energy from light. Excess water not needed by the plant evaporates back into the air in the form of water vapour in a process called transpiration. You can see how much water vapour is transpired by a plant in the first experiment.

When a seed begins to grow we say that it has germinated. Germination occurs when conditions are warm and moist enough for the seed to swell and split its skin. A tiny root grows downwards and a thin shoot pushes upwards towards the light. The second project shows you how to germinate a seed and help it grow into a tree. Germinating a seed in this way takes about two months.

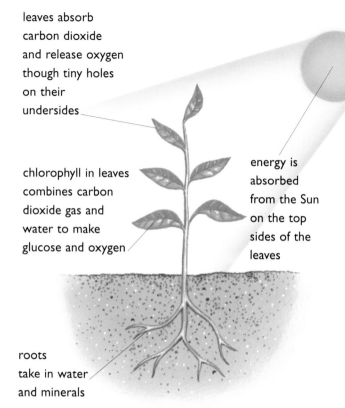

leaves absorb carbon dioxide and release oxygen though tiny holes on their undersides

energy is absorbed from the Sun on the top sides of the leaves

chlorophyll in leaves combines carbon dioxide gas and water to make glucose and oxygen

roots take in water and minerals

▲ Converting energy

Photosynthesis is the process through which plants use the water in the ground and the energy in sunlight to make their food. Leaves take in carbon dioxide and water to make oxygen and glucose (sugar). Glucose flows to all parts of the plant, supplying energy for growth. Oxygen gas escapes through the holes on the underside of the leaves. The oxygen is released back into the air. We need oxygen to breathe.

Survival in the wetlands ▶

Swamps are places where the ground is permanently waterlogged, such as in muddy river estuaries. Most trees cannot survive in swamps because they need fresh water and air around their roots. Some types of mangroves have breathing roots that grow upwards so that their tips are above the surface of the water. Mangrove swamps are home to kingfishers, giant water bugs, crabs, turtles, crocodiles and mudskippers, a type of fish that spends much of its time out of water.

Evaporation in action

1 Water the house plant well using a watering can. Water the plant at the base so the roots can draw the water up. If you water the plant from the top, water just the soil not the plant itself.

2 Place a large, transparent plastic bag over the plant, taking care not to damage the leaves. Tape the bag tightly around the pot. Leave the plant overnight.

◀ Floating water

Trees pass millions of litres of water vapour into the air each day. The vapour forms thick clouds of tiny water droplets over the forest.

3 Have a look at the plant the next day. Inside the bag, water vapour given off by the plant turns back into water. The air inside is warm and moist, like the air in a rainforest.

Germinate an acorn

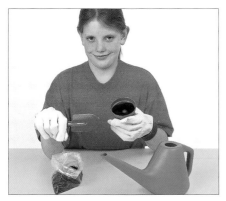

1 Fill the flower pot with compost and bury an acorn just beneath the surface. Put it in a warm place and keep the soil moist. Plant several acorns, as one may not germinate.

2 When a tiny tree starts to grow by itself, it is called a seedling. It needs light and regular watering to grow well. Do not soak the soil with water or the roots will rot and die.

3 Your seedling should grow rapidly for a few weeks and then stop. During winter it will need little water. In spring you can remove the seedling from its pot and plant it outside.

Reaching for light

Look at a leaf and you will see that the top side is usually greener than the underside. This is because there is more chlorophyll, a green substance that traps energy from sunlight. Plants cannot move around to find food as animals do. Instead, they make their own. The green cells work like tiny solar panels, using sunlight to combine carbon dioxide gas from the air and water from the ground. The cells then produce a sugar (glucose) and oxygen gas. This process is called photosynthesis. Without light, plants cannot make their food.

Photosynthesis is the ultimate source of food on Earth, because animals eat plants or other animals that live on plants. Photosynthesis is also the source of all oxygen in our atmosphere. The projects show how plants make special efforts to reach the light. Epiphytes live on high branches in the rainforests to get closer to the light. They need to grow on another plant to survive, but do not draw on the host's resources as a parasite.

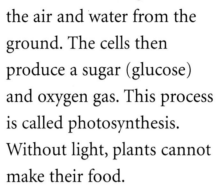

▲ Making energy
Photosynthesis happens near the top surface of a leaf where sunlight has the strongest impact.

▲ Catching the rays
Trees spread their leaves widely to absorb as much energy as they can from sunlight. They use the energy to make a sugary substance called glucose. Liquids flow in and out of leaves through veins. Veins also act like ribs that help to stiffen the leaf and keep it flat.

Grow your own epiphyte

1 Put on a pair of gloves. Wrap moss around one end of the branch or a piece of driftwood. Tie the moss securely in place with cotton thread.

2 Pile some gravel into a sturdy plant pot until the pot is almost full. It needs to be almost full to support the wood. You could use a trowel to help you transfer the gravel.

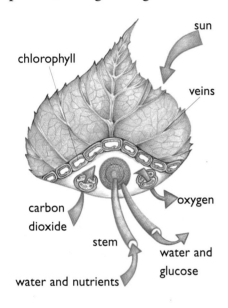

3 Now push the branch or driftwood down into the gravel, until it stands up in the pot without tipping it over. Use a water spray to spray the moss with water.

4 Arrange the epiphytes (available from garden centres) by pressing them gently into the moss. A drop of glue on the base of each plant will help hold it in place.

5 Remember to spray the epiphytes from time to time with water. You could also add few drops of liquid plant food to help the epiphytes to grow.

Epiphytes grow well indoors and make an unusual display. They do not need soil to grow. Instead they wrap their roots around a branch.

Searching for the light

YOU WILL NEED

Grow your own epiphyte:

gardening gloves, sphagnum moss, branch or drfitwood, cotton thread, gravel, plant pot, trowel, water spray, epiphytes, glue, liquid plant food.

Searching for the light: shoe box, scissors, stiff card, sticky tape, black paint, paintbrush, gardening gloves, runner bean, plant pot, compost, water.

1 Watch a plant search for the light as it grows, by making a maze. Cut a hole in the end of a shoe box and stick eight flaps of card inside with sticky tape, as shown here.

2 Paint the inside of the box and lid black all over. The black paint will stop the light that enters through the hole from being reflected around inside the box.

3 Wearing gloves, plant a runner bean in a small pot of compost. Water the soil each day to keep it moist, but not too wet. Some days, no water may be needed.

4 When the plant has a shoot, stand it at the bottom of your maze. Close the lid and place the maze in a sunny spot. Once a day, remove the lid to see if the seedling needs watering.

The plant will find its way through the maze as it steadily moves towards the light. Eventually it will poke out through the hole at the top of the shoe box.

Natural water pumps

When you look at a tree, you only see a part of it. Unseen roots spread out underground as wide as the branches above. These roots anchor a tree in the ground and hold it up against the force of the wind. Roots also help the tree to grow by taking up water and nutrients from the soil through the trunk to the leaves. Trees act like a natural pump – many trees over 50m tall pump hundreds of litres of water a day in order to grow. You can suck a drink up through a straw, but trees cannot do this. They use a method called osmosis to draw the water upwards. The first experiment shows how osmosis works. Water inside the roots (sap) has a higher concentration of sugar than the water outside. The process of osmosis draws water from the soil, where the concentration is low, to inside the root, where concentration is high.

The second experiment uses coloured water to show how water actually travels up a plant's root. All living things are made up of little units called cells. Water can travel through cell walls but sugars cannot. During osmosis, water always moves in a set direction – from the side where there is less sugar dissolved in it to the side where there is more.

▲ Suck it and see

To find out how difficult it is to suck up water, carefully join together straws with sticky tape. The longer the straw, the more difficult it is for you to suck up the drink. The best mechanical pumps can only manage 10m.

How osmosis works

YOU WILL NEED

large potato, ruler, chopping board, peeler, knife, teaspoon, two shallow dishes, water, sugar.

1 You will need a large, smooth potato about 10cm long and 6cm across. Carefully peel the potato over a chopping board to protect the work surface.

2 Cut the peeled potato in half and then slice off the rounded ends. You will now have two round potato slices. Each slice should be about 3cm thick.

3 Use a teaspoon to scoop out a hollow in each potato slice. Place each slice in its own shallow dish and fill the dishes with water to about 1cm in depth.

4 Half fill both hollows with water. Add ½ tsp of sugar to one hollow. Cover and leave the potatoes for one day. (*Dye has been added to the water here to make it show up.*)

5 The level of liquid in the sugary hollow has risen. Osmosis has made more water move into this potato from the dish. The level in the other potato has not risen.

Osmosis in colour

YOU WILL NEED

water, two tall drinking glasses, water-soluble ink or food dye, white carnation, scissors, sticky tape.

1 Pour some water into two tall drinking glasses. Add a few drops of ink or food dye to one of the glasses to give the water a strong, bright colour.

2 Use scissors to split the stem of the carnation lengthwise to about half way up the stem. Bind the stem with tape so that it does not split any further.

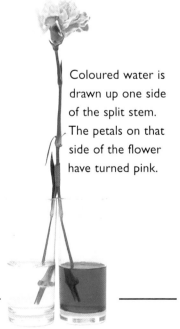

3 Place the glasses side by side on a windowsill, and stand one half of the stem in each glass. Lean the flower against the window if it will not stand up on its own.

4 After a few hours, check to see what has happened. One half of the flower will be coloured with the dye. The other half of the flower will have remained white.

Coloured water is drawn up one side of the split stem. The petals on that side of the flower have turned pink.

Seeds and plant life

Most plants reproduce by making seeds, which sprout and grow into new plants. To produce seeds, plants must be fertilized by pollen, usually from another plant of the same species (kind). Many plants rely on insects such as bees and butterflies to spread pollen. Seeds are mostly spread by animals that eat the fruit produced by plants, and by wind. In some plants, such as those in rainforests, seeds may also be carried by water. The plants in your local area disperse (spread) their seeds in these ways, too. In the company of an adult, you can survey the seeds and plants in your local wood.

YOU WILL NEED

eight pegs, metre ruler or tape measure, string, field guide, pen, notebook, coloured pencils and pens, graph paper.

Carrying out a plant survey

1 Choose a patch of ground to sample and put in a peg. Measure 1m with the ruler and put in another peg. Stretch and tie a piece of string between the pegs.

2 Now measure the remaining sides, pushing in two more pegs and stretching and tying string between them to mark out one square metre.

3 Measure and mark the midpoint of each piece of stretched string with pegs. Stretch more string between these pegs to divide the square into quarters.

4 Use your field guide to help you to identify the plant species growing in each quarter of the square. Do different plants or the same ones grow in each area?

5 Draw a chart on graph paper to record each plant's position. Use different colours for each plant type that you found. Add up the total number of each type of plant.

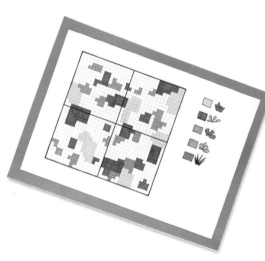

Looking at seed dispersal

1 Look out for nibbled nuts and acorns. These seeds are food for many animals. Collect seeds in a pot, cover with muslin and secure with an elastic band.

2 Visit your local pond or stream to find seeds, such as alders, that are dispersed by water. Use your field guide to identify any seeds you see floating on the water.

3 Maple and sycamore trees have light seeds with wings. As they fall, the wings spin the seed through the air, helping it to fly farther and germinate far from the parent tree.

4 Find a dandelion clock. Plants such as dandelions have very light seeds, each with its own small parachute of fine threads. These are carried away by the wind.

5 Look for the seed capsules of poppies. They are like pepper pots with hundreds of tiny seeds inside. As the wind shakes the capsule, the seeds burst out and scatter widely.

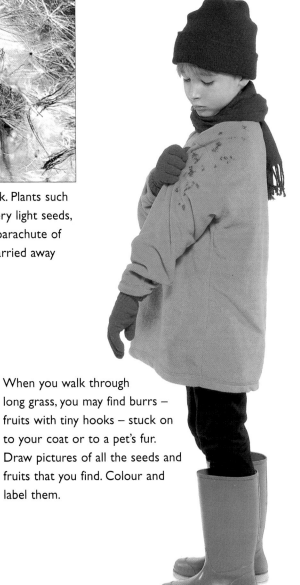

When you walk through long grass, you may find burrs — fruits with tiny hooks — stuck on to your coat or to a pet's fur. Draw pictures of all the seeds and fruits that you find. Colour and label them.

Growing from fruit

There are many kinds of fruits grown in the garden. Some fruits are soft, such as apples and oranges, and others are hard such as acorns and walnuts. Even tough little hawthorn berries and sycamore wings are fruits. Fruits all have seeds protected inside a container. The container may be the soft flesh of a plum or the hard shell of a hazelnut. You can find out the seeds inside different fruits. Some examples are given here. If you want to try others, use fruits bought from your local grocery store since some wild berries are poisonous.

orange

apple

plum

lemon

apricot

◄ **Centre spot**

These fruits are soft, fleshy and sweet. Like most fruits, they have grown from the reproductive ovaries inside female flowers. Open any fruit and inside you will find seeds.

Looking at apple seeds

1 Cut open an apple with a sharp knife. Inside you will find several brown seeds, or pips, in the centre. Use the tweezers to remove as many of the seeds as you want.

2 Use the tweezers to carefully remove the soft outer skin of a seed. Underneath the skin you will find the slippery white seed. Treat it carefully – it is very delicate.

3 Look under a magnifier to see the cotyledon and embryo (at the tip). The cotyledon provides food for the embryo, which will grow into a new root and shoot.

Looking inside a nut

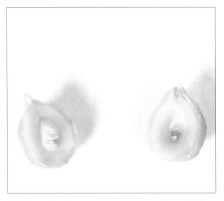

1 Nuts are fruits that have their seeds inside a hard shell. Carefully crack open a hazelnut with a pair of nutcrackers and look for the nut kernel (seed) inside.

2 Use scissors to scrape off the dark outer skin from the kernel. You should then be able to separate the white hazelnut into two halves. Look at these with a magnifying glass.

3 Inside the nut is a tiny embryo. This part grows into roots and a stem. The two larger parts are the cotyledons, which supply energy for the sprouting seed to grow.

How a seed grows

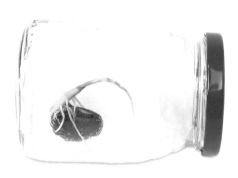

1 Curl blotting paper inside a jar. Push a bean seed halfway down between the paper and the glass. Add water to a depth of 2cm and stand the jar in a light, warm place.

2 When the seed germinates, you will see the root growing downwards. Turn the jar so that the root points to the right. What do you think will happen?

As the root continues to grow, it changes direction so that it is growing downwards again.

Tropical seeds

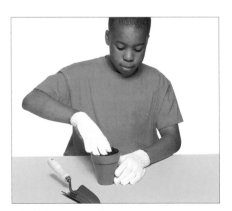

1 An avocado stone is the seed of the avocado plant. Clean off any flesh left on the stone and then carefully push three cocktail sticks into the stone, as shown above.

2 Fill a jar with water and suspend the stone so that it just touches the waterline. Keep the jar in a warm, shady place and top up the water regularly.

3 When roots begin to grow downwards, plant the stone in a pot filled with compost. Place the pot where the air is warm and humid and wait for your seedling to grow.

Life in the forest

People who live in forests build their homes from materials found in the forest. In South America, the Yanomami tribe's large, round huts are made with trees bent into a dome shape, lashed with vines and thatched with palm leaves. The Yanomami sleep on the roof in hammocks made of woven grasses, slung from the rafters. Scientists working in rainforests sometimes build temporary shelters with branches. You can build a shelter by following these instructions, but you may need the help of an adult. When looking for branches to make your shelter with, take an adult with you. Collect the branches from your garden or a public area. Do not cut them from trees – always gather them from the ground, where they have fallen naturally.

▲ Temperate forests

Beech, ash and oak grow in this northern European forest. Birds and squirrels live in the trees. Bluebells and wood anemones grow on the forest floor. Worms, moles and badgers burrow underground. Larger animals include deer, wild pigs and bears.

▲ Conifer forests

Hemlocks, cypresses and giant redwoods grow in conifer forests in North America. Woodpeckers and chipmunks search for food in the trees. Ferns grow on the forest floor. Moose and beavers live near lakes and black bears scavenge for food.

▲ Trees in the savanna

The African savanna is dotted with drought-resistant trees, such as baobabs (bottle trees), and acacias. Herds of zebra, antelope and gazelles feed on grass. Taller giraffes and elephants can reach up into the trees for fresh leaves.

▲ Tropical rainforest

Many trees and climbing plants live in tropical rainforests such as the Amazon of South America. Monkeys and brightly coloured birds live high up in the trees, where there is light and food. Dense rotting vegetation covers the ground.

Build a shelter

1 Lash the ends of two sturdy branches together with rope or string. Stand the branches upright to make an A-frame. You could tie the A-frame to a tree for extra support.

2 Lash two more branches together. Stand them upright about 2m from the first A-frame. Place a lighter branch on top to make a ridge pole and lash it in place.

3 Attach two guy-ropes or strings to each of the A-frames and peg the guy-ropes securely into the ground. Now throw a tarpaulin over the ridge pole to form the roof.

4 Attach guy-ropes or strings to eyeholes in the corners of the tarpaulin and peg them securely into the ground. Stretch the tarpaulin tight to make the roof.

5 Thread string through the eyeholes on opposite sides of the ground sheet to make the sheet into a sort of tube. Push two poles inside the sheet, one on each side.

6 Pull the two poles apart to make a stretcher shape that will fit inside the shelter. This will form the hammock so that you will be able to rest off the ground.

7 Wedge the stretcher inside your shelter, so that the poles rest on the outside of the upright A-frames. Make sure your hammock is secure and will not slip down the poles.

Now it's time to try out your hammock and take a well-earned rest!

Soil erosion

All around the world, rainforests are being cut down at an alarming rate. At the beginning of the 1900s, tropical forests covered about twice the area they do today. Experts estimate that an area of rainforest about the size of England is lost each year. One of the main reasons for this is logging – the felling of trees for timber. Many rainforest trees are made of valuable hardwoods, such as teak and mahogany, which are used for building houses and making furniture. Trees are also cleared to create roads and new pasture for cattle.

The roots of trees and other plants help to hold forest soil together. When the trees are felled, the soil is left bare. In heavy rainfall, the earth is washed away, just as it is in the first project. However, when forests are left alone, they sustain themselves indefinitely, recycling water and nutrients from the soil. You can see how this works by growing a mini-jungle. The bottle or jar reproduces the warm, moist conditions and constant high temperatures of a rainforest. The plants recycle their own moisture so they rarely need watering.

▲ **Vanishing forests**
This illustration shows the effects of deforestation. Tree roots help to hold the soil in place and leaves absorb the force of falling rain. When forests are cut down, soil is washed away and exposed earth dries up and hardens.

> ### YOU WILL NEED
>
> potted plant, two plastic cups,
>
> plant pot, compost or soil, two
>
> watering cans.

Looking at soil erosion

1 Fit the potted plant into the neck of one of the plastic cups. Fill the empty plant pot with compost or soil. Place the pot into the neck of the other plastic cup.

2 Pour water on to the potted plant and into the pot of soil. What happens? You will find that water passes more quickly through the pot without the plant.

Water passing through the pot without the plant is muddy because more soil has been washed through. Water passes more slowly through the pot with the plant. It will trickle through almost clear.

Plant a mini-jungle

1 Wash out your bottle or jar to make sure it is clean. Place handfuls of gravel into the bottom of the bottle, to make the lowest layer of the mini-jungle.

2 Mix a little charcoal with the potting compost. Add a deep layer of compost mixture on top of the gravel and then smooth out the soil so that it is level.

3 Make some quite large holes for the plants in the soil with a spoon or trowel. Then gently lift the plants out of their pots and lower them into the holes you have made.

4 Firm the soil down around the base of each plant. You can use a spoon or a trowel to do this if you find it difficult to reach that far with your fingers.

5 Mist the plants and soil quite thoroughly with water from a plant sprayer, or using a watering can with a sprinkler attachment. This is your tropical rain!

6 Put the lid on the bottle or jar, and your mini-jungle is complete. The water you have sprayed is recycled inside the bottle or jar, so you will not need to water your jungle often. Moisture from the plants condenses on the sides of the bottle or jar. It will then drip down into the soil, to be reused.

The balance of life

Life on Earth is a vast jigsaw of plant and animal activity. The world can be split into vegetation regions according to the kind of plants that thrive there. Scientists often break down the vegetation regions into smaller units, such as tropical rainforests or freshwater lakes. They might go further to identify individual trees or a pond. Each unit, where the creatures living there interact with each other, is called an ecosystem.

An ecosystem is a community of living things, or organisms, that all depend on each other. An aquarium like the one in the project is a miniature freshwater ecosystem. All plants need particular conditions of soil and climate to survive. Animals also survive by adapting to and interacting with their surroundings and the local climate.

If a particular species from an ecosystem is removed, the existence of other living things is threatened. If the plants on which a certain caterpillar feeds are destroyed, the caterpillars die. Eventually, the birds that feed on the caterpillars and the foxes that feed on the birds would starve.

▲ Building an ecosystem

When there is enough warmth and moisture in an area of bare, rocky land, simple plants grow. The first to take hold are mosses and lichens. They are followed by tough grasses, which hold the soil together. As they die and rot, they add nutrients to the soil, preparing it for bigger plants to grow. Soon there is enough to support small shrubs and tough trees, such as pines, and eventually deciduous trees such as oaks. This process is called vegetation succession. It would take about 200 years for deciduous woodland to evolve from the moss and lichen stage.

Feeding habits ▶

Humans and animals depend on other living things for food. This picture shows how this food chain or web works. A grasshopper eats a leaf of grass, a thrush may eat the grasshopper and a kestrel may eat the thrush. When the kestrel dies, bacteria break its body down and add nutrients to the soil so that new plants can grow. Herbivorous animals eat plants only. Carnivores are meat eaters, and omnivores eat both animals and plants. Plants make their own food from sunlight, and so are called autotrophs (self-feeders).

Make your own aquarium ecosystem

YOU WILL NEED

gravel, net, plastic bowl, jug, water, aquarium tank, rocks and pieces of wood, water plants, pondwater, water animals.

1 Put the gravel in a net. Rinse it in a plastic bowl of water or run it under the cold water tap in the sink. This will discourage the formation of green algae.

2 Spread the gravel unevenly over base of the tank to a depth of about 3cm. Add rocks and pieces of wood. These give surfaces for snails to feed on.

3 Fill the tank to about the halfway mark with tap water. Pour the water gently from a jug to avoid disturbing the landscape and churning up the gravel.

4 Add some water plants from an aquarium centre. Keep some of them in their pots, but take the others out gently. Then root them in the gravel.

5 Now add a jugful of pondwater. This will contain organisms, such as *daphnia* (water fleas), which add to the life of your aquarium. You can buy pondwater in a garden centre.

6 Add a few water animals you have collected from local ponds, such as tadpoles in frog spawn or water snails. Take care not to overcrowd the aquarium.

7 Place the tank in bright light, but not in direct sunlight. You can watch the plants in the tank grow. Keep the water clean by removing dead matter off the gravel every few weeks.

Animal tracks and footprints

Wild creatures in the forest usually run away when humans approach. However, you can learn a lot about birds and other animals by looking at their tracks. You could go to a wood with an adult to hunt for animal tracks in soft or wet ground. The banks of streams and rivers are often criss-crossed by prints from animals who have gone there to drink.

Different groups of animals (mammals, birds, reptiles and amphibians) leave different tracks. The first project shows you how to look for these prints. Tracks give clues about the size and weight of the animal. They also show how animals move – whether they run, hop, slide or slither. Large, heavy birds for example, such as geese, waddle along – shifting their weight from side to side. Their prints show that they place one foot in front of the other and slightly to the side, rather like the way humans walk. Small birds, such as tits and finches, hop along on thin legs and feet. They leave tracks of tiny prints running side by side. Draw the prints or take a photograph and record in a notebook the date and place, ground conditions and other observations. The second project shows you how to make casts of the most interesting footprints.

▲ **Out and about**
Study the tracks that you have found very carefully. What do they tell you about the way the animal that made them moved – did it hop, run or waddle? Use a field guide to animal tracks to help you identify the animals that left them.

> ### YOU WILL NEED
> magnifying glass, camera, notebook, pencil, field guide.

Animal tracks

1 When you find a footprint, count the number of toes. Can you see any claws? A fox's paw is rounded, with four toes and claws. Take photos or make drawings of animal tracks you see.

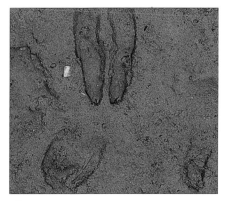

2 Deer have narrow, split hooves with just two toes. They leave deep tracks because they walk with all their weight on their toes, rather than evenly spread throughout their feet.

3 Most birds have long, spindly feet, with either three or four toes. All ducks and some wading birds have webbed feet. The web shows up in the outline of the print.

Footprint cast

YOU WILL NEED

protective gloves, field guide, card,

paper clip, plaster of Paris, water,

mixing bowl, spoon, trowel,

scrubbing brush, paintbrush,

paints or varnish, water pot.

1 Find a clear animal track either in sand or dry mud. Remove any loose twigs or leaves around the print. (Remember to wear gloves if you are working in soil.)

2 Look for bird footprints in wet sand or mud. Tracks show the size of the bird that made it and what group of birds it belongs to. Use a field guide to identify the bird that made the print.

3 Bend a strip of card into a ring large enough to fit around the print and secure the card ring with a paper clip. Place the ring over the print.

4 Mix the plaster of Paris with a little water in a bowl, according to the instructions on the packet. Stir the mixture until it is a thick and even paste with no lumps.

5 Carefully spoon enough plaster of Paris on to the print to cover it completely. After 15 minutes the cast will be dry enough for you to pick it up.

6 Use a trowel to prise the cast loose. Carefully peel away the paper ring. Clean up the cast by brushing off any loose soil or sand with a scrubbing brush.

7 Allow the plaster cast to dry for 24 hours. After this you could paint or varnish the cast. Try painting the raised footprint one colour and the background another colour.

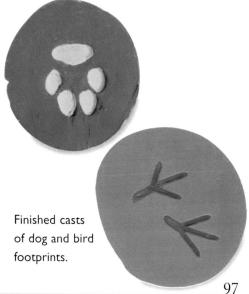

Finished casts of dog and bird footprints.

Searching for insects

Insects make up three-quarters of all animal species (kinds) on the Earth. Insects are everywhere so they are easy to find. The best place to start is your garden or a local park. If there is a good range of plants, up to 300 species of beetles can be found in a very small area, such as gardens. There may be up to 200 kinds of flies, 90 different bugs and many species of bees, ants, wasps, moths and butterflies.

To identify the species living in a particular area, scientists mark off a square, and search all the places where creatures hide – under leaves, stones and logs, and in tiny crevices in trees. Scientists may leave pitfall traps in the ground, or hang traps in the trees. You can find creatures locally using the type of trap demonstrated in the first project. The second project shows you how to make a simple pooter, that enables you to collect insects without harming them. Wear gloves when handling insects as some may sting or bite. Always take an adult out with you.

▲ Feet tasters

The housefly has taste sensors on its feet. It sucks up its liquid through spongy mouthparts as soon as it lands.

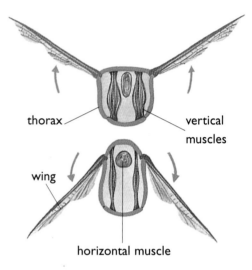

▲ How insects fly

Insects have no muscles in their wings. Instead the wings are hinged to the insect's thorax. They move up and down as the thorax changes shape. As the roof of the thorax is pulled down, the wings flick up. As the ends of the thorax are pulled in, the wings flick down.

Pitfall trap

1 If you have a garden, ask an adult to show you a place where you can dig a small hole. Use a trowel to dig a hole in damp earth, large enough for the jar to fit in.

2 Place the jar in the hole. Firm the earth back around the sides of the jar with your hands. Put small, fresh leaves in the bottom of the jar for minibeast bait.

3 Place some small stones around the trap and balance a large flat stone or tile on top, to prevent the minibeast trap from filling up with rain. Leave it overnight.

4 In the morning, remove the jar. Place a piece of muslin over the top and secure it with an elastic band. Study any minibeasts you have caught using a magnifying glass.

5 Use a field guide to identify the minibeasts you have caught. When you have finished, remember to release the creatures near to where you found them.

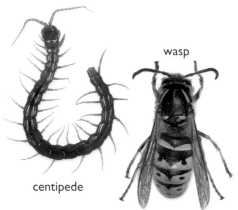

wasp

centipede

▲ Show a leg

Centipedes, like insects, are members of the arthropod group. They have many legs, one pair on each body segment. Adult insects, such as this queen wasp, have bodies in three main sections and six legs. Most also have wings.

Make a pooter

YOU WILL NEED

Pitfall trap: gardening gloves, trowel, glass jar, small fresh leaves, small stones, large flat stone or tile, muslin, elastic band, magnifying glass, field guide.

Make a pooter: small plastic bottle, scissors, non-hardening modelling material, wide bendy straws, small piece of muslin, elastic band, sharp pencil.

1 Cut off the bottom of the plastic bottle. Roll out one large and one small ball of modelling material. Flatten out the large ball and mould it over the bottom of the bottle.

2 To make a filter, cut a short piece of straw. Secure a piece of muslin around the straw with an elastic band. Push the other end through the small lump of modelling material.

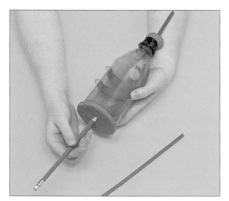

3 Fit the filter into the neck of the bottle by moulding the modelling material. Make a hole in the bottom flap with a sharp pencil. Fit a long straw into the hole you have made.

4 Look for a small insect to study. (Big insects would get damaged.) Aim the end of the long straw over the insect. Suck on the short straw to draw the insect safely into the pooter.

5 When you have finished studying your insect, take it back to where you found it. To release the insect, carefully remove the bottom flap and shake the insect out.

What is an insect?

Birds, reptiles and mammals all have internal skeletons to provide a framework for their bodies. Insects are different – they have skeletons on the outside. Their soft body parts are protected by a hard case called an exoskeleton. This forms a waterproof barrier around the insect. It prevents the insect from drying out and air from passing through. Unlike birds and mammals, insects are cold-blooded animals. This means the temperature of an insect's body is about the same as its surroundings. To warm up, an insect basks in the sunshine. When it gets too hot, it moves into the shade.

Insects are fragile. It can be difficult to pick them up and examine them without harming them. When studying insects, use a notebook to record what you see. Write down the date, time, weather conditions and place where you found the insect. Use a field guide to help you make an identification. The projects here show you how to keep a record of the insects that you see. Look at the mouthparts and antennae. Think about the shape of the insect's body. Is it short or long? Does the insect have hard wing cases, or long legs?

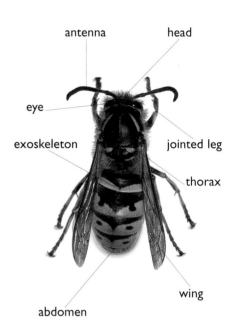

antenna   head
eye
exoskeleton   jointed leg
thorax
wing
abdomen

▲ Wasp sections

The bodies of adult insects have three sections – head, thorax and abdomen. Like this wasp, each section is made of small plates that fit together at flexible joints. The head carries the mouth parts, antennae and eyes. The legs and wings are attached to the thorax. The abdomen contains the reproductive organs and part of the digestive system.

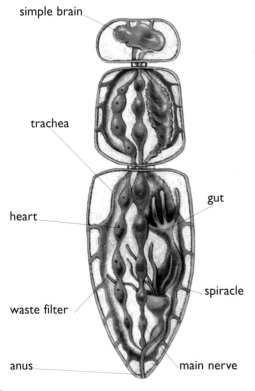

simple brain
trachea
heart
gut
waste filter
spiracle
anus
main nerve

◀ Inside the insect

An insect's internal systems are protected by its hard exoskeleton. This diagram shows the main systems separated out and coloured to make them clear. The nervous system (purple) sends messages from the senses to the brain. In the respiratory system (grey), air enters the body through tiny holes along each side of the insect's body, called spiracles. Pipes called tracheae carry the air to other parts of the body. In the circulatory system (red) several hearts, arranged in a row, pump blood around the body. The digestive system (green, orange) processes food.

Drawing insects

1 Find an insect and use the magnifying glass to study it closely. Start by drawing three ovals to show the head, the thorax and the abdomen of the insect.

2 Can you see the insect's legs? Copy them on your drawing. Now copy the size and shape of the insect's antennae. Draw in the eyes and add the outline of the wings.

3 Now draw any markings that you notice on the insect's body and wings (if it has them). Finish off your drawing by colouring it in as accurately as you can.

Insect survey

1 Find an area of long grass. Wearing gloves, use the tent pegs, a measuring tape and string to mark out a square measuring one metre on each side.

2 What insects can you find inside the square? Use a collecting jar and a magnifying glass to study them. Write down what you have found in a notebook.

3 Now mark out a square metre in a different place. Try an area with flowers or a hedge. You may find aphids and ladybirds on plant stems, and shieldbugs under leaves.

4 Move a fallen log to see what kinds of insects live underneath. Make sure you wear gloves to protect your hands. You may find beetles under logs and woodlice and earwigs under bark.

5 Still wearing gloves, carefully look under some stones. What kinds of creatures prefer this dark, damp habitat? You may find worms, snails, ground beetles or an ants' nest.

Use your field guide to identify your finds. How many different species did you find in each area? Make a chart to record the results of your survey.

Studying insect life

▲ Insect pollination

This wasp is visiting a flower to feed on its sugary nectar. It sucks up the nectar with its tongue to feed the larvae (young) in its nest. As the wasp reaches into the centre of the flower, pollen from the flower rubs off on the insect's body. This is then carried by the wasp to next flower.

Woods are great places to go insect watching. Trees offer food and shelter from the weather so are an ideal habitat for insects. The number of insects you find may depend on the season. In spring, wild flowers bloom and attract insects. In summer, the woods offer insects sunny clearings and cool shade. Choose a large tree and make a survey of all the insects you can find on a single branch. Make a tree trap to catch insects active at night.

Many insects depend on plants, but many plants depend on insects too. Insects help to pollinate plants by carrying pollen from the same plant to another of its species. Many plants have pink, red or orange flowers because these are the colours that butterflies see well. Other flowers have special markings called nectar guides, leading from the base of the petals. Some show up only in ultraviolet light. Insects such as bees have eyes that are sensitive to this light and they follow these guides to the middle of the flower.

Human vision

Insect vision

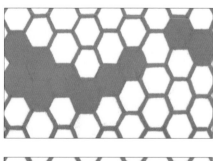

◀ Seeing is believing

Insect vision is very different from ours. Experts think each lens of an insect's compound eye sees a small part of a scene. This gives a mosaic-like view that is built up into a bigger picture. These diagrams compare how we see a moving insect and what experts think an insect sees. An insect can sense tiny movements our eyes would hardly notice because they have many more lenses that are affected.

Make a tree trap

1 Using a pair of sharp scissors, carefully cut the plastic bottle in half widthways. Ask an adult to help you to do this if you find it too difficult.

2 Turn the neck half of the bottle around and push it inside the bottom half. Now tape the two halves of the bottle together using sticky tape.

3 Cut a long piece of string. Loop the string around the open end of the trap and secure it with a knot. Place a small piece of ham inside the trap as insect bait.

4 Carefully tie the trap along the branch of a tree, or hang the trap down underneath the branch. Leave the trap out overnight. Go back the next morning to check it.

5 Use your field guide to identify the insects that you have caught. Record your findings in a notebook. Release the insects when you have identified them.

Life on a branch

1 Spread out the white sheet below a branch. Shake the branch to dislodge the insects on to the sheet. If the branch is high, tap it with a stick. Be sure not to damage the tree.

2 Sweep the insects that drop on to the sheet into collecting jars for you to study. Use a paintbrush to carefully transfer the insects without harming them.

Use a field guide to identify the insects. Try surveying another type of tree. Make a chart, as above, to show the different species found on the different trees.

Insects in disguise

Most insects try to escape from predators by flying away. But it is even better not to be seen at all. Insects that hunt other creatures also need to be invisible to creep up unnoticed on their prey. Many insects have special colours and patterns on their bodies to help them look like leaves, seeds, twigs or stones. These natural disguises are known as camouflage.

Stick insects change their body colour to match their surroundings and so remain hidden almost anywhere. Their long slender bodies and stick-like legs make them hard to see among twigs and leaves. Stick insects are easy to look after at home. You can buy them at some pet shops. Try the test opposite to find out more about camouflage.

You could look outside for ways in which insects disguise themselves. The last project shows you how to attract insects such as butterflies and wasps by planting flowers and herbs. Remember to ask permission from an adult before you start.

▲ **Hidden hunter**
Insects are attracted by the bright colours and sweet scent of flowers. This wasp is almost the same colour as the flower it is feeding on.

YOU WILL NEED

Camouflage test: scissors, light and dark green paper, two cardboard boxes, sticky tape, stick insects, paintbrush, privet or ivy leaves, kitchen paper, muslin, non-hardening modelling material, notebook, coloured pencils.

Rearing stick insects: earth, small tank or large jar, privet or ivy leaves, glass of water, sticks, stick insects, kitchen paper.

Plant a window box: gardening gloves, window box or large tub, earth, compost (optional), packet of wild flower seeds, watering can, notebook, pencil, field guide.

▲ **Prickles and bristles**
A pair of giant prickly leaf insects with the green female (*right*) and the smaller male (*left*). The wings of the male are folded along its back. The safest way to pick up leaf or stick insects is by placing your fingers on each side of the body.

Camouflage test

1 Cut pieces of coloured paper to line the insides of the cardboard boxes. Make one box light green and the other dark green. Attach the paper with sticky tape.

2 Transfer your stick insects with a paintbrush to the light green box. Add leaves and damp kitchen paper. Cover with muslin weighted at the corners with modelling material.

3 Leave the box in a light place for a day. Record the insects' colour with coloured pencils. Put the insects in the darker box. After a day, check to see if they have changed colour.

Rearing stick insects

1 Put a layer of earth in the bottom of a tank or a large jar with a tight-fitting lid with small air holes. Add privet or ivy leaves in a glass of water, some sticks and your stick insects.

2 Put some wet kitchen paper in a corner so that the insects have enough moisture. Remember to replace the paper regularly. Ask the pet shop if your insects need anything else.

Plant a window box

1 Wearing gloves, fill a window box or large tub with earth. You could add some compost to the earth and mix it in. The container should be about three-quarters full of earth.

2 Scatter wild flower seeds over the soil. You can buy seeds such as daisy and bird's-foot trefoil at a nursery. Do not dig up wild plants. Cover the seeds with more earth.

3 The seedlings will come up in a few weeks. Water the young plants regularly. As the plants grow, record in your notebook which insects visit and feed on them.

Insects to watch

As insects eat they leave behind damaged plants and other signs of feeding. Sometimes these signs are easier to spot than the insects themselves. Look in a small area, such as a fallen log, a shrub or a bush. Hundreds of insects will be near, but most are small and wary. Discover the eating habits and preferences of different insects in the first project.

Look for freshwater insects such as beetles and bugs in ponds or streams. Spring and summer are good times to look, because the young insects turn into adults at these times. You could even make a small pool for insects in your garden. Ask a responsible adult if you may dig the pond. To catch water insects you will need a net, which you can make easily yourself. When you catch insects at the pond, take an adult with you for safety. Approach the water quietly to disturb the wildlife as little as possible. Different insects live in various places in the pond or stream. Some live near the surface, while others swim near the bottom. Gently lift up stones and pebbles to find the creatures that lurk on the underside. Always replace them carefully so that you disturb the habitat as little as possible.

▲ **Mmm, my favourite ...**
Most plant-eating insects prefer one particular food and may eat only a part of that food plant. Some insects leave ragged holes in leaves. Aphids and other bugs leave brown or yellow lines on crops when they suck out the sap.

Food samples

YOU WILL NEED

stiff card, pair of compasses and pencil, scissors, four garden sticks, small samples of food (such as jam, meat, cheese and fruit), notebook, field guide.

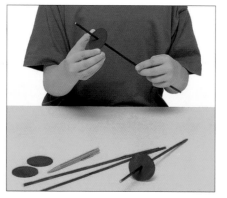

1 Make four circles on the card with the compasses. Cut them out. Use the point of the compasses or a pencil to make holes in the centres of the circles. Push the sticks through the holes.

2 Plant the sticks in the ground. Push the food samples on the sticks, so they rest on the circles. Do insects prefer certain foods? Are there more insects around at different times of day?

Insect pool

1 Wear gloves when you are making your insect pool. Dig a hollow in the ground with the trowel. The hole should be big enough to fit an old plastic bowl inside.

2 Place the bowl in the hollow and press it down firmly. Spread gravel on the bottom and put in the water plants. Place stones arond the edge of the bowl and inside it.

3 Then fill the bowl with water, using a watering can. Your pool is now finished and ready for occupation. Insects and other animal life will soon be attracted to the pool.

Make a pond net

YOU WILL NEED

Insect pool: gardening gloves, trowel, plastic bowl, gravel, water plants, large stones, watering can.

Make a pond net: wire, thin sock, pliers, long pole or broom handle, jubilee clip from a hardware shop, screwdriver, jug, empty plastic ice-cream container, magnifying glass, field guide.

1 Begin your pond net by threading wire in and out through the top of a thin sock. You may need to use a pair of pliers to bend the wire into a circle.

2 Use the pair of pliers to twist the ends of the wire together to make the net secure. Ask an adult to help if you need to. Now position the net at the end of a long pole.

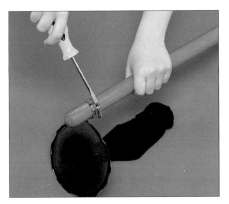

3 Carefully thread the jubilee clip over the pole and push the twisted wires under the clip, as shown above. Tighten the clip using a screwdriver. Ask an adult to help you do this.

4 Down at the pond, capture insects by sweeping your net gently through the water. Lightly tap the stems of plants to knock other insects into your net.

5 Empty a jug of pond water into a container. Empty your net into it. Study the creatures you have caught. Tip the water and creatures back into the pond when you have finished.

Moths and butterflies

All butterflies and moths go through a metamorphosis (change). They start as caterpillars then, as pupae, encase themselves in a cocoon, where a remarkable change takes place and they finally emerge as adults. Caterpillars feed on leafy plants, such as grasses and nettles. Adult moths and butterflies gather on plants with nectar-bearing flowers. As you will see from the projects here, bright lights and a mixture of fruit and sugar will bring moths fluttering. Some butterflies have wings with warning colours. The markings tell predators that they are poisonous to eat. Other butterflies are harmless, but mimic (copy) poisonous species. Their colours fool predators into avoiding them as well. The best way to attract butterflies is to plant a butterfly garden. Choose plants that bloom at various times of the year.

▲ Beating around the bush
The sweet-smelling purple buddleia is a popular plant with butterflies and so has gained the nickname butterfly bush. Butterflies attracted to buddleia include small tortoiseshells (*shown here*), peacocks, painted ladies, commas and red admirals.

▲ Antennae ID
You can tell a butterfly from a moth by looking at the antennae (feelers). Many butterflies have antennae with clubbed tips, like this Swallowdale. Moths' antennae vary but most are straight or feathered.

Torchlight attraction

1 Wearing gloves, dig a small hole in the garden with a trowel. Do this in daylight and remember to ask an adult's permission first before you start to dig.

2 Check that your torch fits inside the hole. At dusk turn on the torch and put it inside the hole. Fill any gaps with earth to hold the torch securely in position.

3 Step back and watch the moths flutter around the light. You could try taking flash photographs of the insects with a camera. How did your photos turn out?

Sweet moth feast

1 Begin by measuring out about 500g of brown sugar with a spoon into your scales or a measuring bowl. Pour the measured sugar into your mixing bowl.

2 Add the overripe fruit to the mixing bowl and mash it with a fork. Keep mashing until the fruit has become a pulp. Add some warm water until the mixture becomes runny.

3 Paint the mixture on to a tree trunk or fence post. Return when it is dark. Take a torch to help you see the moths feeding and a field guide to help you to identify them.

Butterfly garden

YOU WILL NEED

Torchlight attraction: gardening gloves, trowel, small torch, camera.

Sweet moth feast: brown sugar, spoon, weighing scales, mixing bowl, soft over-ripe fruit, fork, warm water, paintbrush, torch, field guide.

Butterfly garden: seeds or young plants, gloves, trowel, rake, watering can, notebook, pencil, field guide.

1 First you need to grow some plants from seed – or buy young plants. Wearing a pair of gloves, dig over your chosen patch of earth with a trowel.

2 Break up any large clods of earth with a rake or trowel. Now start to rake over the top of your plot so that the earth is evenly spread and crumbly.

3 Dig several small holes for your plants with the trowel. Place the plants in the holes and press the earth down firmly with gloved hands around the base of each plant.

4 Water the plants well. They will need to be watered regularly through the spring and summer. The sun will scorch wet leaves during the day, so water your plants at dusk.

5 Record which butterflies you see visiting your flowers. A field guide will help you to identify them. Which species prefer which flowers? And which is the most popular plant?

Watching a caterpillar grow

These projects show you how to prepare a home for caterpillars. Look for caterpillars on plants where you see half-eaten leaves – they may be hiding on the undersides. Take some of these leaves with the caterpillars you find. Use a field guide to identify the species you have found and which plants they prefer. Try not to touch caterpillars directly with your fingers, as some species may sting. Pick them up with a paintbrush, or encourage them to climb on to a leaf. Carry them in a jar. At home, keep caterpillars out of direct sunlight, in a moist, cool place. Try not to disturb them. Clean the box regularly and replace old leaves with fresh ones.

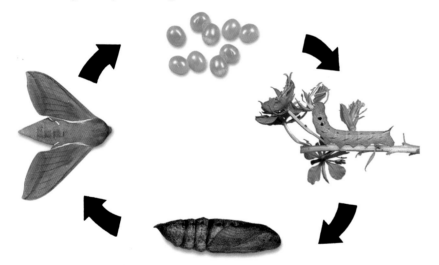

Keeping caterpillars

YOU WILL NEED
scissors, cardboard box, strong sticky tape, muslin or netting, non-hardening modelling material, rubber gloves, fresh leaves, kitchen paper, collecting jar containing caterpillars, ruler, pencil, notebook, field guide, coloured pencils.

◄ **Complete metamorphosis**

When butterflies, moths, ants and bees change during their lives, it is called complete metamorphosis. The life cycle of the elephant hawk moth shown here has four separate stages. The moth begins life as an egg. The egg hatches out a caterpillar, which spends almost all of its time feeding. When the caterpillar is fully grown, it burrows into the ground and sheds its skin to reveal a pupa, a stage at which the larva changes into the adult insect while cocooned in a protective case. Finally the case splits and the adult moth emerges.

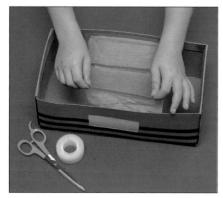

1 Cut holes in the sides of the box for windows. Using strong sticky tape, stick pieces of muslin or netting over the windows to cover them securely.

2 Now cut a large piece of muslin to make the cage lid. Weight the corners of the muslin lid down with modelling material to prevent the caterpillars from escaping.

3 Wearing a pair of gloves, put some fresh leaves inside the box. Make sure that they are from a plant your caterpillars eat. Be sure to provide fresh leaves daily.

4 Put some damp kitchen paper in a corner of the box to provide moisture. Carefully transfer your caterpillars from the collecting jar to the box. Cover with the lid.

5 Check your caterpillars every day and replace the damp kitchen paper. Record how much they eat and how big they are. Remember to replace the leaves daily.

6 Watch how your caterpillars feed and move about on the leaves. Record the dates when you see them moulting (shedding skin). How many times did they shed their skins?

7 When it has finished growing, the caterpillar will change into a pupa, or chrysalis. It will attach itself to the stem of a food plant and form a new skin. Make a note of the date.

8 Check your pupa every day and write down the date when you see the case splitting. Compare your two dates. How long did the insect spend as a pupa?

When the caterpillars become adult moths or butterflies it is time to let them go. Take the insects back to where you found them. Lift the lid off the box and let them fly away.

9 You will see a butterfly or moth struggle out of the old skin. The insect rests and pumps blood into its crumpled wings to straighten them out before flying off.

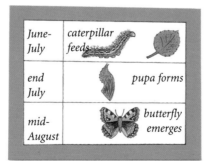

June-July	caterpillar feeds	
end July		pupa forms
mid-August		butterfly emerges

Keep a chart of the life cycles of your insects.

Crawling colonies

Unlike most insects, ants live in colonies. They are known as social insects as opposed to solitary insects. Ants are different to flying insects, such as butterflies and bees, yet they behave in a similar way. An ant colony is like an underground city with millions of insects, each with its own role to play. Queen ants (of which there may be several in one nest) lay eggs. Undeveloped females called workers carry out the essential tasks of the colony. They scurry around, searching for food and bring it to the nest.

The key to the smooth running of the colony is good communication. Ants cannot see well, so they communicate by touch and smell. When two ants meet, they touch antennae (feelers). When an ant finds a food source, it hurries back to the nest, pressing its body on to the ground as it runs. This leaves a trail of scent, which the other ants can follow to reach the food.

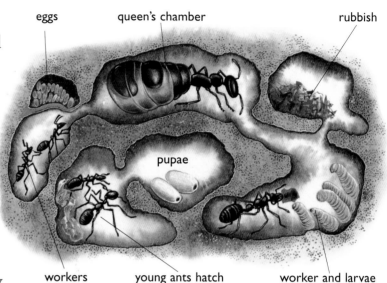

eggs   queen's chamber   rubbish

pupae

workers   young ants hatch   worker and larvae

▲ **Inside an ants' nest**

Ants' nests are usually underground. A nest has many chambers, or rooms, and passages. Different chambers contain the eggs, larvae (young), pupae and the queen. Other chambers are used to store food and rubbish. Worker ants alter the temperature of the nest by opening or closing passages.

YOU WILL NEED

gardening gloves, peeled ripe fruit,

piece of paper, magnifying glass.

Watching ant trails

1 Wearing gloves, find a trail of ants. Follow the trail to find out where the ants are going. Does the trail lead to food? Rub out part of the trail and see what happens.

2 Now put fruit down on a piece of paper near the trail of ants. The paper will make it easier to see the ants. When the workers find the fruit, watch to see what happens.

3 Once an ant has laid a scent trail to the fruit, others will follow. Move the fruit to another part of the paper. What happens next? Do the ants go straight to the new food site?

Make an ant home

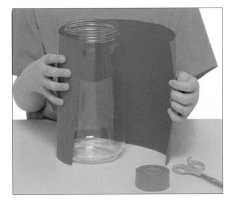

1 Measure and cut a piece of dark-coloured paper that is large enough to fit around the jar. Fix the paper in position around the jar with sticky tape.

2 Wearing a pair of gloves, use the trowel to fill the jar with earth until the jar is almost full. Carefully place a few leaves on top of the earth.

3 Capture some garden ants using a paintbrush and collecting jar. Let the ants crawl on to the paintbrush. Then tap the jar so that the ants fall in. Transfer the ants to their new home.

4 Feed your ants with a piece of ripe fruit or jam. Some damp kitchen paper will provide moisture. Feed your ants daily and refresh the leaves and moist paper regularly.

5 Cover the top of the jar with a piece of muslin, so that the ants cannot escape. Secure the muslin with sticky tape. Keep your ant home in a cool place.

6 After a few days, remove the sticky tape and lift the paper to observe your ant home. There will now be winding tunnels, built by the ants, against the sides of the jar.

If you have caught a queen ant, you may see the workers tending eggs or larvae in special chambers.

Discovering birds

There are birds living in all areas of the world. They inhabit icy polar regions, tropical wet rainforests and scorching hot deserts. Birds are also found in crowded cities, on high mountains and remote islands.

Birds vary in size. The tiny hummingbird of Cuba is no larger than a bumblebee. The African ostrich, at the other extreme, stands 2.5m high. Birds are warm-blooded creatures like mammals, but they lay eggs, as reptiles and amphibians do. Unlike other animals, birds' bodies are covered with strong, lightweight feathers. These help birds to fly, although there are a few species that cannot fly.

There are more than 8,600 different species (kinds) of birds. Scientist divide all these birds into groups called orders. The 28 bird orders are divided into smaller groups, called families, and each family contains several species. Species in the same family tend to have a similar body shape, which makes them suited to a certain way of life. For example, ducks have wide bodies and webbed feet to help them move through water.

The largest bird species often live the longest. Giant albatrosses can live for 80 years. Small songbird species, such as blue tits and sparrows, may live for just one year.

skull
nostril
neck
backbone
keel
wingbone
ribcage
ankle
toe

▲ Body shape

Birds have a basic body shape that varies in size and colour according to species. All birds have a beak, instead of jaws with teeth, and scaly legs and feet. Flying birds have a skeleton that is geared for efficient flight. Powerful wings and a feathered tail help with stability and steering. The wings and legs are arranged close to the centre of the body, to help with balance.

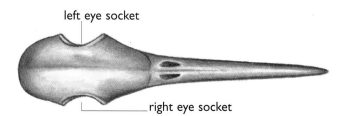

left eye socket

right eye socket

▲ Field of vision for a woodcock

A woodcock eats earthworms and insects. It does not need to spot prey like an owl does but must look out for enemies. Its eyes are on the side of its head. This enables it to see all around itself.

Looking at diving birds

1 Choose a pond or lake for bird-watching. See where different species feed. Notice where they dive and reappear. Use a field guide to help you to identify species.

2 Now find out how long the different birds spend under the water. Use your stopwatch to time their dives. Do they feed under water, or bring food to the surface?

3 Record the times in your notebook. Which bird stays under water for the longest time? Do you think that this is affected by the depth of the water?

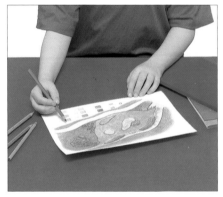

4 In your notebook, make a rough map of the pond or lake. When you get home, do a neater version and colour it in. Show vegetation such as grass or reeds.

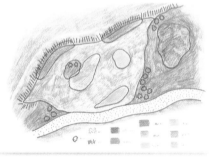

5 On your map, use different coloured pencils to mark where various species of birds swim and feed. Remember to draw a key to explain which bird each colour represents.

Drawing birds

1 You do not have to be a great artist to draw birds. Study the shape of the bird. Notice how long the neck is. Start with simple ovals for the head and body.

2 Look at the shape of the bird's beak, and at its neck and tail. If you can see the legs, how long are they? Can you see the feet? Add these details to your drawing.

Now add a pair of wings and other details, such as the face and tail. Make notes about the bird's colouring. so that you can colour your drawing in later.

Bird-watching

Birds are among the easiest animals to spot and study from your home or school. To see a wider range of species (kinds), you could try bird-watching in a local park, pond or woodland area. Always take an adult with you. Birds are shy creatures with sharp eyesight and hearing. They are always on the lookout for enemies, so keep very quiet and still when bird-watching. If you make yourself a hide, like the one shown, bird-watching will be much easier.

YOU WILL NEED

Using binoculars: binoculars.

Build a hide: eight short canes or poles, six longer canes, string, scissors, canvas or tarpaulin, safety pins, four tent pegs, leaves and twigs, lightweight binoculars.

Using binoculars

1 Lightweight binoculars are very useful on bird-watching trips. Remove them from the case and hang them around your neck so you are ready to use them.

2 When you see a bird, do not look down, or you may lose sight of it. Keep watching it, and slowly raise the binoculars to your eyes. Try to avoid sudden movements.

3 Now adjust the focusing wheel on your binoculars to bring the bird into focus. You may find this difficult to do at first, but it will become easier with practice.

Build a hide

1 You will need a friend to help you. Lay four short canes on the ground in a square. Tie the ends with string. Make another square the same size, to form the roof.

2 Get your friend to stand inside the base. Your friend should hold the roof in position while you tie four long canes to the base and roof to form the sides.

3 Now strengthen the structure of your hide. Add two long canes to make cross-pieces on opposite sides of the hide. Tie the canes in place with string.

4 Drape your hide with the canvas or tarpaulin. Add a smaller piece for the roof. Fasten the edges with safety pins. For extra security, fix the base to the ground with tent pegs.

5 Now cover the cloth with some leaves and twigs. These will camouflage your hide, so that it will blend in with the woods and will be less obvious to birds.

6 Once inside the hide, look out through the gaps in the seams, between the safety pins. Try using your binoculars. Keep still and quiet, and birds will soon approach.

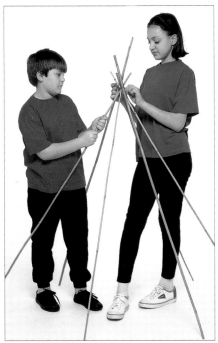

A tipi is another, simpler kind of hide. You will need four to six canes, string, a tarpaulin, safety pins and possibly tent pegs. Fan out the canes to form a pyramid shape and tie the top ends with string. Drape the tarpaulin over this and fasten it with safety pins.

Camouflage the tipi with leaves and twigs. Leave a gap to look through the cover with your binoculars.

Listening to birds

The voices of singing birds that seem beautiful to us often have many meanings. A bird's song identifies what species (kind) it is as well as each bird as an individual. Male birds sing to establish their own territories. A territory is a patch of ground where the birds intend to breed or feed. In Antarctica, a parent penguin finds its chick among . thousands of other chicks by its cry. Birds also call to warn of danger and to attract a mate. Birds that flock together use contact calls to keep in a tight group.

You can make a birdbath for the birds visiting your garden in the first project. Listening to birdsong is a good way of identifying birds. The best times of the day to listen to birds are dawn and dusk, when they sing the loudest. It is fun to make recordings of the different bird songs that you come across. Use a portable tape recorder with a long lead, so that you can position the microphone farther away. Tape the microphone to a stick, so that the sounds of your hands will not be recorded. Headphones allow you to check what you are recording. To achieve even better results, make yourself a sound reflector, as shown in the third project.

▲ Hooters of the night

An owl's night-time hooting is a well-recognized sound. Owls have excellent eyesight. This makes them good hunters in the dark. Some have flat disc shaped faces. These help direct sound into the ears at the side of the head.

YOU WILL NEED

trowel, rubber gloves, large dish

or old dustbin lid, stones,

bucket of water.

Build a birdbath

1 Use your trowel to dig a hollow in the earth. It should be big enough to fit your dustbin lid or dish. Place the dish in the hollow and press it down firmly, making sure it is flat.

2 Now place a few large stones in your dustbin lid or dish. Birds coming to your garden will use these stones to stand on to get in and out of your bird-bath.

3 Pour water into the bath, to a depth of about 10–15cm. The tops of the stones should stick up above the water, so that birds can spot them and land on them easily.

Taping birdsong

I Become familiar with the songs of birds that live in your area by listening to recordings on CD or cassette tape. You can borrow these from your local library.

2 Outside, position yourself behind a tree or bush, if possible. Set up the microphone on a long lead by a bird-table, or near a perch where you see a bird singing.

3 To record, press the record and pause buttons, releasing the pause button when you want to record. Listen with headphones and also note down the time, place and weather.

When you get home, listen to the calls you have recorded very carefully. Most field guides give details of bird-calls and will be able to help you to identify the songs.

Sound reflector

I Cover the inside of an old umbrella with sheets of foil. Carefully bend the foil over the edges of the umbrella and tape it down securely with sticky tape.

2 Fix the mike to the stem of the umbrella, with the mike head pointing towards the shade. Try the mike in different positions – about 15–20cm away from the shade.

3 Set up your reflector where birds are singing. The reflector will channel sounds and amplify them (make them louder). Give birds time to get to used to this strange object.

Birds' nests

Nests are warm, safe places where birds lay eggs and where the nestlings (baby birds) develop after they have hatched. Birds do not sleep in their nests at night. Instead, they roost on perches in sheltered places such as hedges and trees.

Constructing the nest is usually the female's job. The first step is to choose a good site. Then the materials are gathered. Twigs, leaves, feathers, moss, wool and mud are all used by various birds. The nest-building bird pushes the materials into place and hollows out the inside with her body. The finished nest may be lined with soft materials such as feathers to protect the eggs.

Nesting birds are fascinating to study. Attract birds into your garden and help them to nest and raise their young by building a nesting box in early spring. You may see birds fly by with nesting materials in their beaks, looking for a place to build. Many birds build their nests wedged in the forks of tree branches. Nest-building uses up a lot of time and energy. It may take between a week and a month, yet most nests last for just one breeding season, and are ruined by winter weather.

▲ **Nesting materials**

In spring, try hanging nesting material from branches or a windowsill. You can use wool, string, grass, moss and feathers. You could also try paper tissue, straw or animal hair. Different bird species like different materials. Keep a look-out to see which materials are chosen by various birds.

Template for nesting box

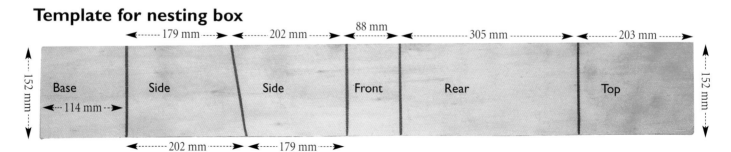

Use 15mm thick pine or plywood. Ask an adult to cut pieces to the sizes and shapes shown above.

Build a nesting box

YOU WILL NEED

wood (cut into pieces by an adult as shown), wood glue, hammer, nails or panel pins, pencil, strip of sacking or rubber (for the hinge), varnish, brush.

1 When all the pieces of wood have been cut by an adult, arrange them in position to make sure that they all fit properly. Glue the low front of the box to the base.

2 Now add one of the side pieces to the base of your nesting box. Glue it in place. Next add the other side piece to the opposite edge of the base and glue that into position, as well.

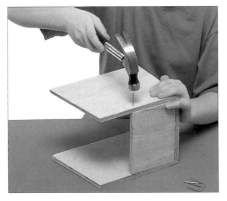

3 Nail all the pieces together. Take great care with the hammer. You could ask an adult to help. Place the box in the middle of the rear board, and draw around it in pencil.

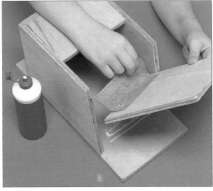

4 Using your pencil guidelines, nail the rear board to the box. Add the roof by gluing and nailing on the sacking hinge. Now your nesting box is ready to use.

5 Your nesting box will last much longer if you give it a coat of varnish inside and out to protect it. Leave the box overnight to let the varnish dry completely.

Nail your box to a tree, shed or post, about 2m from the ground. Face the box away from any direct sunlight, as this may harm very young birds.

Feed the birds

Put bird food out in a safe place and you will discover one of the best ways of studying birds close up. You can make your own bird cake, such as the one here, and put out kitchen scraps such as stale breadcrumbs, cheese, fruit, cooked rice or pasta, uncooked pastry and bacon rind. Birds will really appreciate these titbits, particularly in cold weather, when the ground is hard to peck at for worms and trees are bare of fruit and berries. Count how many different kinds of birds visit. Also, notice which species (kind) prefer each kind of food. Note down the date, time and weather when you first see a new species. Do the birds feed quietly together, or do they fight over scraps?

▲ Winter feed

Fruit is an important food for many birds, particularly in winter. Garden birds such as thrushes and blackbirds will peck at apples, leaving large, irregular holes.

◄ Shells and nuts

Look out for nut shells gnawed by animals. Squirrels and mice leave neat holes and teethmarks. Birds leave peck-marks or jagged edges or crack nuts in half, such as the top two nuts here. Song thrushes feed on snails. They smash the shell against a stone. The stone is known as the thrush's anvil. You may be lucky and find shell remains beside a stone.

Make a bird cake

1 Soften the fat on a radiator or get an adult to help you melt it in a pan. Mix the nuts, oatmeal and crumbs in a bowl. Add the fat and mix together.

2 Cut a long piece of string. Tie a really big knot in one end. Put the string into the cup so that the knotted end is at the bottom, and spoon the mixture into the cup.

3 Ensure that the end of the string comes out through the middle of the mixture. When the mixture is set, pull the string to remove the cake. Hang it on a tree branch or windowsill.

Build a bird table

1 Lay the wooden strips along the edges of your plywood board, as shown. Now glue the strips of wood into position, so that the ends fit together neatly.

2 When the glue is dry, turn the board over. Carefully hammer nails through it into the strips. If you find using a hammer difficult, you could ask an adult to help you to do this.

3 Paint the top surface of your bird table with a coat of varnish, to make it waterproof. When this coat is dry, turn the table over and coat the underside too.

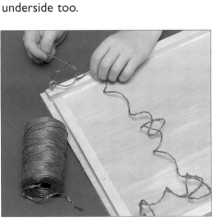

4 Screw eye-hooks into the strips at the four corners of the table. Now cut two pieces of string about 30cm long. Tie the ends of the strings to the hooks.

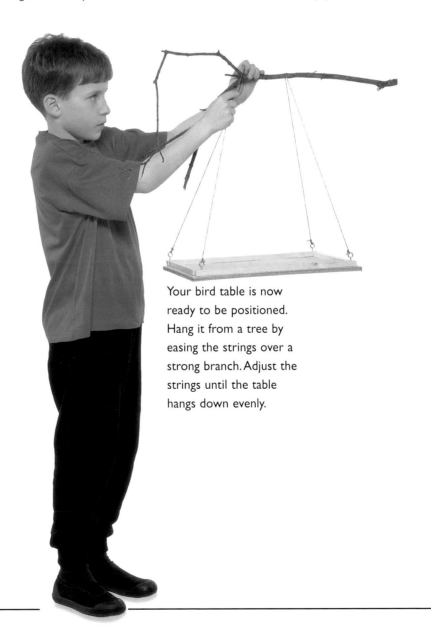

Your bird table is now ready to be positioned. Hang it from a tree by easing the strings over a strong branch. Adjust the strings until the table hangs down evenly.

Tell-tale bird traces

In nature, birds peck at nuts, fruit and berries. Their beaks leave tell-tale marks. These signs can help you to identify the birds that made them. A good field guide will help you to find out whether food remains have been left by birds rather than small animals, such as mice and squirrels. Hunters, such as owls, leave special food remains behind. They swallow voles, mice and even small birds whole. Once or twice a day, the bird chokes up the remains that it cannot digest, in a tightly packed ball, or as pellets. By examining a a pellet closely, as in the second project, you can discover exactly what the hunting animal caught the previous day.

Bird feathers are made of a flexible substance, called keratin, that is also found in human hair and nails. They are amazingly strong, but weigh almost nothing. Feathers are windproof and most are waterproof. Feathers are used in flying and to help keep birds warm and dry. Some male birds use brightly coloured plumage (feathers) to attract a mate. The colour of plumage may also help to camouflage a bird from predators. Keep a look out for dropped feathers around your bird table.

▲ Searching for pellets
Look around the base of trees for all kinds of interesting animal remains. Pellets left by hunting birds are found under trees with low branches, where the birds may perch.

▾ Mounting feathers
Cut slits in a page of a notebook and slide them in. This also makes the feathers easy to remove.

▲ Light as air
Down feathers are light and fluffy. They lie next to the bird's skin, and help keep the bird warm.

▲ Flying high
Flight feathers are found on the wings and tail and are strong and stiff. Tail feathers help with steering.

◂ Flight aid
Body or contour feathers cover the bird's body and give it a streamlined shape, which helps it fly well.

Finding out about feathers

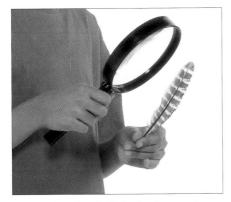

1 Study a bird's flight feather under a magnifying glass. Split the feather's barbs (individual strands). You can now observe the barbules (the fringed edges).

2 Repair the feather's surface, just as a bird does during preening. Smooth the barbs between your finger and thumb so that they join back together properly.

3 Now try another experiment. Add a little water to some paint and brush it on to your flight feather. What happens to the paint? Why do you think this is?

Dissect an owl pellet

YOU WILL NEED

Finding out about feathers:

feathers, magnifying glass, water, paint, waterpot, paintbrush.

Dissect an owl pellet: rubber gloves, owl pellet, bowl, warm water, washing-up liquid, tweezers, paper towel, small box, tissue paper.

1 Wear rubber gloves for this project. First, soak the owl pellet in a bowl of warm water with a little washing-up liquid added. Leave the pellet until it has softened.

2 Using a pair of tweezers, gently begin to pull the pellet apart. Inside, you will find the fur, teeth, skulls and other bones of small animals that the owl has eaten.

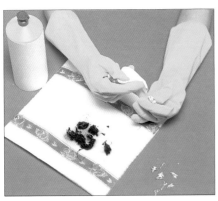

3 Use the tweezers to carefully separate the bones from the fur. Wash the bones in warm, soapy water and pat them gently dry with a paper towel.

Line a small box with tissue paper. Choose a bright colour that will make the bones show up. Now arrange your bones. Can you identify the animal remains that you have found? There may be remains of voles, including skulls, jawbones and leg bones. It can also contain small stones that the owl had swallowed to help with digestion.

Bird travel and flight

Many birds travel vast distances each year. They may travel to escape the chill of winter, to find food or a safe nesting site. Departure is often triggered by the shortening daylight hours of autumn. In spring, the birds travel back again. These journeys are called migrations. Many species (kinds) do not feed while they travel, so must fatten up before they leave. Migrating birds face many dangers. They may get lost in storms or be killed by predators. Thousands die of hunger, thirst and exhaustion.

Flying takes up a lot of energy but has many advantages for birds. Hovering uses the most energy of all. However, birds are able to save their energy by gliding on air currents. Large birds soar upwards into air currents with their wings outstretched to trap as much air as possible. Making your own aerofoil in the project opposite shows you how the shape of a wing produces lift. Then build a spiral model to see how birds circle in warm air currents without flapping their wings.

▲ Lift and flight

A bird's wing is slightly curved at the top, and flatter underneath. A shape like this that is designed to provide uplift in flight is called an aerofoil. As the bird moves through the air, the curved shape makes the air travel faster over the wing than beneath it. This makes an area of low air pressure above the wing, which allows the bird to rise. Aircraft are able to fly because their wings are a similar shape to a bird's wings.

Migration routes

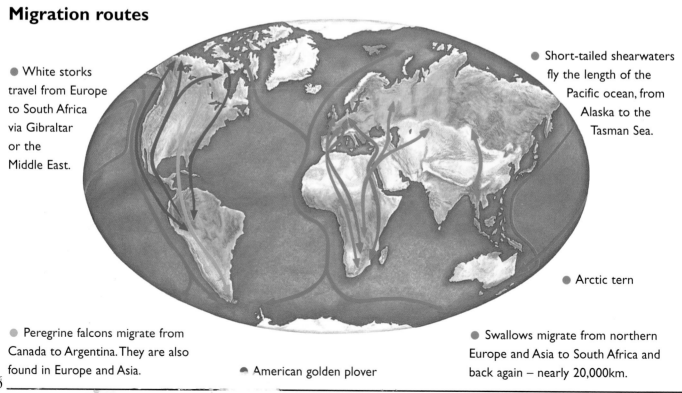

● White storks travel from Europe to South Africa via Gibraltar or the Middle East.

● Short-tailed shearwaters fly the length of the Pacific ocean, from Alaska to the Tasman Sea.

● Arctic tern

● Peregrine falcons migrate from Canada to Argentina. They are also found in Europe and Asia.

▲ American golden plover

● Swallows migrate from northern Europe and Asia to South Africa and back again – nearly 20,000km.

How a wing works

1 Cut a strip of paper about 30cm long. Glue the ends together firmly. When the glue is dry, bend the paper into a wing shape, curved on top and flat underneath.

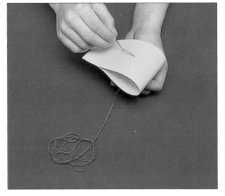

2 Mark the centre of the wing. Thread a long piece of cotton on to a needle and push it through the centre of the wing. Gently pull the aerofoil down the thread.

3 Now get a friend to hold the thread taut. Blow hard against the curved edge of the aerofoil, and watch the wing rise up the thread – just as an aeroplane or a bird's wing lifts.

Soaring spiral

YOU WILL NEED

How a wing works: paper, scissors, glue, pencil, needle, thread.

Soaring spiral: thick paper, pair of compasses, pencil, coloured pencils/felt-tipped pens, scissors, pencil with rubber on end, cotton reel, pin, thimble.

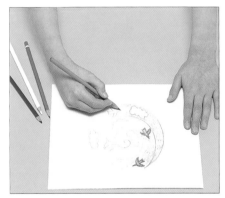

1 Use a pair of compasses and a pencil to draw a circle on a piece of paper. Now draw and colour in a spiral shape with buzzards (or other birds) flying around it.

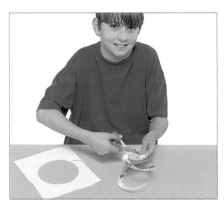

2 Carefully cut out the decorated paper spiral. Use a pencil to make the hole left in the centre of the spiral by your compasses big enough to fit over the thimble.

3 Fit the pencil point into the cotton reel. Put the pin in the rubber. Push the thimble through the hole in the paper spiral, so that it sits over the thimble. Balance the thimble on the pin.

4 Stand your model on a radiator. Now watch the buzzards circling around in the warm air currents rising from the radiator. Your model must be well-balanced to work properly.

Physical and Material Marvels

We live in a world of engineering marvels – of soaring tower blocks, wide-spanning bridges and massive dams. We can communicate with almost everyone, anywhere on the Earth, and even in Space. This section shows the part that science and technology have played in setting the pace of change. Science accumulates knowledge about the world by observation, study and experiment. Technology puts the knowledge into practical use as inventions to improve the quality of life.

Chemical change

Over the past 100 years, scientists have invented many substances, such as plastics, medicines and detergents, that we take for granted today. These substances are created by chemical reactions. In a chemical reaction, a new substance (called a product) is made as a result of other substances (called reactants) undergoing chemical change. Many chemical reactions happen naturally, such as oil (petrol) and gas, which form from the remains of animals and plants. They are called hydrocarbons, because they are mixtures of hydrogen and carbon.

The following experiments demonstrate the three main ways in which chemical reactions can happen – by passing electricity through substances, by heating them, or simply by mixing them together. In the first, electricity breaks down salty water to make chlorine (the disinfectant often used in swimming pools). In the second, heat turns sugar, which is made from carbon, hydrogen and oxygen, into pure carbon. Finally, you make the gas used in some fire extinguishers by mixing bicarbonate of soda and vinegar together.

▲ **Checking up**
A technician is ensuring all the bottles of chemicals are correctly labelled. Accuracy is very important in science.

WARNING!
Please take care when using electrical equipment. Always have an adult present.

YOU WILL NEED

Electrolysis: battery (4–6 volts), bulb and holder, wires, wirestrippers, screwdriver, paper clips, salt, jar, water.

Heat changes: old saucepan, teaspoon, sugar, cooker.

Getting a reaction: teaspoon, bicarbonate of soda, glass bowl, spirit vinegar, matches.

How oil is formed

The story of oil begins in warm seas full of living things. As they die, they fall to the bottom of the sea floor to decay into thick, black mud.

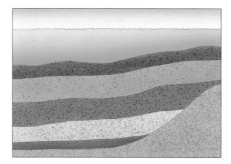

In time, mud is buried beneath many layers of sand with clay in between. The sediments (deposits) sink deeper and deeper, and also become hotter.

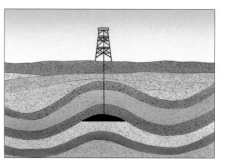

After millions of years, the sediments fold under pressure. Oil from the black mud is forced into sandstones and trapped under the layers of clay.

Electrolysis

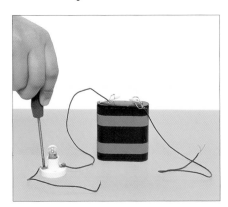

1 Connect the battery and bulb holder with wires, as shown here. Remove 1cm of insulation from each end of wire. Use the paper clips to join the wires to the battery.

2 Stir salt into a jar of water until no more dissolves. Dip the two bare wire ends into the mixture and hold them about 1cm apart. Look for bubbles forming around them.

3 The bulb should light to show that electricity is passing through. Carefully sniff the jar from 20cm away. What does it smell of? The smell is like swimming pools!

Heat changes

1 Make sure the saucepan is completely dry. Spread one teaspoonful of sugar across the bottom of the pan. Aim for a thin layer a few millimetres thick.

2 Place the pan on a cooker set to low heat. After a few minutes, the sugar will start to melt to give a brown treacly liquid. You may begin to see a few wisps of steam.

3 The sugar starts to bubble as it breaks down and gives off steam. If you carry on heating the sugar, the brown sticky liquid will change to solid black carbon.

Getting a reaction

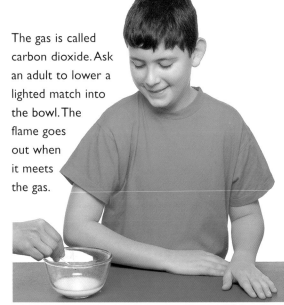

The gas is called carbon dioxide. Ask an adult to lower a lighted match into the bowl. The flame goes out when it meets the gas.

1 Place three heaped spoonfuls of bicarbonate of soda in the bowl. Cooks often add this white powder to vegetables such as peas and carrots. It helps to keep their natural colour.

2 Carefully pour vinegar into the bowl. As the liquid mixes with the bicarbonate of soda, a chemical reaction happens. The mixture bubbles as a gas is given off.

Tests with yeast

For thousands of years, people all over the world have used yeast for brewing beer and baking bread. Yeast is a type of fungus that lives on the skins of many fruits. Just a spoonful of yeast contains millions of separate, single-celled (very simple) organisms. Each one works like a tiny chemical factory, taking in sugar, and giving out alcohol and carbon dioxide gas. While they feed, the yeast cells grow larger and then reproduce by splitting in half.

▲ Kneading dough
Bread is kneaded into a soft dough and then left in a warm place to rise. The dough is then kneaded again before baking. This process ensures that the yeast produces as many bubbles of gas as possible, so that the bread is light.

Yeast turns grape juice into alcoholic wine and makes beer from mixtures of grain and water. When added to uncooked dough, yeast produces gas bubbles that make the bread light and soft. Brewing and baking are important modern industries that depend on yeast working quickly.

This project consists of four separate experiments. By comparing the results you can discover the best conditions for yeast to grow. It needs a moist environment to be active. Lack of moisture makes the cells dry out and hibernate (sleep). Add water to dried, powdered yeast and, even after many years, it will become active again.

Finding the best conditions

YOU WILL NEED

measuring jug, water, kettle, sticky coloured labels, four small glass jars, teaspoon, dried yeast granules, sugar, scissors, clear film, three elastic bands, two heatproof bowls, ice cubes.

1 Half fill a kettle with water. Ask an adult to boil it for you and then put it aside to cool. Boiling the water kills all living organisms that might stop the yeast from growing.

2 Label the glass jars one to four. Put a level teaspoonful of dried yeast into each jar as shown here. Then put the same amount of sugar into each jar.

3 Pour 150ml of the cooled boiled water into the first three jars. Stir the mixture to dissolve the sugar. Do not pour water into the fourth jar. Put this jar away in a warm place.

4 Cut out pieces of clear film about twice a jar's width. Stretch one across the neck of each remaining jar and secure it with an elastic band. Put the first jar in a warm place.

5 Place the second jar in a glass bowl. Put some ice cubes and cold water into the bowl. This mixture will keep the jar's temperature close to freezing.

6 Place the third jar in another glass bowl. Pour in some hot water that is almost too hot to touch. Be careful not to use boiling water or the jar may crack.

high temperature

warm temperature

7 Regularly check all four jars over the next two hours. As the ice around the second jar melts, add more to keep the temperature low. Add more hot water to keep the third jar hot.

cold temperature

dry jar

In the jar that was kept hot, the yeast is a cloudy layer at the bottom, killed by the heat. The jar that was kept cold has only a little froth on the surface because the cold has slowed down the yeast.

The yeast that was kept warm has fed on the water and sugar, and its gas is pushing up the clear film. In the dry jar, there are no signs of activity, because the yeast is hibernating.

Preservation and decay

Decay is the breaking up of dead organic matter, such as animals and plants. It results when invisible creatures called bacteria, and tiny fungi called moulds, breed. The bodies of living plants and animals fight these agents of destruction, but as soon as the animals die, decay begins. Bacteria and moulds that cause decay need water to live, so decay happens best in damp conditions.

The process of preserving something aims to stop it from decaying. The ancient Egyptians were skilled at mummifying (preserving) their kings' bodies. They removed moist internal organs, such as the intestines, heart, liver and brain. Then they buried the body in natron, a kind of salt. This dried out all the fluids that speed up decay. The body was then wrapped in bandages. The bandages had been soaked in oily resins that killed bacteria and moulds in a similar way to modern antiseptic creams. You can practise slowing down and speeding up the process of decay in these two experiments.

▲ Protected by the gods
Turning the body of a great Egyptian pharaoh into a mummy was an complicated process. In addition to the preserving process, a jackal-masked priest performed sacred rituals.

peeled carrot

unpeeled carrot

plastic

stone

unpeeled apple

peeled apple

wood

What decays?

1 Peel one of the apples and one of the carrots. Line the tray with some newspaper. Add a layer of compost and place all the items on top. Add more compost to cover the items.

2 Dig a shallow hole in a shady spot and put the tray in it. Cover it with earth so that you can just see its top edges. Buried like this, the items will stay damp. Dig the tray up after a week.

Examine the results. Fruit and vegetables are attacked quickly by bacteria and moulds, especially if they have no skins. Wood takes months to decay. Stone and plastic do not decay.

Preventing decay

1 Put one slice of ordinary bread into a plastic bag and seal it with a tie. Now toast another slice of bread until it is crisp and dry. Seal the toast in another plastic bag.

2 Spread some antiseptic cream, which is designed to kill germs, over one side of a third slice. Seal the antiseptic cream-coated third slice in another plastic bag.

3 Label each plastic bag. Leave them in a warm place and check them once a day. Bacteria and moulds are everywhere. What will they do inside your plastic bags?

▲ **Dry toast**
Look at the slices. Mould and bacteria cannot grow on the dry toast as there is no moisture.

Do not open the bags when you have finished looking at the results. Keep the moulds and bacteria wrapped safely inside their plastic bags and drop the bags into a dustbin.

▲ **Antiseptic cream**
The chemicals in the antiseptic cream have killed any germs on the cream-covered slice of bread.

▲ **Ordinary bread**
The ordinary slice of bread is very mouldy. Mould and bacteria have thrived in the moist conditions.

Stone and concrete

Buildings made of hard stone last much longer than those made of dried earth or bricks. The people who lived in early civilizations carved stone with simple hammers and chisels – rather as you will try to do in the first experiment. When the ancient Egyptians built the pyramids more than 3,000 years ago, they had to drive large wedges into cracks in the rock face to lever off blocks of stone.

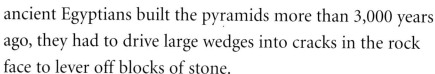

Nelson's Column

Sydney Opera House

Statue of Liberty

Great Pyramid, Giza

Ancient peoples used stone that they found locally, and gradually learned to use different rocks for different jobs. The Inca people of South America built with granite, a hard, igneous (volcanic) rock. The ancient Egyptians also used granite, but limestone, a softer, more easily carved sedimentary rock, was common too. Certain rocks, such as marble, were selected for decorative effects because of their beautiful patterns and colours. Many modern buildings are made of concrete, a mixture of ground-down rocks and minerals. You can test its strength in the second experiment.

▲ Ancient scale

The Great Pyramid in Egypt is the largest stone building in the world, even though it was built over 4,000 years ago. It is made up of over 2 million blocks of stone, each one weighing an average of 2½ tonnes.

YOU WILL NEED

blunt round-ended knife,

solid foam block used by flower-arrangers, foamed concrete

(fairly soft) type of building block.

Cutting and carving

1 Could you be a sculptor? Practise by marking out a simple shape on the flower-arranging block. Use the knife to cut around it. How easy is it to use this material?

2 Now do the same with your building block. This is much harder, but it is still softer than stone. Make sure that the knife blade is pointed away from you.

Now you know how hard it is to carve material that is much softer than stone. How long do you think it would take you to carve real stone with simple tools?

Mix your own concrete

YOU WILL NEED
rubber gloves, measuring cup, sand, bucket, cement, gravel, water, stirring stick, old metal tray, small thin box, foil.

1 Place one cupful of sand in a bucket. Add two cups of cement and a handful of gravel. Take care not to touch the cement with your bare hands.

2 Add some water to the mixture little by little. Keep stirring all the time until the mixture has the consistency of porridge. Mix it well with the stick.

3 Pour the wet concrete on to a shallow metal tray and spread it out. Leave it to solidify for about half an hour. Wash all the other equipment you have used straight away.

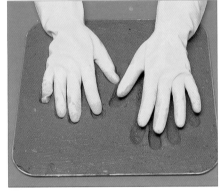

4 Now you can shape the concrete. Make impressions of your hands, or write with the stick. The marks will be permanent once the concrete has set. Do not use your bare hands.

hand prints
in concrete

5 You could make a concrete block like those used in the construction industry. Line a small but strong box with kitchen foil. Pour in the concrete and smooth the top with the stick.

How strong is the concrete block once it has set? Test its strength by trying to bend it. Can you rest a heavy weight on top of the block without breaking it?

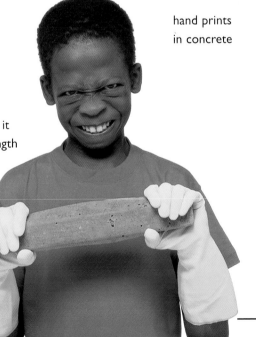

Building bridges

A platform bridge was a very early human invention, dating from tens of thousands of years ago. The simplest platform bridges were just a tree trunk or a single slab of stone laid across a narrow river or steep gully so that people could get across. Many modern platform bridges are hollow and made of steel. The model here shows how thin folded sheets make platform bridges stronger.

If you stand on a simple platform bridge, the downward force of your weight makes it sag in the middle. Too much weight can snap a flat wooden plank or crack a stone slab. Arch bridges, however, as the second experiment shows, do not sag when loaded. They curve up and over the gap that they span, and the forces acting on the arch squeeze it together. Weight from above is pushed outwards so that the load spreads to the side supports. The Romans were among the first to build arch bridges.

Make a platform

1 Cut out four strips of card 40cm x 10cm. With a ruler and pen, draw lines 1cm apart across each card. Fold each card back and forth across the lines to form zigzag pleats.

2 Lay one board flat on the table. Stand a piece of pleated card upright along the board's edges. Repeat for the other three sides. Use modelling clay to secure each corner.

3 When all sides of the platform are in place, lay the second board on top. Push downwards with your hand. Pleating the card has made the platform very strong. Your platform is stronger than a platform bridge because it is supported on four sides. Without this support it would sag in the middle.

Make an arch

1 Although it is not shown in this picture, it would be a good idea to cover the work surface with newspaper first. Place the two bricks on the work surface about 20cm apart.

2 Pile sand between the bricks and smooth it with your hands to make a curved mound. Place the wooden blocks side by side across the sand. They should touch the outer blocks.

3 The inner blocks touch each other but have V-shaped gaps between them. Mix the plaster with water until it forms a stiff paste. Use the knife to fill gaps between the blocks with paste.

4 Make sure you have filled each space where the arch meets the bricks. Wait for the plaster to dry. Once dry, remove the sand from underneath the arch.

5 Push down on the arch and feel how firm it is. The weight that you are putting on the bridge is supported by the two bricks at the side. This bridge is stronger than a platform bridge and does not sag in the middle. Like stone blocks in real bridges, the wooden toy blocks make a remarkably strong curve.

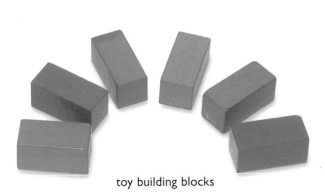

toy building blocks

Tunnel construction

A tunnel has to bear the weight of millions of tonnes of rocks and earth – or even water – above it. One way of doing this is to make lots of brick arches that together run the length of the tunnel. An arched roof is much stronger than a flat one because weight from above is pushed out sideways, as the first experiment shows. In the second project, you place a wedge-shaped keystone at the peak of the arch. In real life, this keystone locks the whole structure together. It compresses (squeezes) the bricks on either side to make the arch self-supporting and very strong.

Today, a long, train-like machine is used to bore tunnels. A big drill carves out the hole, sending the waste backwards on a conveyor belt. Behind it, robotic cranes lift pre-cast concrete sections of the tube-shaped tunnel into place.

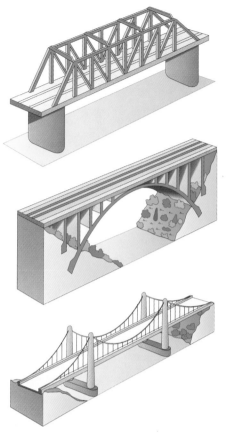

▲ Bridge types
The beam bridge (*top*) is made of horizontal platform supported on two or more piers (pillars). Arch bridges (*centre*) are built over steep valleys or rivers. Suspension bridges (*bottom*) support the longest bridges. The weight of the platform is carried by steel wires that hang from cables. The cables are held up by concrete towers and anchored firmly at valley sides.

Templates

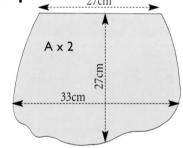

A x 2 — 27cm, 27cm, 33cm

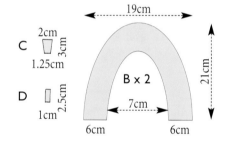

C — 2cm, 3cm, 1.25cm
D — 1cm, 2.5cm

B x 2 — 19cm, 21cm, 7cm, 6cm, 6cm

Strength test

YOU WILL NEED

two pieces of thick card (width roughly the same as the length of the blocks or bricks), two wooden building blocks or house bricks, a few heavy pebbles.

1 Place one of the pieces of card on top of the building blocks. Place pebbles on top as shown above. You will see that the tunnel roof sags under the weight.

2 Curve a second piece of card under the flat roof as shown. The roof supports the weight of the pebbles because the arch supports the flat section, making it stronger.

Tunnel in a landscape

YOU WILL NEED

masking tape, two pieces of thick card measuring 36 x 30cm and 46 x 27cm, ruler, pencil, scissors, thin card measuring 44 x 40cm, newspaper, cup of flour, ½ cup of water, acrylic paints, paintbrush, water pot, thin card (A4 size), PVA glue, glue brush, old sponge.

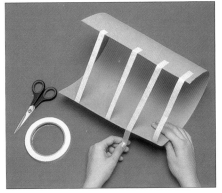

1 Tear off about four long strips of masking tape. Curve the 46 x 27cm rectangle of cardboard lengthways. Use the tape to hold the curve in place as shown above.

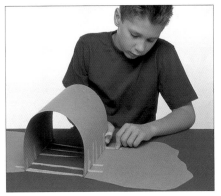

2 Copy the two templates A on to two 36 x 30cm pieces of thick card. Cut out the shapes. Attach each one to the sides of the tunnel and secure with tape as shown above.

3 Fold the 44 x 40cm thin card in half. Copy the arch template B on to the card. Cut out to make two tunnel entrances. Stick these to the tunnel with masking tape as shown.

4 Scrunch newspaper into balls and tape to the tunnel and landscape. Mix the flour and water to make a thick paste. Dip newspaper strips in the paste. Lay them over the tunnel.

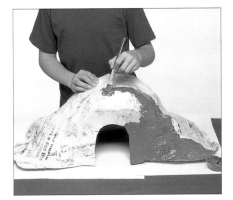

5 Leave to dry overnight. When completely dry and hard, paint the tunnel and landscape green. Apply up to three coats, letting each one dry before you apply the next.

6 Paint the A4 thin card to look like brick. Draw and cut out templates C and D. Draw around them on to the brick card to make the keystone and lots of bricks. Allow paint to dry.

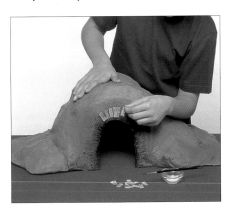

8 Dip pieces of old sponge into green acrylic paint to make bushes. Leave to dry. Stick them on the landscape. Apply three coats of paint to the whole landscape.

7 Glue the keystone at the top of the tunnel entrance. Then glue bricks around the arch either side of the keystone. In real tunnels, there are keystones along the tunnel length.

The strength of a pyramid

Over a period of more than 4,500 years, people in different parts of the world built huge pyramids. The oldest Egyptian pyramids were started almost 4,600 years ago, while the youngest pyramids in Central America were finished about 600 years ago. Each one took a long time to build, sometimes over 50 years, and involved thousands of people.

Why did these civilizations opt for a pyramidal structure rather than a cube or a rectangle for their monuments? These experiments will help you to find out. In the first, by changing a cube into a pyramid, you end up with a structure that is three times taller than the original cube. A pyramid makes good use of material by making the structure as high as possible. The second project shows that triangular shapes are more rigid than squares and do not collapse as easily. When an earthquake destroyed the Egyptian city of Cairo 700 years ago, the pyramids stood firm. Modern materials and technology make it possible to build tall, rectangular buildings that are strong and stable.

▲ Steep challenge

The Egyptians had no cranes to help them move the enormous blocks of stone used to build the pyramids. Workers built ramps of hard-packed earth. They hauled the blocks up these using plant-fibre ropes and wooden rollers. As the pyramid grew, so the ramps became longer and steeper. When the pyramid was finished, the ramps were removed.

Bases and heights

1 Make two cubes from modelling material. The faces should measure about 3cm to 4cm, but they must all be the same. Use a ruler to check your measurements.

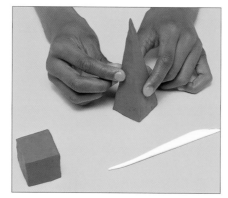

2 Reshape one of the cubes to form a tall, square-based pyramid. Its base must be the same size as the original cube. You now have a cube and a pyramid.

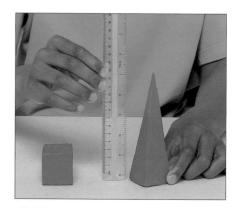

3 Now measure the cube and pyramid. They have the same volume and the same size base. The pyramid is three times taller, but is strong and more stable.

4 Make the cube into a long block. Place the block and the pyramid on a book. Slowly tilt the book, to imitate the effect of an earthquake. The block topples over before the pyramid does.

5 Make another smaller cube and pyramid from modelling material. Make sure that they are the same height. Their bases must also be the same size.

6 Do the same book test with the two smaller shapes. You should still find that the pyramid is the more stable of the two shapes. It is the second of the two shapes to fall over.

A question of strength

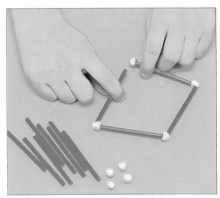

1 For this project, you will need two models – a cube and a square-based pyramid. Make them out of large plastic drinking straws and reusable adhesive. First, make the cube.

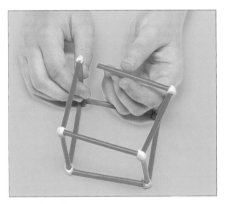

2 After fixing four straws to make the base of your cube, you need eight more to finish it. Make sure that your cube is even, with each face the same size.

3 Now make a square-based pyramid. The base should be the same size as the base of your cube. Make the base and just fix four more straws to it to complete your pyramid.

4 Push down gently with your hand over the centre of the cube. Move your hand slightly to one side as you push down and you will feel the cube start to collapse.

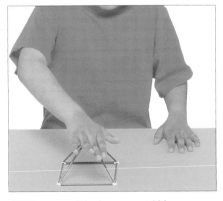

5 Repeat with the pyramid. You can feel how much more rigid this shape is, and it does not collapse. This is because a pyramid has triangular-shaped faces that meet at a central point.

Surveying a site

Making precise measurements in order to put up a building is called surveying. Accurate building requires two things. There must be a level base to the building, and building blocks must be laid absolutely flat, with their sides perfectly vertical, at right angles to the ground. Builders use plumb lines to check that verticals are absolutely true. A plumb line is a weight on the end of a line, which holds the line straight. These experiments show how to use water levels or a plumb line to measure differences in heights on a site.

▲ **The lie of the land**
A modern surveyor makes a detailed examination of the land before building work can start.

Is it vertical?

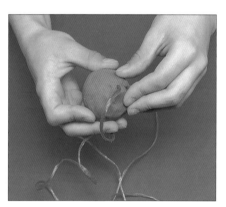

1 Make your own plumb line by fixing a 3cm ball of modelling material to a piece of string. Make a large knot in the string and model the material around it.

2 Push your stick into the ground. Make it as vertical as possible (pointing straight upwards). Keep moving it slightly until you are sure it is straight.

3 Now use your plumb line to check how straight your stick is. Get a friend to hold the line next to the stick. Measure between the stick and line at the top and farther down. If the measurements are the same, your stick is vertical.

Is your site level?

1 Here, you are making a simple version of a surveyor's level. To start, nail the short plank of wood to the top of the long wooden stick. Take care with the hammer.

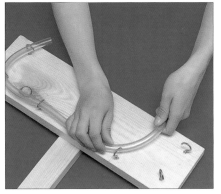

2 Now screw the hooks in along the bottom and up the sides of the plank. Thread the piping through the hooks. About 2cm of piping should stick up above the plank.

3 Get a friend to hold the device upright. Now, very carefully, pour the water into the pipe, using a funnel. The water level should come just above the piece of wood.

4 The friend holds the pole up 5m away. You look along the water levels so they line up, and also line up with the pole. The friend moves a finger up and down the pole. Shout out when the friend's finger lines up with the water levels.

5 The friend marks this on the pole, then moves to another spot. Repeat step 4. The distance between the two marks on the pole shows the difference in level between the two places.

Powerful levers

One of the simplest and oldest gadgets in the world is the lever. Any rod or stick can act as a lever, helping to move heavy objects or prise things apart. Levers are also used for lifting, cutting and squashing. The action of a lever can make a push more forceful, or make it a smaller push. It can also change the direction of a push. The difference between the size of the push you make on a lever (the effort) and the push the lever itself makes (the load) is called mechanical advantage.

A lever on a central pivot can also be used as a balance. The lever balances if the effect of the force (push) on one side of the pivot is the same as the effect of the force on the other. A see-saw is one sort of balancing lever. It is a plank balanced on a central post or pivot. A big person can balance someone small and light if they sit nearer to the central pivot of the see-saw.

▲ Using a simple lever

A spoon can be a lever. This girl is using the spoon as a simple lever to lift the lid off a can of paint. The lever arm pivots on the lip of the can. As the girl pushes down on the long end, the shorter end wedged under the lid lifts it up with greater force, making the stiff lid move.

▲ Cracking a nut

The strong crushing action of the nutcracker's jaws is produced by pressing the two lever arms together. A pair of nutcrackers, like a pair of scissors or a pair of pliers, has two lever arms joined at a pivot. The levers make the effort you use about four times bigger, allowing you to break the nut easily. Putting the pivot at the end of the nutcracker rather than towards the centre (as in a pair of scissors) means that the arms of the cracker can be shorter but still create a force just as big.

lever arm

jaws

pivot

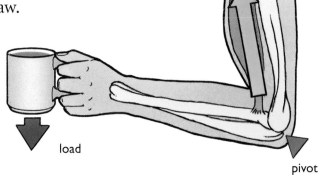

effort

load

pivot

▲ Body levers

Did you know that some parts of your body are levers? Every time you brush your hair or get up from a chair, the bones in your arms and legs act as levers. As your arm lifts up an object, your elbow is the pivot. Effort from the upper arm is transferred to your lower arm so that you can pick up the load in your hand.

Levers and lifting

1 A ruler can be used as a lever to lift a book. With the pivot (the box) near the book, only a small effort is needed to lift the book up. The lever makes the push greater.

2 When the pivot is moved to the middle of the lever, the effort needed to lift the book up is equal to the book's weight. The effort and the load are the same.

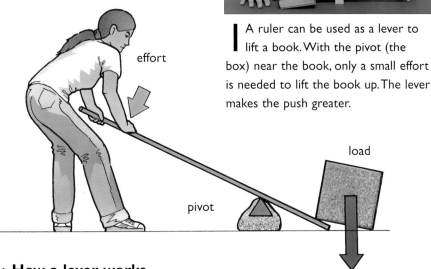

▲ How a lever works

A lever tilts on a pivot, which is nearer to the end of the lever with the load on it. The effort, or force, is the push you make on the long end of the lever to lift the weight of the load.

3 When the pivot is near where you are pressing, more effort is needed to lift the book. The force of the push needed to lift the book is now larger than the book's weight.

Balancing a see-saw

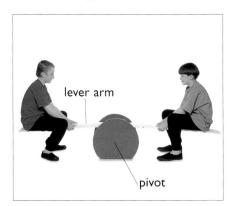

1 Ask a friend of equal weight to sit on one side of the see-saw, while you sit on the other side. If you sit the same distance from the pivot, you make the see-saw balance.

2 Ask another friend to join you on the see-saw. By adding another person, that side of the see-saw will overbalance. The pair's greater weight will easily lift the lighter person.

3 Get the pair to move nearer to the pivot of the see-saw. Their weight can be balanced by the lighter person moving farther away from the pivot. The see-saw will be equally balanced.

Levers at work

Find out how to make three different kinds of lever in these experiments. The first is a can crusher that uses a lever action to squash a can. The second is a gripper for picking up small objects, rather like a pair of tweezers. It can also work as a nutcracker. In a pair of nutcrackers, the load (in this case a sweet or a nut) is between the pivot (the pencil) and the effort (where you push). In a pair of tweezers, the effort is between the pivot and the load.

The third experiment is a balance scale. It is like the ones used by the Romans about 2,000 years ago. It works by balancing the weight of an object against a known weight, in this case a bag of coins. The coins are moved along the lever arm until they balance the object being weighed. The farther away from the pivot the weighed bag is, the greater turning effect it has on the lever arm. The heavier the weight being measured, the farther away the bag must be moved to balance the arm. The weight is read off against the scale along the arm.

Can crusher

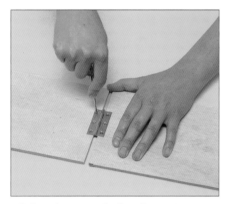

1 Lay the two planks of wood end to end. Ask an adult to help you screw them together with a hinge, using screws and a screwdriver. Make sure the hinge is secure.

2 Glue a jar lid to the inside edge of each plank of wood with the top of the lid face down. The lids should be about halfway along each plank and the same distance from the hinge.

To crush a can, put the can in between the lids so that it is held in place. Press down hard on the top piece of wood.

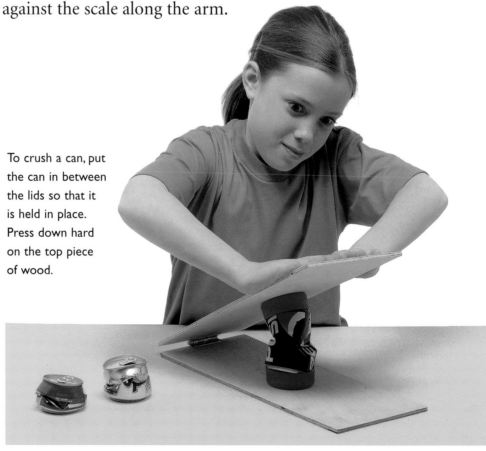

Gripper

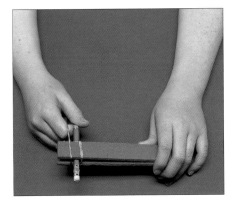

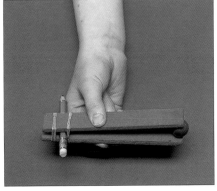

1 Put the pencil between the two pieces of wood, near one end. Wrap the elastic bands tightly around the pieces of wood to make a pivot. You have now made the gripper.

2 Hold the gripper near the pivot to make it act like a pair of tweezers. See if you can pick up a delicate object, such as a sweet or a grape, without crushing the object.

3 Hold the gripper at the end farthest away from the pivot. Now your lever operates as a pair of nutcrackers. The effort at the point you push is increased.

Balance scale

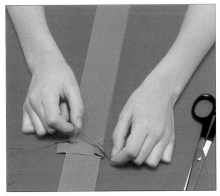

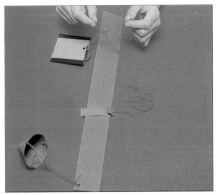

YOU WILL NEED

Gripper: short pencil, two pieces of wood each about 15cm long, thick elastic bands, objects to pick up or squash such as sweets or nuts.

Balance scale: thick card about 50cm x 8cm, thin card, scissors, string, ruler, hole punch, 12cm circle of card, sticky tape, 100g of coins, felt-tipped pen, objects to weigh.

1 Make the arm by folding the thick card in two. Make a loop of thin card and fold it loosely around the arm 11cm from one end. Tie a piece of string to this support.

2 Make a hole 1cm from the arm's end. Make the card circle into a cone. Tie it to the hole. Make an envelope from thin card and tie it to a loop so that it hangs over the arm.

To weigh an object, put it in the cone and slide the envelope of coins backwards and forwards along the arm until the arm balances. Each mark along the scale equals 50g. In this picture, the object being weighed is about 75g.

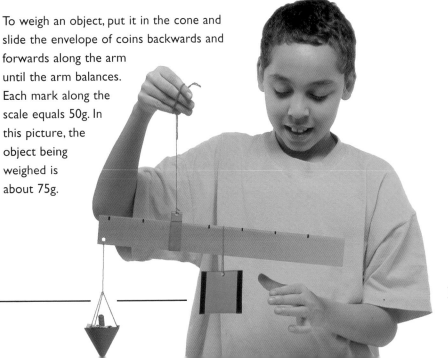

3 Put the coins in the envelope and seal it up. Starting from the centre of the support, make a mark every 5cm along the arm. This scale will tell you the weight of an object.

The power of energy

Nothing can happen without energy. Energy is needed to do work, such as making things move. To make something move, a source of energy is needed. For example, an engine works by burning fuel – a storage of chemical energy. The two experiments here explore different ways in which energy can be captured to make something move.

The turbine experiment shows how the energy in flowing water makes a bottle spin. This energy is used in hydroelectric power stations to generate electricity. The second project shows how electrical energy from a battery spins a motor. Electric motors are used in many household appliances such as vacuum cleaners and washing machines.

The development of the steam engine and the electric motor in the 1800s provided new sources of energy that were able to power ships and railway engines, for example, and later to light homes and streets.

▲ **Strike a light**

Lightning is a massive discharge of energy from a thundercloud. The cloud gets overloaded with electrically charged particles of water and ice.

YOU WILL NEED
scissors, plastic drinks bottle, pencil, two wide drinking straws, plastic sticky tape, thin string, tray, water.

3 Hold your turbine over a tray, or outdoors, so that you will not make a mess with the water. Fill the bottle with water. It will squirt out through the straws, causing the bottle to spin.

Turbine

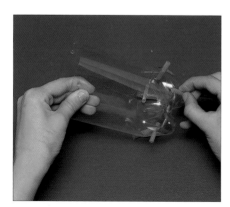

1 Cut off the bottle's top. Use the pencil to poke holes around its base. Cut the straws and push them through the holes. Use sticky tape to hold the straws in place.

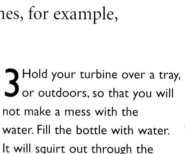

2 Poke three holes around the top of the bottle. Tie three equal lengths of string through the holes and join them to one long piece of string.

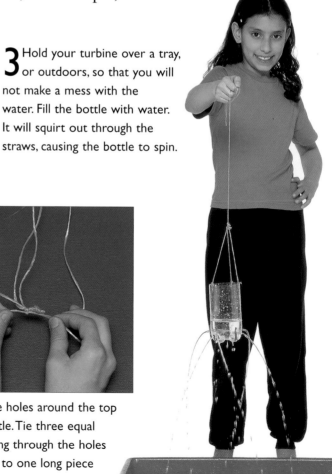

Electric motor

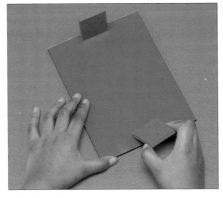

1 Use the bradawl to make a hole 1cm from the top of each of the two end supports. Glue them to the base board, 1cm inwards from the shorter edges.

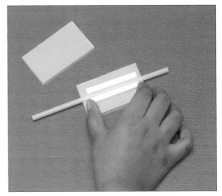

2 Cut a length of straw 12cm long. Glue the straw to one coil support. Fix the two coil support spacers either side of the straw. Glue the second support over the top.

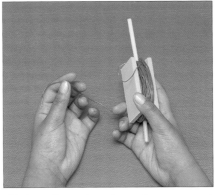

3 Strip 2cm of insulation from one end of the wire and 3cm from the other. Wind wire between the coil supports. Slide the reel on to the straw, with the longest part of the straw showing.

6 Place the magnets on the supports so that the coil and reel spin freely. Unbend two paper clips to make hooks. Join one end of each to a connecting wire and fix to the base with thick tape. Using paper clips, join the ends of the wires to the battery. The reel should start spinning around.

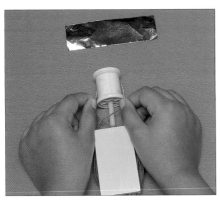

4 Cut a foil strip the width of the reel to fit three-quarters of the way around the reel. Cut it in half. Put the wire ends against the reel. Tape foil over each wire so it is under the foil's centre.

5 Stick the reel to the straw. Hold it between the end supports. Slide the knitting needle through the hole in each end support. Secure the coil support with green magnet supports.

Wind and water power

Modern windmills called wind turbines are used to generate electricity. The most efficient wind turbines only have two or three blades, like the propeller of an aircraft. Sometimes just a couple of large turbines can generate enough electricity to meet all the power needs of a small community.

There are several shapes of wind turbine. One of the most efficient is the vertical-axis type. This has an axle like the dowelling one in the first project. It is very efficient because it works no matter which way the wind is blowing. The second experiment shows you how to make a water wheel that captures the energy of falling water to lift a small weight. Pour water from different heights to see if it makes a difference to the wheel's speed.

sails

simple gears

grinding stones

▲ Wind for milling

A windmill uses the power of the wind to turn heavy mill stones that grind grain to make flour. The whole building can be turned around so that it faces into the wind. The speed of the mill is controlled by opening and closing slots in the sails. Inside a windmill is an arrangement of gear wheels, which transfers power from the sails to the grinding stones.

To make the windmill spin, hold it vertically with your fingers on the drawing pins at each end of the dowelling. Blow on the vanes. The windmill will spin easily.

YOU WILL NEED

plastic bottle, scissors, sticky tape, ruler, thin dowelling, drawing pins.

Make a windmill

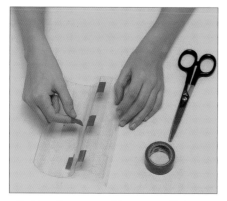

1 Cut the top and bottom off the bottle to leave a tube. Cut the tube in half lengthwise, then stick the two halves together in an S shape, so that the edges overlap by 2cm.

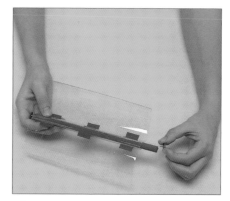

2 The piece of dowelling should be about 4cm longer than the vanes. Slide it into the slot between the vanes. Press a drawing pin gently into each end of the dowelling.

Make a water-wheel

YOU WILL NEED

large plastic bottle, scissors, wire
(ask an adult to cut the bottom out
of a coat hanger), cork, craft knife,
sticky tape, string, small weight,
jug, water, large plate.

1 Cut the top third off the plastic bottle. Cut a small hole in the bottom piece near the base (this is to let the water out). Cut a V-shape on each side of the rim.

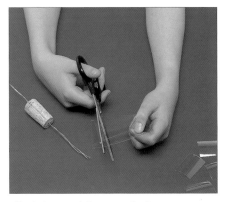

2 Ask an adult to push the wire through the centre of the cork to make an axle. From the top third of the plastic bottle, cut six small curved vanes (blades) as shown.

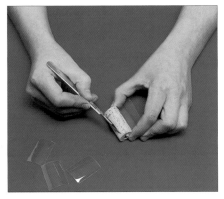

3 Ask an adult to cut six slots in the cork with a craft knife. (This might be easier without the wire.) Push the plastic vanes into the slots to make the water wheel.

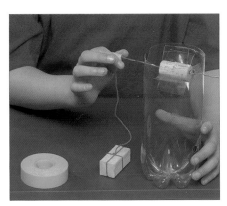

4 Rest the wheel's axle in the V-shaped slots. Tape a length of string towards one end of the axle and tie a small weight to the end of the string. Fill a jug with water.

5 Put the water wheel on a large plate or in the sink. Pour water on to the wheel so that it hits the upward-curving vanes. As the wheel turns, the weight should be lifted up.

Energy from liquid and air

Hydraulic machines have parts that are moved by liquid. Pneumatic machines have parts that are moved by a gas such as air. A hydraulic system has a pipe filled with a liquid such as oil and a piston that moves to and fro within the pipe. Pushing liquid into the pipe forces the piston to move, transmitting power from one end of the pipe to the other. In a simple pneumatic system, compressed air forces a piston to move.

In the first experiment you make a simple hydraulic machine powered by water pressure. Water is poured from a central reservoir (the jug of water) into a pipe. The water fills up a plastic bag. The bag expands and forces up the piston (the lid), which in turn raises a heavy object. Many cranes and trucks use this principle to lift heavy loads. In the air pump project, you discover the basic principles of how vacuum cleaners work. Finally, you make a miniature vacuum cleaner. Air is sucked in one hole and pushed out of another. A valve stops it being sucked in and pushed out of the wrong holes.

◀ **Filling an empty space**
Modern vacuum cleaners have an air pump operated by an electric motor. The pump creates a vacuum inside the cleaner. Dust rushes in from the outside to fill the vacuum.

YOU WILL NEED

large plastic bottle, scissors, airtight plastic bag, plastic tubing, sticky tape, plastic funnel, spray can lid, heavy book, jug of water.

Make an hydraulic lifter

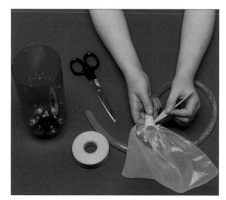

1 Cut the top off the large plastic bottle. Make sure the plastic bag is airtight and wrap its neck over the end of a length of plastic tubing. Seal the bag to the tube with tape.

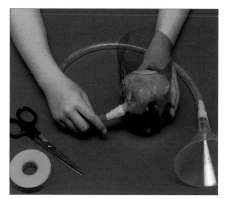

2 Fix a funnel to the other end of the tube. Make a hole at the base of the bottle and feed the bag and tubing through. The bag should sit in the bottom of the bottle.

3 Put the spray can lid on top of the bag and rest a heavy book on top of the bottle. Lift the funnel end of the tubing up, and slowly pour in water. What happens to the lid and the book?

Make an air pump

1 Cut around the large plastic bottle, about one third up from the bottom. Cut a slit down the side of the bottom part of the bottle so that it will slide inside the top part.

2 Ask an adult to help you nail the bottom of the bottle to the end of a wooden stick or piece of dowelling. You have now made a piston for your air pump.

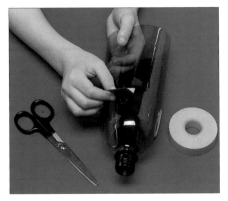

3 Cut a hole about 1cm across near the neck of the bottle. Cut a piece of card about 2cm x 2cm. Tape one edge of the card to the bottle to form a flap over the hole.

4 Drop a table tennis ball into the top part of the bottle so that it rests in the neck. Push the bottom part of the bottle (the piston) into the top part (the cylinder).

5 Move the piston in and out to suck air into the bottle and out of the hole. Can you see how both the valves work? The flap should automatically close when you pull the piston out.

Make a vacuum cleaner

1 Make the air pump from the project above without the card flap. Tape string to the ball, feed it through the bottle's neck and tape it down so that the ball is held near the neck.

2 Make a tissue paper bag and glue it over the hole near the neck of the bottle. Air from the pump will go through the bag and anything the vacuum picks up should be trapped.

3 Try picking up tiny bits of paper with the vacuum. Pull the piston out sharply to suck the bits of paper into the bottle. Push the piston back in gently to pump the paper into the bag.

How magnets work

Magnets are usually made of the metal iron, or another material that has lots of iron in it, such as steel. Magnets can be various shapes, but all of them have the ability to pull things towards themselves. This invisible force is called magnetism. Magnets only attract (pull) metals that are made of iron or that contain iron.

Magnetism is concentrated around the poles (ends) of a magnet. A magnet has two poles, called the north pole and the south pole. The two poles may look the same but they behave differently. Put one pole of a magnet near to a pole of another magnet and watch what happens. You may feel an attraction (pulling) force as the two poles stick together. Alternatively, you may feel a repulsion (pushing) force, as the two poles push away from each other. In all magnets, identical poles will repel (push away) each other, while different poles will pull towards each other.

Is a big magnet more powerful than a small one? Not always. You cannot tell how powerful a magnet is just by looking at it. Compare the strength and power of different magnets in the projects opposite.

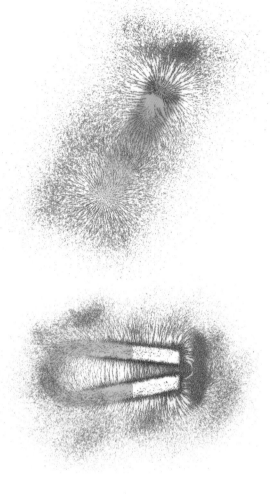

▲ Seeing magnetism
You cannot see the magnetic force around a magnet but you can see the effects of its presence when an iron nail sticks to a magnet. You can see the shape of a magnetic field by using tiny, powder-like pieces of iron, called iron filings. Iron filings reveal that the lines and strength of the magnetic force are concentrated around and between the poles at the end of the horseshoe magnet. On a bar magnet, they line up to show how the magnetic force spreads out from the poles (ends).

Tiny magnets ▶
Think of a bar of iron as having millions of micromagnets inside it. These are called domains. If they are all jumbled up, the bar is not a magnet. If the micromagnets in a bar are lined up and point the same way, it is a magnet.

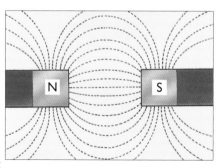

◀ Attraction and repulsion ▶
The poles of two magnets that are different or opposite will attract. Magnetic lines of force from north and south poles pull together and join. The poles of two magnets that are the same will repel or push each other apart.

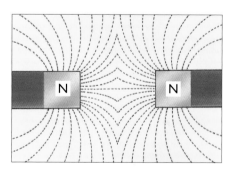

Strength of a magnet

1 Cut off a length of sticky tape and use it to fix the round container firmly to the work surface. The round container will act as the pivot, or the balancer.

2 Attach a magnet to one end of the ruler with an elastic band and some washers to the other end of the ruler. Position the middle of the ruler on the balancer.

3 Hold another magnet above the first. Lower it until the ruler tips over. Measure its height above the table. The higher it is when the ruler tips over, the stronger the magnet.

YOU WILL NEED

Strength of a magnet: scissors, sticky tape, round plastic container, two magnets, ruler, elastic bands, steel washers.

Power of a magnet: pencil, drawing pins, strong thread, card, ruler with holes at either end and in the middle, scissors, sticky tape, elastic bands, sticky dots, pen, two small bar magnets.

Power of a magnet

1 Attach one end of a piece of thread to a pin and the other to a pencil. Draw two large quarter-circles on card. The distance from the pin to curved edge should be as long as the ruler.

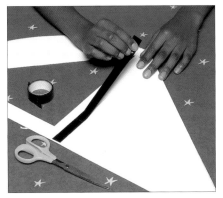

2 Draw a triangle in one quarter-circle and cut it out. Using the triangle as a template, cut out a triangle from the other quarter-circle. Tape them together.

3 Push a pin through the ruler's end hole so that it pivots. Attach elastic bands from the ruler's middle hole to the quarter-circle's side. Add dots labelled N and S to each end of the ruler.

Stand the magnet measurer upright. Fix one magnet to the ruler's top end with an elastic band. Bring the unlike pole of another magnet near it. How far can it pull the ruler? Stronger magnets pull it farther.

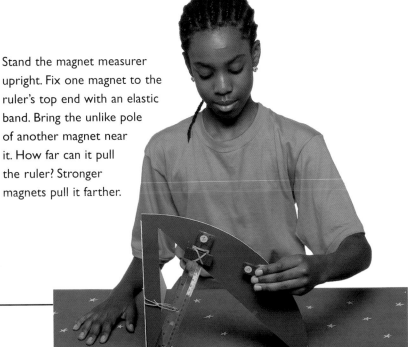

157

Magnetic Earth

The Earth behaves as if there is a giant bar magnet running through its middle from pole to pole. This affects every magnetic material that comes within its reach. If you hold a magnet so that it can rotate freely, it always ends up with one end pointing to the Earth's North Pole and the other to the South Pole. This is how a compass works – the needle automatically swings to the North. The Earth's magnetism comes from its inner core of iron and nickel.

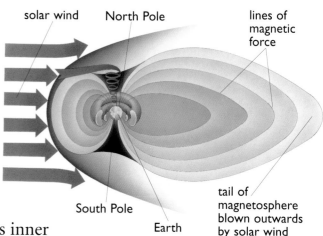

solar wind   North Pole   lines of magnetic force

South Pole

Earth

tail of magnetosphere blown outwards by solar wind

You can use the compass you make here to plot a magnetic field like the Earth's. The Earth's magnetic field is slightly tilted, so compasses do not swing exactly towards the North Pole, but to a point a little way off northern Canada. This direction is known as magnetic north.

Make a compass

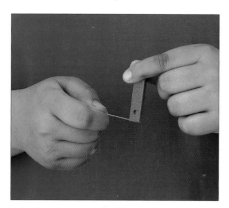

1 To turn the needle into a magnet, stroke the end of the magnet slowly along it. Repeat this in the same direction for about 45 seconds. This magnetizes the needle.

▲ Magnetic protection

The effects of Earth's magnetism extend 60,000km out into space. In fact, there is a vast magnetic force field around the Earth called the magnetosphere. This traps electrically charged particles and so protects the Earth from the solar wind – the deadly stream of charged particles whizzing from the Sun.

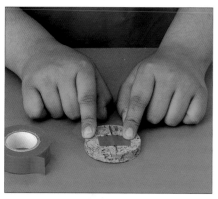

2 Place the magnetized needle on the slice of cork. Make sure that it is exactly in the middle, otherwise it will not spin evenly. Tape the needle into position.

3 Fill the bowl nearly to the brim with water and float the cork in it. Make sure the cork is exactly in the middle and can turn without rubbing on the edges of the bowl.

The Earth's magnetic field should now swivel the needle on the cork. One end of the needle will always point to the north. That end is its north pole.

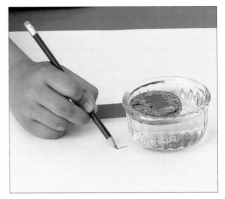

Magnetic field

1 Lay a large sheet of paper on a table. Put the magnet in the middle of the paper. Set up your needle compass a few centimetres away from one end of the magnet.

2 Wait as the compass needle settles in a particular direction as it is swivelled by the magnet. Make a pencil mark on the paper to show which way it is pointing.

3 Move the compass a little way towards the other end of the magnet. Mark a line on the paper to show which way the needle is pointing now.

4 Repeat Step 3 for about 25 different positions around the magnet. Try the compass both near the magnet and farther away. You should now have a pattern of marks.

Look at the pattern of marks you have made on the paper. They should form a series of rings around the magnet, like layers of an onion. Earth's magnetic field is shaped like this.

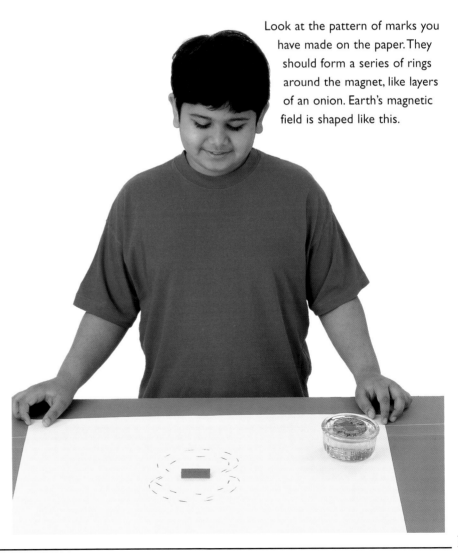

Magnets and maps

Look at a map – which way up does it go? Maps are important. They let us know our location. Without magnets, we would not know how to use a map or find our way around an area. Compass needles are tiny magnets that rotate to point to the Earth's magnetic north. Look on a local map to find a diagram of the compass points, an arrow or 'N' that indicates north. Then set a compass so that the needle points north. Turn the map so that its north faces the same way as the compass north. Now the map is lined up accurately in relation to the landscape. If you are on a hilltop with wide views, you can see how the map is a tiny plan of the countryside around.

▲ Magnetic migration

The yellow arrows show the migration routes of the Arctic tern. The routes follow the Earth's magnetic force. The tern flies from north to south and then, later in the year, from south to north. Birds may also use rivers, mountains, coastlines, the Sun, Moon and stars to help them find their way.

▲ Which way up? ▶

We are so familiar with maps having north at the top that they look odd when they are turned around. Can you recognize this country (top) when it is turned upside down? Can you find it on the globe (right)?

Loop compass

I Straighten out a paper clip. Magnetize it by stroking it with the strong magnet. Cut a disc of card, bend the wire into a large loop and insert it into holes in the card.

2 Tape the paper clip to the piece of cork and to the card circle. Tie the thread to the top of the wire loop. Let it hang and twirl around freely. It is now ready to test.

3 Does the paper clip magnet work as a compass needle and point north and south? Check it with the ready-made compass. What do you find happens?

Drawing a maze

YOU WILL NEED

Loop compass: paper clip, strong magnet, card, scissors, thin wire, sticky tape, cork tile, thread, ready-made compass.

Drawing a maze: cardboard, coloured pens, compass.

I Draw a maze on cardboard. Make it colourful and fun. Put in some dead ends and false turns. Make sure one route leads all the way through from one end of the maze to another!

2 Record your course through the maze, using compass points for the direction. You can limit the information to north, south, east and west or include north-east, south-west and so on.

Can you find your way through this maze? When you have made it to the other side, try recording your route with compass points. At the beginning of the journey, you head east, turn north and then go east again. Can you complete these instructions for the entire journey?

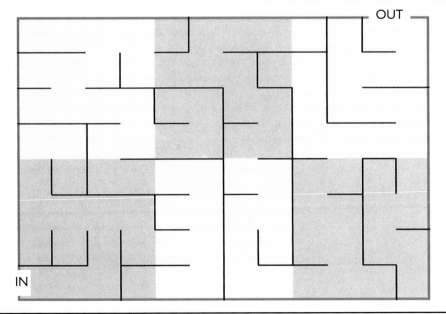

Electric magnets

Some magnets, such as bar and horseshoe magnets, are permanent. They have what scientists call 'spontaneous permanent magnetism'. Their magnetism needs no outside force or energy to create it. A way of making magnetism is by using electricity. When electricity flows through a wire or another similar conducting (carrying) material, it produces a magnetic field around the wire. This is called electromagnetism or EM. In fact, magnetism and electricity are very closely linked. Each can be used to make the other. EM is used in many tools, machines and devices. Some electromagnetic machines use the electricity from batteries. Others need the much more powerful mains electricity from wall sockets.

The first practical electromagnets were made by British bootmaker and spare-time scientist William Sturgeon. He used them to amaze audiences at his science shows in the 1820s. The basic design has hardly changed since. You can make a similar electromagnet in the projects opposite.

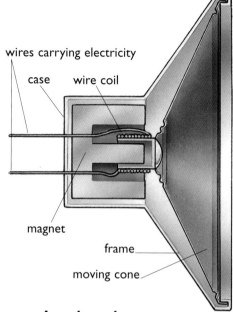

wires carrying electricity

case   wire coil

magnet

frame

moving cone

▲ Loudspeaker
Electrical signals are transferred to the loudspeaker along a connecting wire (speaker lead). Electricity flows through the wire coil, which is attached to the plastic speaker cone. The signals make the coil into an electromagnet that varies in strength. This magnetic field is itself inside the field of a strong permanent magnet. The two fields interact, with like poles repelling. This makes the coil move or vibrate, and the loudspeaker cone vibrates, too. This in turn sends out sound waves.

▶ Creating a magnetic field
As electricity flows through a wire, a magnetic field is created around it. The magnetic lines of force flow in circles around the wire. This is called an electromagnetic field. As soon as the electricity is switched off, the magnetism stops.

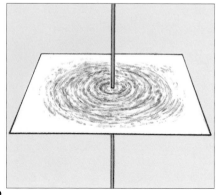

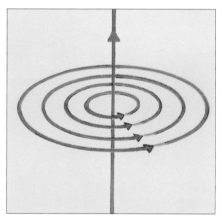

◀ Seeing electromagnetism
If iron filings are sprinkled on to a piece of cardboard that has an electricity-carrying wire through it, the filings are affected by the magnetic field. They arrange themselves in circles to show the lines of magnetic force, as they do with an ordinary magnet.

▼ Are you receiving me?
The earpiece of a telephone receives varying electrical signals from the mouthpiece of the telephone held at other end of the line. The earpiece works like a simple loudspeaker to recreate the sounds of the speaking person's voice.

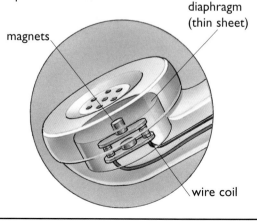

diaphragm (thin sheet)

magnets

wire coil

Electromagnet

1 Using the wirestrippers, carefully remove a few centimetres of plastic insulation from each end of the wire. These bare ends will connect to the battery.

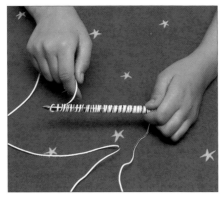

2 Carefully wrap the wire in a tight coil around the iron nail. The plastic insulation around the wire conducts the electricity around the iron nail.

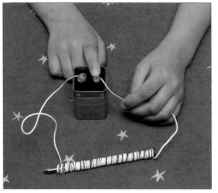

3 Connect the wire's ends to the battery terminals. (It does not matter which is positive or negative.) Test your electromagnet by picking up paper clips.

Adding a switch

YOU WILL NEED

Electromagnet: wirestrippers, 2m of wire (insulated, plastic-coated, multistrand copper), large iron nail, 9-volt battery, paper clips.

Adding a switch: hole punch piece of card, brass fasteners.

1 Make two equal-sized holes in the piece of card. Push the brass fasteners into them. Push one of the fasteners through a paper clip first. Open out the legs of the fasteners.

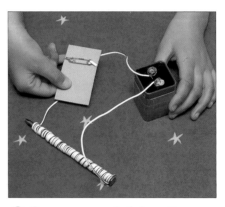

2 Connect one end of electromagnet wire to the fastener. Connect the other to a battery terminal. Attach the remaining fastener to the other terminal with short wire. Turn the card over.

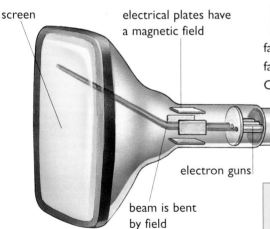

screen — electrical plates have a magnetic field

electron guns

beam is bent by field

▲ Inside a television

Television sets, computer monitors and other similar screens have electromagnet-type devices inside. These are usually shaped like flat plates. They bend the beam that scans across the screen line by line, to build up the picture. This occurs many times every second.

WARNING!

NEVER use electricity from wall sockets. It is too dangerous and could kill you. Ask an adult for help with this project.

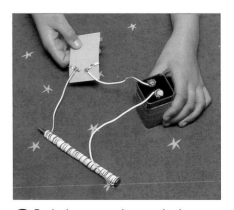

3 Push the paper clip attached to one fastener away from the other fastener. No electricity flows. Turn the clip to touch the fastener. Electricity flows, switching on the electromagnet.

Computer data storage

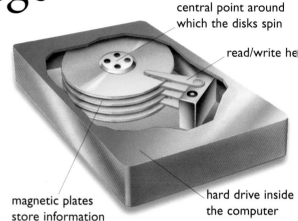

central point around which the disks spin

read/write he[ad]

magnetic plates store information

hard drive inside the computer

The hard disk of a computer consists of a number of flat, circular plates. Each one of these plates is coated with tiny magnetic particles. The hard disk also contains a controlling mechanism called the read/write head. This is positioned slightly above the magnetic plates. Data (information) is sent to the disk as a series of electrical pulses. These are sent to the read/write head, which contains a tiny electromagnet. The head magnetizes the tiny magnetic particles on the surface of the plates. This pattern of particles on the disk represents the data. You can see how this happens in the project.

When reading information, the magnetized particles on the hard disk create a small current in the head as the plates spin under it. This is then converted by circuits into binary code, a number system that computers use. The code is based on just two numbers (binary means two), 0 and 1. Different combinations represent the letters of the alphabet.

▲ Inside the hard drive

A typical drive consists of a stack of thin disks, called a platter. The upper surface of each disk is coated with tiny magnetic particles, and each disk has its own read/write head on a movable arm. When storing and reading information, the disks spin at very high speeds (up to 100 revolutions a second).

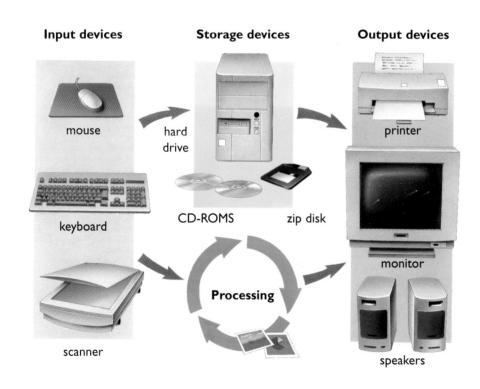

Input devices

mouse

keyboard

scanner

Storage devices

hard drive

CD-ROMS   zip disk

Processing

Output devices

printer

monitor

speakers

◄ Using computers

When people use a computer, they are doing four different things:

1. Inputting data (information) using an input device.

2. Storing the data so that it can be reused (often called data storage).

3. Working with the data they put in (often called processing).

4. Retrieving and looking at the data using an output device.

Storing data on disk

1 Draw a circle with a diameter of 20cm on the piece of white card. Draw three more circles inside, each with a diameter 2cm smaller than the one before. Cut out the largest circle.

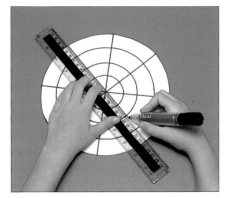

2 Position a ruler at the centre of the circle where the compass point has made a hole. Draw four lines through the middle to divide the circle into eight equal parts.

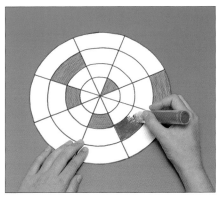

3 Use a red marker to colour in six or seven sections as shown above. Leave the remaining section white. The white areas represent full disk space. Red areas are empty disk space.

4 Attach some modelling material to the rim of a plastic cup. Then turn it upside down on a smooth surface. Press it down gently to make sure it is secure. Place the disk on top.

5 Push the drawing pin through the middle of the disk into the cup. Make sure the disk can turn. Scatter paper clips on the surface. Hold the magnet under the disk. Move it around.

The paper clips will move around the surface of the disk, and all line up in one section of the disk. This is what happens to the magnetic particles on a hard disk when an electric current is passed through them by the read/write head. In a computer, the way the magnetic particles line up is a record of the data stored on the hard disk. Remove the paper clips from the disk. Spin the disk clockwise with one hand and with a finger of the other hand touch areas of the disk. If you stop the disk on a white part you have found data. If you stop on a red section you have found empty disk space.

Fun with magnets

Many tricks rely on the invisible power of magnets. For example, did you know that you can easily remove paper clips from water without getting your fingers wet? The first project shows you how to make a paper bat that hovers in mid air.

Magnets are used to recover pieces of wrecked ships from awkward or dangerous places on the sea bed, where the water might be murky. The magnetic fishing game opposite demonstrates how magnets are used in this way.

▲ **Floating trick**
Put paper clips in a beaker of water and slide the magnet up the side. The paper clips will follow, dragged along by the magnet, until they reach the rim.

YOU WILL NEED

Bat magnet: black paper, white pencil, scissors, stiff paper, sticky tape, stiff wire, string, paper clips, strong magnet.

Magnetic fishing: different coloured plastic bags, felt tipped marker, scissors, paper clips, magnets, string, wooden dowelling, sticky tape, deep plate or shallow bowl, water, jug or watering can.

Bat magnet

1 Draw a large bat shape onto a sheet of black paper with the white pencil. (You could fold the paper in half first to make sure that your bat is symmetrical.) Cut out the bat shape.

2 Tape pieces of stiff paper to the bat's underside, as shown. Then tape lengths of stiff wire across each of the wings. Secure the wire with a piece of string.

3 Place several paper clips on the pieces of paper that you have used to stiffen the bat. Cover each paper clip with a piece of sticky tape to keep it secure.

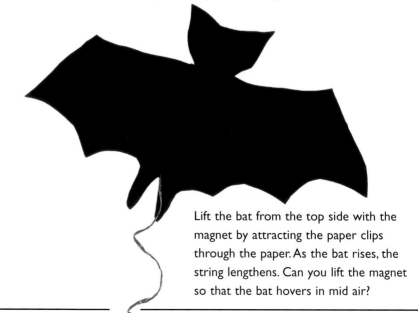

Lift the bat from the top side with the magnet by attracting the paper clips through the paper. As the bat rises, the string lengthens. Can you lift the magnet so that the bat hovers in mid air?

Magnetic fishing

1 Draw some fish shapes on to the coloured plastic bags with the felt tipped marker. Keep the bags as still as possible while you do this. Cut out the shapes carefully with the scissors.

2 Decorate each of the fish with the marker. Draw scales and a face on one side of each fish and write a different number on the other side of each fish.

3 Attach a steel paper clip to each fish. Make sure the paper clips are firmly attached. This will allow you to catch the fish with a magnetic rod.

4 Tie a magnet to one end of a piece of string. If you tie the string around the middle of the magnet, it will be quite secure and the magnet won't fall out.

5 Tape the string that is attached to the magnet, to the end of some wooden dowelling with sticky tape. Make sure it is stuck on securely or it may float off in the water.

6 Put all of your fish, scale side up, in a plate or bowl and fill with water from a jug or watering can. You are now ready to start the fishing game.

WARNING!

Keep plastic bags away from small children as they can be very dangerous.

Lower your fishing rods into the water to catch the fish. The paper clips will be attracted to the magnets on the ends of the rods. Lift your fish out of the pond. When there are no fish left, count up the points on the back of your fish, and the highest score wins.

Magnet sports

You can make your own table-top car race, using some magnets. Small, flat, bar or ring magnets are best. The trick is to stay on the track and speed along, but not so fast that the magnet loses your car! If that happens, the race is over. The second project shows you how to create your own Olympic Games using an electromagnet. A washer represents a discus, a nut a shot put and a nail a javelin. Use the electromagnet to throw each of them. When you switch off the electromagnet, it releases the iron or steel object.

Magnetic racing

1 Carefully glue a magnet to the end of each ruler or strip of wood. Use 30cm rulers if you can, or if these are unavailable, use similar-sized strips of wood.

2 Draw the shapes of some racing cars on the coloured card. You can make the wheels a different colour and perhaps add stripes, too, so that each car looks different.

3 Carefully cut out the racing car shapes with scissors. Decorate the cars with stick-on shapes, such as stars, to make up your own racing team.

4 Glue a steel paper clip to the underside of each racing car. Let the glue dry thoroughly while you draw a racing track on a large sheet of cardboard.

Put the track on two books so it is raised all around the edges. Place your racing cars on the start line. Push the ruler underneath so the magnet faces upward and attracts the paper clip on the base of your car. Move the ruler slowly so the magnet drags the paper clip and car along. Practise driving like this for a while before you race your opponent.

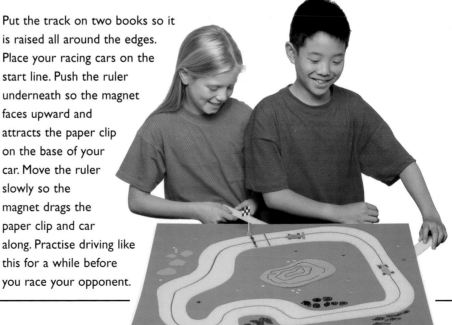

Electromagnetic Olympics

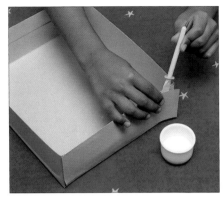

1 Cut a sheet of card into a base about 50 x 40cm. Cut four strips the same length and 10–15cm deep, for the sides. Glue the sides and base together.

2 Cut out squares of card for the scoreboard and tape them together to make a sheet that will fit neatly into the box. Write scores on them and decorate them.

3 Fit the scoreboard into the box. It is best not to glue it, since you may wish to take it out and alter the scores, or make a new scoreboard as you become an expert at the games.

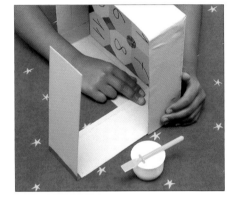

4 Cut two more card strips. Tape them together at one each of their short edges. Glue the other short edges inside the box, on opposite sides. Position this 'arch' at one end of the box.

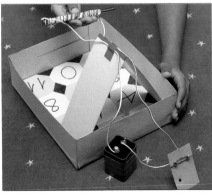

5 Make an electromagnet from the nail and wire. Tape it to the arch so it hangs below by its wires. Connect the free ends of the wire to the battery. Use a paper clip as a battery switch.

Push the nail hanging below the wires to test that it swings back and forth. Switch on the nail electromagnet using the paper clip switch. It should attract an iron or steel object such as the nail, which is the javelin. Push the nail electromagnet so it swings back and forth. Turn off the switch and the javelin will be released. Note where this lands on the scoreboard.

Images from light

The picture on a television screen is made up of thin lines of light. In the first project you will see that a television picture is made up from rows of glowing dots of coloured light. The picture consists of just three colours – red, green and blue. Viewed from a distance, these colours mix to produce the full range of colours that we see naturally around us – as the second experiment demonstrates.

Fax machines work in a similar way to television, only more slowly. When you feed a sheet of paper into a fax machine, a beam of light moves back and forth across it. Dark places absorb the light and pale places reflect it. The reflected light enters a detector that produces an electric current. The electric current is changed into a code made up of chirping sounds. These travel down the line to the receiving fax machine. This code controls a scanner that moves across heat-sensitive paper and produces a facsimile (copy) of the original. The final project shows how a fax machine breaks an image into tiny squares that are black or white.

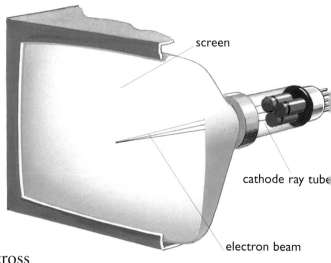

screen

cathode ray tube

electron beam

▲ **Tube travel**
The cathode ray tube is the heart of a television. Pictures are received in the form of electrical impulses. These impulses control a stream of electrons inside the cathode ray tube. The electron beam scans across the screen and creates the pictures as points of coloured light. This is the picture that the viewer sees.

TV screen

YOU WILL NEED

TV screen: TV set, torch, powerful magnifying glass.

Secondary colours: red, green, and blue transparent plastic film, 3 powerful torches, 3 elastic bands, black card.

Digital images: ruler, pencil, tracing paper, photograph, black felt-tipped pen.

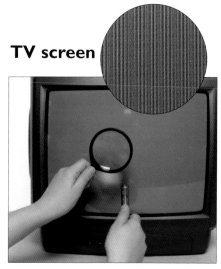

1 Turn off the TV. Shine the torch close to the screen and look through the magnifying glass. You will see that the screen is covered in very fine lines.

2 Turn on the TV and view the screen through the lens. The picture is made up of minute rectangles of light coloured red, green or blue.

Secondary colours

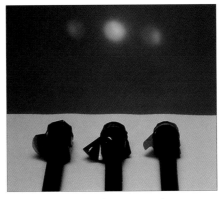

1 Attach a piece of coloured film over the end of each of your three torches. Stretch the film tightly and use an elastic band to hold it firmly in place.

2 Shine the torches on to the black card. You can see the three different primary colours of red, green and blue.

3 Position the torches so that the three circles of coloured light overlap in a cloverleaf pattern. Overlapping colours mix to give new, secondary colours.

Digital images

1 Rule lines 5mm apart to cover the tracing paper in squares. Put the paper over the photograph. Use the pen to fill each dark square. Leave each light square blank.

The picture is made from squares that are either black or white.

The result is a 'digitized' image, which means it can be represented by numbers – the digit 1 for white squares and the digit 0 for black squares. The digitized image contains less detail than the original photo. You could increase the detail of the image by using a greater number of smaller squares.

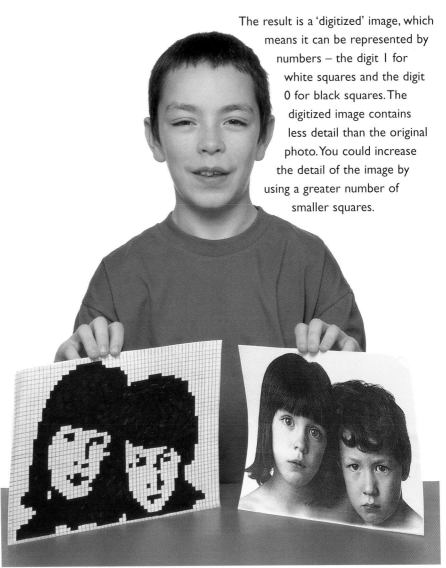

Cameras and light

What is the vital piece of equipment you must not forget if you are off on holiday or having a birthday party? Your camera! To most people, a camera is simply a device for taking snapshots of their favourite people or places. In fact, modern cameras are sophisticated light-recording machines that make use of the very latest breakthroughs in technology and computer science.

Cameras work in a similar way to your eyes, but they make a permanent record of a scene that you can share with other people. They record scenes on film or digitally by collecting light from that scene and turning it into a picture. Although light appears to be white, it is actually made up of light of many colours like a rainbow. The first experiment shows you how to break the light spectrum into its component parts by shining light through water.

Cameras have three basic parts. The camera body holds the film. The shutter opens to allow light to come through to the lens. The lens bends rays of light and directs them on to the film to make a picture. In the second experiment you can collect light from a scene to make a picture, in the same way that a camera works.

YOU WILL NEED

Split light into a rainbow:
mirror, dish, reusable adhesive, jug of water, torch, piece of white card.
Make your own viewer: small cardboard box, scissors, ruler, thin card, sharp pencil, sticky tape, tracing paper.

Split light into a rainbow

1 Carefully lean the mirror against the inner side of the dish. Use two pieces of reusable adhesive to stick either side of the mirror to the dish at an angle as shown.

2 Pour water into the dish until it is about 4cm in depth. Notice that as you fill the dish, a wedge-shaped volume of water is created alongside the mirror.

3 Switch on the torch. Shine the beam from the torch on to the surface of the water in front of the mirror. This should produce a spectrum or 'rainbow'.

4 In dim light, hold up the piece of white card above the dish to look at your rainbow. You may need to alter the positions of the card and torch before you can see it properly.

Make your own viewer

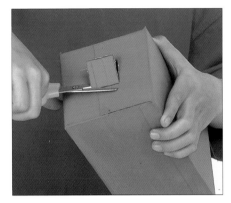

1 Use a pair of sharp scissors to cut a small square hole, approximately 1.5cm x 1.5cm, in one end of the cardboard box. You may need an adult's help to do this.

2 Now cut a much larger square hole in the other end of your cardboard box. Cut away most of the end of the box, as shown in the picture.

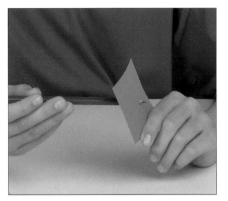

3 Cut a square of thin card about 4cm x 4cm. Find the centre of the card using a ruler. Use a sharp pencil to pierce a tiny hole in the centre of the card.

4 Place the piece of thin card over the outside of the smaller hole on the box. Make sure that the pencil hole is centred over the square hole. Now tape it into place.

5 Cut a square of tracing paper slightly bigger than the larger hole at the other end of the box. Stick it securely over that hole. Your viewer is now ready to use.

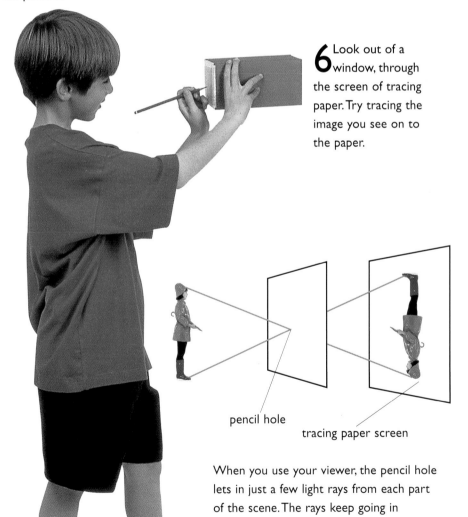

6 Look out of a window, through the screen of tracing paper. Try tracing the image you see on to the paper.

pencil hole

tracing paper screen

When you use your viewer, the pencil hole lets in just a few light rays from each part of the scene. The rays keep going in straight lines and hit the tracing paper screen, making an upside-down image of the scene.

A photographic image

The camera's job is to create a focused image of a scene, but this would be no use without a way of recording the image. This is the job of the film. There are three basic types of film – colour negative, colour-reversal, and black-and-white. Film comes in different sizes (called formats) and lengths. Most cameras take 35mm film, and the usual lengths are 24 and 36 exposures.

Film is coated with a chemicals that are affected by light. When an image strikes the film, the coating records the patterns of light, dark and colour. Film has to be developed with chemicals before you can see the recorded pictures. Until then, it must be kept in complete darkness. When undeveloped film is exposed to direct light, it turns black.

This project shows that you do not need to have a camera to see how film works. In fact, you do not even need a film! You can use black and white photographic paper instead. Photographic paper is the paper that prints are made on. It works in the same way as film. Here, you can see how to make a picture called a photogram. It is made by covering some parts of a sheet of photographic paper with objects and then shining light on the sheet. When the paper is developed, the areas that were hit by the light turn black, leaving you an image of the objects.

▲ Danger!
This symbol, on photographic chemical bottles, means that they can be dangerous if not used with care. Always wear protective gloves and goggles.

◄ Photographic paper
For black and white prints, you need a paper called monochrome paper. Buy the smallest size you can, and choose grade 2 if possible, with a gloss (shiny) finish. The paper comes in a light-proof envelope or box. Only open the envelope in complete darkness. The paper is in a second, black polythene envelope. You will also need two photographic chemicals – developer for paper (not film) and fixer. Buy them from a photographic supplier, and ask an adult to help you use them safely.

Make your own photogram

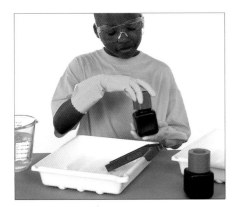

1 Ask an adult to help you follow the instructions to dilute the chemicals with water. Protect your eyes and hands when handling them. Store the diluted chemicals in plastic bottles.

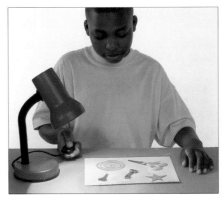

2 Turn off the lamp. Lay a sheet of photographic paper down, shiny side up. Put some objects on it. Then turn the lamp on again for a few seconds.

3 Pick up the paper with the tongs and put it into the dish of developer. Push the paper down so that it is completely underneath the liquid.

4 After a minute, use the tongs to move the paper into the fixer. Leave the paper right under the liquid for a minute, until the image is fixed.

images made on photographic paper

5 Now you can turn the light back on. Using the tongs, lift the paper out of the fixer and wash it with running water for a few minutes. Then lay the paper on a flat surface to dry. This technique is an excellent way of producing unique invitations or greetings cards quickly and effectively.

Getting in focus

Before taking a photograph, you need to make sure that your subject is in focus. When it is, all the rays of light that leave a point on the subject are bent by the lens so that they hit the correct place on the film. This makes a clear, sharp image. Parts of the scene inside or behind the subject may not be in focus. On some cameras you have to choose the part of the scene that you want to be in focus. Autofocus cameras focus the lens by automatically choosing the object at the centre of the image to be taken.

This experiment involves making a simple camera with just a few basic pieces of equipment. It uses photographic paper (paper with a light-sensitive coating on one side) instead of film and a pinhole instead of a lens. When the paper is processed, you will have a negative. The 'Easy prints' project on the next page shows you how to develop it.

viewfinder

lens *pentaprism*

light ray *mirror*

▲ Focusing SLRs

With an SLR (single lens reflex) camera, you can see exactly what the image looks like through the viewfinder. On a manual-focus SLR, you turn a ring around the lens until your subject comes into focus. When the subject is in focus, the light rays meet on the film focal plane. This is the exposed part of the film that is held flat at the back of the camera by a pressure plate. You can see it if you open the back of your camera when it is empty.

YOU WILL NEED

pinhole box viewer, kitchen foil, scissors, sticky tape, pencil, black paper, thin card, ruler, heavy light-proof cloth or plastic sheet, photographic paper, elastic band.

◄ Get it sharp

In this photograph (*left*), the subject is in sharp focus. You can see all the fine detail. When the same shot is out of focus (*below*), it makes the subject look blurred. Autofocus cameras focus on the object in the centre of the viewfinder and do the job of focusing for you.

Making a pinhole camera

1 Make the pin-hole viewer from the 'Make your own viewer' project, but remove the tracing-paper screen. Replace the 4cm card square with kitchen foil.

2 Pierce a hole, about 2mm across, in the centre of the foil using a sharp pencil. Open the back of the box. Roll up some black paper and fit it through the large hole to line the inside.

3 Cut a square of card large enough to cover the kitchen foil. Tape just the top edge of the square of card to the box, so that it will act as a shutter.

4 Measure and cut a square of card to fit right across the other end of the box. Tape it to one edge so that it closes over the hole like a door or flap.

5 Lay the heavy, light-proof cloth or light-proof plastic sheet on the working surface. Cut a piece of the cloth or sheet large enough to fold around the end of the box.

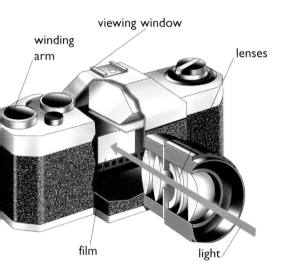

winding arm

viewing window

lenses

film

light

▲ Reflex action

In a single lens reflex camera, light enters through the lenses at the front and strikes the film at the back. Users can see clearly what they are photographing by means of a prism mounted in the camera.

6 In a completely dark room, and feeling with your fingers, put a piece of the photographic paper underneath the flap at the end of the box.

7 Close the flap, then, still feeling with your fingers, wrap the cloth or plastic sheet tightly over it. Next, put an elastic band tightly around the box to secure it.

8 Now you can turn the light on. Point the camera at a well-lit object and open the shutter. Leave the camera perfectly still for about five minutes and then close the shutter.

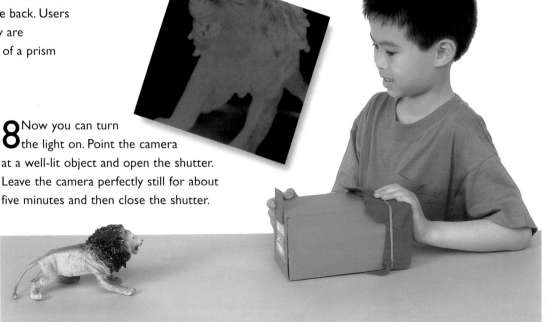

Letting in the light

Exposure is the word for the amount of light that reaches the film in your camera. The aperture (opening) is a hole behind the lens that can be adjusted to let more or less light on to the film. Changing the aperture affects both the brightness of an image and the depth of field that is in focus. Your eyes work in the same way. If the light is bright, your pupils get smaller to protect your retinas. If the light is dim, then the pupils enlarge to let in more light. In the experiment opposite you can investigate different apertures for yourself.

One of the first things photographers want to do is to get their films developed so that they can see how the pictures have turned out. If you have just taken a photograph with the pinhole camera you made in an earlier project, you can find out how easy it is to turn it into a photographic print in the project below.

> ## YOU WILL NEED
>
> **Easy prints:** photographic paper and chemicals, negative from pinhole camera, torch or desk lamp, safety goggles, rubber gloves, plastic dishes, plastic tongs or tweezers.
>
> **Amazing apertures:** magnifying glass, cardboard tube, sticky tape, scissors, thin card, tracing paper, desk lamp.

▲ How does a shutter work?

Open the back of your camera (when there is no film inside). Place a small strip of tracing paper where your film usually goes. Aim the camera at a subject and press the shutter release button. You should see a brief flash of the image on your tracing paper.

Easy prints

1 In a totally dark room, lay a fresh sheet of photographic paper on a flat surface, shiny side up. Lay the negative from your pinhole camera face down on top.

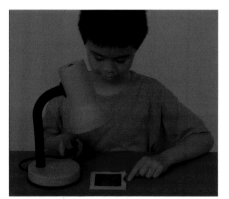

2 Shine a torch or a desk lamp on to the top of the two papers for a few seconds. Turn the light off and remove your paper negative. Put on the goggles and gloves.

3 Put the fresh paper into a tray of developing fluid, then fix and wash the paper (see the project on 'Making your own photogram'). You should end up with a print of the original image.

Amazing apertures

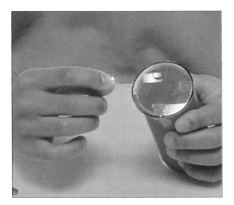

1 Make sure that your magnifying glass fits into your cardboard tube. Then carefully attach the magnifying glass to one end of the tube using small pieces of sticky tape.

2 Roll a piece of thin card around the other end of the cardboard tube. Tape the top edge down so that it makes another tube that slides on and off the first one.

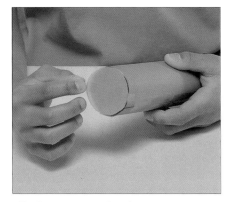

3 Cut out a circle of tracing paper with a diameter the same as the sliding card tube. Use sticky tape to attach it across the end of the tube. This will form your viewing screen.

4 With the viewing screen facing towards you, aim your tube at a desk lamp that is turned on. Can you see an image of the bulb on the screen?

5 Slide the tubes slowly together until the image of the bulb is clear and in focus. Now adjust the tubes again so that the image is slightly out of focus.

6 Cut a hole (about 5mm wide) in a piece of card, to make a small aperture. Look at the light bulb again and hold the card in front of the lens. The smaller aperture will bring the light bulb into focus. Is it clearer? Can you read the writing on the bulb?

How telescopes work

Optical telescopes use lenses or mirrors to make distant objects look bigger and brighter. Lens telescopes are also called refractors. Mirror telescopes are called reflectors. Most large astronomical telescopes for looking at stars are reflectors.

The first experiment shows you how to make a reflecting telescope, using a mirror. A reflecting telescope's main mirror is curved, so that light rays bounce off at an angle.

The refracting telescope in the second experiment uses lenses. There are difficulties involved in making big lenses, which is why most of the telescopes used in astronomy are reflectors. Our brains work out how big an object is by analyzing the angle of the light rays from it as the rays enter our eyes. Telescopes use lenses or mirrors to change this angle. Bending light rays from distant objects makes them seem larger than they would appear to the naked eye.

YOU WILL NEED

desk lamp, thick purple paper, marker pen, scissors, sticky tape, small mirror, non-hardening modelling material, magnifying glass.

eyepiece lens

starlight

primary mirror reflects an upside-down image

secondary mirror corrects image

▲ **Reflecting telescope**
Light reflects off the primary mirror. The light rays bounce off a small secondary mirror and are focused and magnified by an eyepiece lens. Astronomers use telescopes to help them study the stars and other planets. Telescopes are often built on top of mountains, for the clearest views. There, the air is thin and there are no lights from towns. The William Herschel Telescope (WHT) is located 2,400m above sea level on top of an extinct volcano on La Palma, in the Canary Islands.

Make a single-mirror reflecting telescope

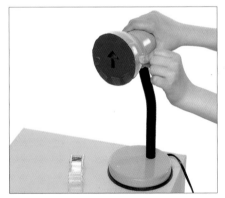

1 Draw a circle around the front of the desk lamp on a sheet of purple paper. Cut it out. Then cut out an arrow in the centre. Stick the circle on to the front of the lamp.

2 Set up the desk lamp and mirror so that the mirror reflects the light from the lamp on to a nearby wall. Use modelling clay to help support the mirror, if necessary.

3 Set up the magnifying glass so that light reflecting from the mirror passes through it. The lens magnifies and focuses the light, projecting an upside-down arrow.

Make a refracting telescope

YOU WILL NEED

desk lamp, thick red paper,

marker pen, scissors, sticky tape,

two magnifying glasses,

non-hardening modelling material.

1 Draw around the front of the desk lamp on to a sheet of red paper. Using scissors, cut out a star in the middle of the circle. Then cut out the circle, as shown.

2 Using sticky tape, fasten the circle of paper securely over the front of the desk lamp. Make sure that it does not touch the bulb, as this could cause the paper to burn.

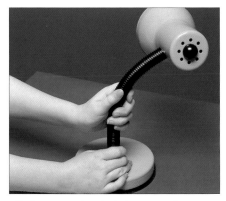

3 Position the desk lamp so that it shines on a nearby wall. Adjust the angle of the lamp if necessary. Make sure that the lamp's base is stable to prevent it from overbalancing.

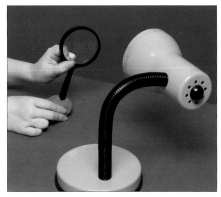

4 Position a magnifying glass between the lamp and the wall. To support the glass and fix it in place, take the handle and wedge it firmly in a lump of modelling material.

5 Turn on the lamp. Adjust the magnifying glass so that the light passing through it appears as a blurred patch of light on the wall. The glass acts like a telescope's objective lens.

6 Position the second lens behind the first lens. This acts as an eyepiece lens. Adjust the eyepiece lens until the light is focused to form the sharp image of the star.

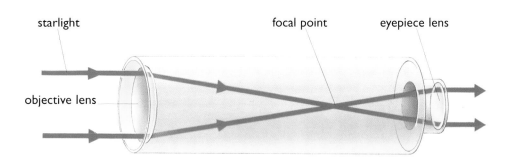

starlight

focal point

eyepiece lens

objective lens

▲ Refracting telescope

Light from a distant star passes through the objective lens. The light rays from distant objects change direction as they enter the lens and again as they leave it. A magnified, blurry image of the star appears. The image is brought into focus by the lens in the eyepiece.

Satellites and orbits

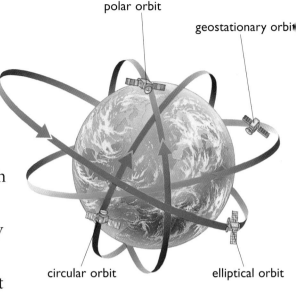

polar orbit

geostationary orbit

circular orbit

elliptical orbit

The movement of a satellite around the Earth is fixed in either a circular or an elliptical (oval) orbit. The satellite can be positioned in a polar orbit, circling the Earth from pole to pole, or placed in an equatorial orbit around the Equator, or in any orbit in between. It may cross the sky several times a day in a low Earth orbit (LEO), or it may hang in one place, in geostationary orbit. In the first project you can see for yourself how geostationary orbits work.

The type of orbit is chosen according to the job the satellite is there to do. Most communications and weather satellites are placed in geostationary orbit 36,000km above the Equator. A satellite in this orbit keeps pace with the turning Earth and appears to hang motionless over the same spot on the ground. Once a radio dish on the ground is aimed at the satellite the dish need not be moved again. Other satellites have to be tracked using movable radio dishes that follow the satellite as it crosses the sky. The second project demonstrates the way in which satellites relay signals from one place to another.

▲ Types of orbits

Weather satellites are often placed in geostationary orbits. They always face the same part of the Earth. Polar orbits are often chosen for scientific-survey satellites. As the satellite orbits from pole to pole, the Earth turns below it. In time, the satellite passes over every point on the Earth's surface.

YOU WILL NEED

about 15 strips of blue card, about 30 strips of red card, rope, a friend.

Geostationary orbit

1 Use the card strips to mark a blue circle with a larger red circle around it on the ground. Hold one end of the rope and ask a friend to hold the other end.

2 Walk around the inner circle, while your friend walks around the outer circle. The blue inner circle represents the Earth, and the outer circle represents the orbit of a satellite around the Earth. If your orbiting friend keeps pace with you as you walk, your human satellite is in a geostationary orbit.

Make a satellite relay

1 Using the scissors, cut out a rectangle of blue paper just big enough to wrap around the tin can. Tape it in place. The tin can will act as a ground-based radio receiver.

2 Measure out a 10cm x 10cm piece of card with the ruler. Cut it out and stick it to one side of the tin can. This will act as an antenna on your tin-can receiver.

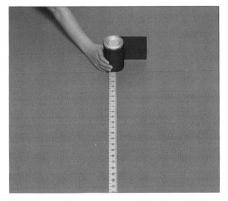

3 Place the tin can on the floor. Take the metre ruler and lay it on the floor directly in front of the tin can. Place it on the opposite side to the antenna, as shown.

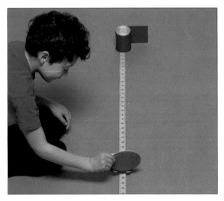

4 Place the mirror on the ruler about 75cm from the tin can. The mirror will act like a satellite in geostationary orbit relaying signals. Fix in place with modelling material.

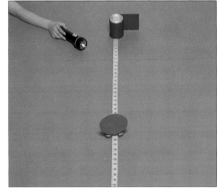

5 Darken the room. Place the torch beside the can, as shown. The torch will send out light beams in the same way that a ground-based transmitter sends out radio waves.

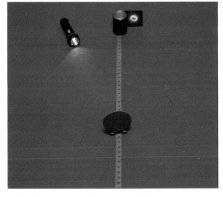

6 Switch on the torch. Move the mirror along the ruler. Keep moving it until the light beams are reflected off the mirror satellite and on to the antenna of the tin can.

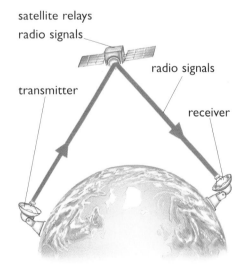

satellite relays radio signals

radio signals

transmitter

receiver

◄ Redirecting radio waves

Comsats (communication satellites) in geostationary orbit above the Equator enable radio transmissions to be sent to anywhere on the Earth's surface. Radio signals are transmitted from one side of the planet and aimed at the orbiting satellite. The comsat then relays (redirects) the signal to a receiver on the opposite side of the Earth.

Power boost in Space

Some space probes, including *Pioneer 10* and *11*, used gravity boosts to help them travel through the Solar System. To get a boost, a probe passes by a planet and becomes attracted by its gravity. It is pulled by the planet on its orbit around the Sun. Some of the planet's orbital speed is transferred to the probe, which is then catapulted towards the next planet to be visited. This slingshot effect is vital, as robot spacecraft would not be able to carry enough fuel to change course from planet to planet. The first project shows how the slingshot effect works. Space probes send back information to Earth by radio signals. These are collected by large dish antennae on Earth. The second project shows why many of the radio antennae used are dish-shaped.

▼ **Pioneering probes**

Probes have landed on or flown past almost every planet in the Solar System. The most widely travelled deep space probes are *Pioneer 10* and *11*, and *Voyager 1* and *2*, which have toured most of the Solar System's outer planets. They used the pull of gravity from each planet they passed to change their course and speed them on to the next planet. *Pioneer 10* flew past Jupiter, while the flight path of the *Pioneer 11* probe took it past Jupiter and then on to Saturn.

YOU WILL NEED

two thick books (of equal thickness), 60 x 30cm piece of thick card, marble-sized steel ball, strong magnet, sticky tape, two 30cm lengths of wooden dowelling.

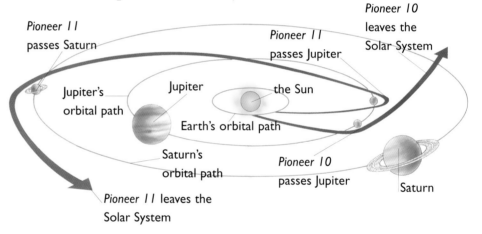

Pioneer 11 passes Saturn

Pioneer 11 passes Jupiter

Pioneer 10 leaves the Solar System

Jupiter's orbital path

Jupiter

the Sun

Earth's orbital path

Saturn's orbital path

Pioneer 10 passes Jupiter

Saturn

Pioneer 11 leaves the Solar System

Gravity boost

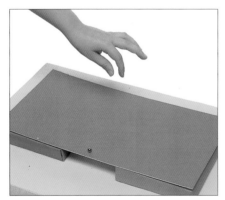

1 Place the books flat on a table about 15cm apart. Lay the piece of card on top of the books, then roll the steel-ball space probe across it. It moves smoothly across the surface.

2 Place the magnet under the card. Roll the steel-ball probe across the card. It is drawn towards the magnet planet by the gravity-like pull of its magnetic field.

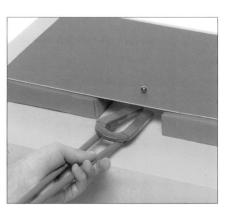

3 Tape the magnet to the dowelling. Roll the ball and then pull the magnet away. The ball speeds up and is pulled along by the magnet planet, like a probe getting a gravity boost.

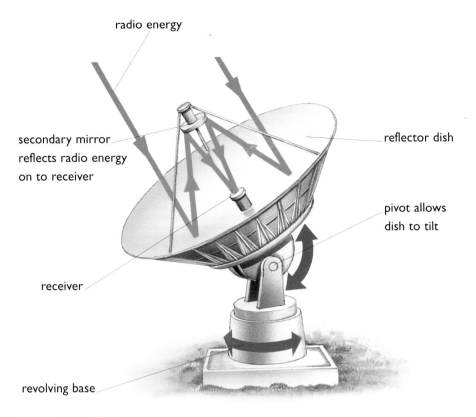

radio energy

secondary mirror
reflects radio energy
on to receiver

reflector dish

pivot allows
dish to tilt

receiver

revolving base

◄ Beaming waves

Dish antennae reflect their collected radio energy on to the receiver. Space probes use their antennae to receive radio signals from mission control on Earth. The receiver can also act as a transmitter, enabling the probe to send back its findings to Earth.

YOU WILL NEED

plain postcard, pencil, ruler, scissors, 60 x 100cm piece of thick card, non-hardening modelling material, 20 x 50cm strip of mirror board, torch.

Make a dish antenna

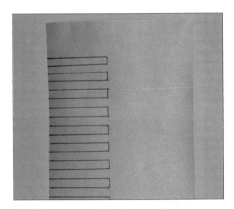

1 Draw nine thin slits on the postcard using the pencil and ruler. Each slit should measure 2.5cm x 0.5cm. They should be equally spaced out from each other at 0.5cm apart.

2 Using the scissors, carefully cut out the slits in the postcard. The slits in the card will filter light, splitting it up into thin rays that will reflect off the curve of the antenna.

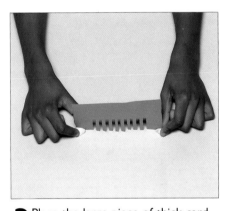

3 Place the large piece of thick card on a table. Stand the postcard 40cm from one end of the card, with the slits facing down. Fix it in position with modelling material.

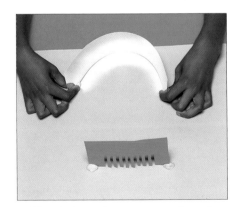

4 Bend the reflective mirror board to form a semicircular antenna, as shown. Stand it at one end of the thick card base. Then fix it firmly in position using modelling material.

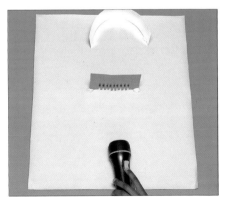

5 Switch on the torch. Direct the light beam so that it shines through the slits in the postcard. The light is split into thin rays, which reflect off the mirror board.

6 Darken the room. Move the torch until the light rays reflecting off the curved mirror are brought together at one spot, like radio waves on a dish antenna.

Listen to this

Sound is energy that moves back and forth through the air in the form of vibrations. These vibrations spread outwards as waves, like the ripples caused by a stone when it is dropped into rather still water.

The first experiment demonstrates the existence and energy of sound waves. Channelling the sound inside a tube concentrates the waves in the direction of the tube. By channelling sound towards a candle, you can use the energy to blow out the flame.

The second experiment is all about the strength of sound waves. It shows that sounds get quieter if their waves are allowed to spread out. Scientists say that loud sounds have large amplitudes (variations of range).

In the final project, you can investigate pitch or the range of sounds by making a set of panpipes. Low sounds consist of a small number of vibrations every second. Musicians describe these sounds as having 'low pitch' but scientists report the sounds as 'low frequency'. The panpipes show that pitch depends on the length of each pipe.

▲ **Play it again, Sam!**
You can play deep notes or low notes on a bass guitar. The sound waves vibrate slowly with a frequency as low as 50 times each second. High notes vibrate much more rapidly.

How sound travels

1 Stretch the clear film tightly over the end of the tube. Use the elastic band to fasten it in place. You could also use a flat piece of rubber cut from a balloon instead of the clear film.

2 Ask an adult to light the candle. Point the tube at the candle, with the open end 10cm from the flame. Give the clear film a sharp tap with the flat of your hand.

You will hear the sound coming out of the tube. It consists of pressure waves in the air. The tube concentrates the sound waves towards the candle flame and puts it out.

Sound waves

1 Place the watch close to your ear. You can hear a ticking sound coming from it. The sound becomes fainter when you move the watch away from your ear.

2 Place one end of the tube over a friend's ear and hold the watch at the other end. The tube concentrates the sound and does not let it spread out. She can hear the watch clearly.

How to make panpipes

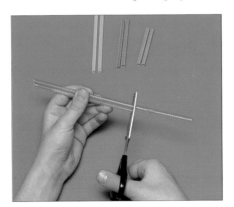

1 Cut the drinking straws so that you have four pairs that are 9cm, 8cm, 7cm and 6cm long. Block one end of each straw with a small piece of modelling material.

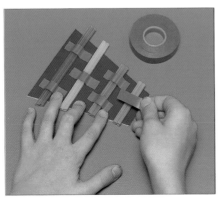

2 Carefully cut out the card to the same shape as the blue piece shown above. Fix the straws into place with the sticky tape from long to short to align with card as shown.

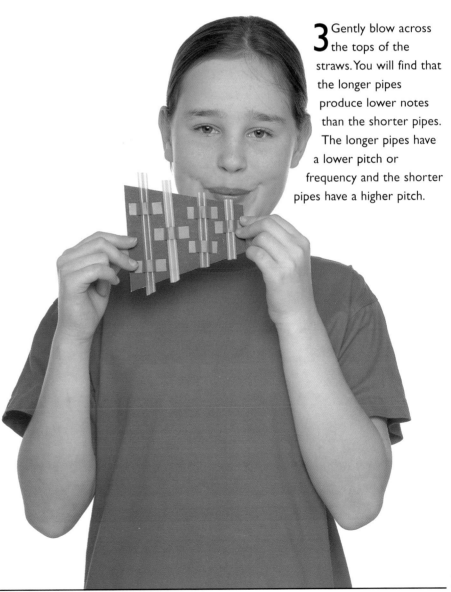

3 Gently blow across the tops of the straws. You will find that the longer pipes produce lower notes than the shorter pipes. The longer pipes have a lower pitch or frequency and the shorter pipes have a higher pitch.

Travel and Transport

The most powerful, luxurious and specialized forms of transport today all evolved from simple scientific principles. The trick of keeping a luxury passenger liner or a massive oil tanker afloat is basically the same as it was for early humans with their canoes and coracles. Many of the secrets of super-powered vehicles are the result of learning to make use of simple forces such as jet propulsion, thrust, and lift, and combining them with other inventions and new materials. On the following pages, you will discover how boats, trains, cars, planes and spacecraft work by experimenting with the forces that make them go.

Simple boats

Some of the earliest – simplest – types of boat are still made today. Small reed boats are still built in southern Iraq and on Lake Titicaca in South America in a similar way to the one in the project below. Reed boats are made by tying thousands of river reeds together into huge bundles. The bundles are then tied together to make hull shapes. In ancient Egypt, quite large boats were made like this, from papyrus reeds. Some historians believe that Egyptians may have made long ocean crossings in papyrus craft.

The model in the second project is of a coracle. This is a round boat made by covering a light wooden frame with animal hides. Coracles are also still made but are now covered with canvas treated with tar instead of animal hide. Coracles were small enough for one person to paddle along a river and were used for fishing. When you are out and about, take photographs or make drawings of other simple craft, such as canoes and punts. See if you can make working models of them, too.

◄ **Afterlife evidence**
This boat was found in a pit alongside the Great Pyramid of Egypt in 1954. It is believed to have been used as a pharaoh's funeral boat, which ferried the dead pharaoh to the afterlife.

Make a reed craft

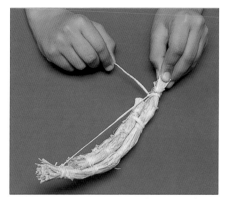

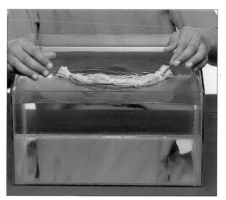

1 Make bundles of raffia by tying a few dozen strands together with a short length of raffia. You will need two bundles about 20cm long and two more about 25cm long.

2 Tie the two long bundles and the two short bundles together. Tie the short bundles on top of the long ones. Fix a strand between each end to make the ends bend up.

3 Gently lower the reed boat on to the surface of a tank of water. How well does it float? Does it stay upright? Try leaving it in the water to see if it becomes waterlogged.

Make a coracle

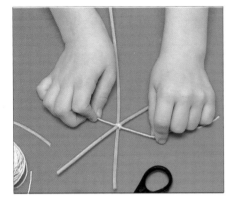

1 Cut one long piece of cane and three short pieces. Using short lengths of string, tie all three of the short pieces to the long piece to make a triple-armed cross.

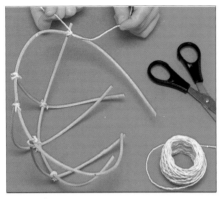

2 Cut a much longer piece of cane. Form it into a loop and tie it to all the ends of the triple cross shape. Bend the ends of the cross up as you tie them to form a dish shape.

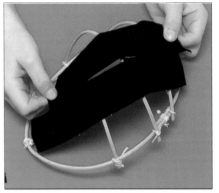

3 Cut pieces of cotton cloth about 15cm x 5cm. Apply glue to the outside of the frame and place the pieces over it. Glue the pieces to each other where they overlap.

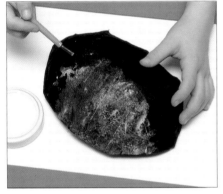

4 Glue down the cloth where it folds over the top of the frame. Put two coats of glue on the outside of the cloth to waterproof it. Leave the glue to dry completely.

When the model is dry, put the finished coracle into a tank of water. How well does it float? Why not try making a person from modelling material to sit in your model coracle?

Early Britons used coracles 9,000 years ago. Coracles are light to carry, easy to use and stable enough to fish from.

Sail power

When you launch your model sailing boat, you can get an idea of how it is propelled by the wind. To sail in the direction they want to go, sailors must be aware of wind direction, so that they can adjust the position of the sails to make best use of it. If sailing boats face straight into the wind, the sails flap uselessly, and the boat is in a 'no-go zone'. They can, however, sail into oncoming wind by taking a zig-zag course. This is called tacking. The wind blows against one side of the sail to propel the boat diagonally upwind. When the boat changes tack, the wind blows against the other side of the sail, and the boat goes forward on the opposite diagonal. If the wind is blowing from behind the boat, the sail is set at right angles to the boat like an open wing, so that it is filled by the wind.

▲ Parts of a sailboat

Sailboats usually have a crew of two people. A helmsman operates the tiller and the mainsail, and a crew who works the jib and centreboard (which stops the boat from drifting sideways).

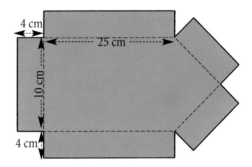

Template ▶

YOU WILL NEED

pencil, ruler, thick card, scissors, sticky tape, plastic sheet, stapler, bradawl, non-hardening modelling material, thin garden canes, coloured paper, plastic straw, small plastic bottle, string, paper clip, sheet of paper.

Make a sailboat

1 Cut out your hull shape from thick card, using the template above as a guide. Score along the dotted lines with the scissors. Use sticky tape to fix the sides together.

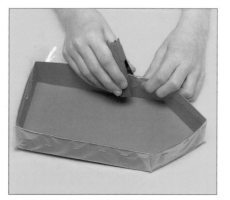

2 Lay the hull on a plastic sheet. Cut the plastic around the hull, allowing enough to cover the sides and overlap them at the top by 5cm. Fold the sheet over the hull and staple it in place.

3 Pierce a hole in the middle of a strip of card a little wider than the hull. Staple in place. Put modelling material under the hole, and push a 30cm cane through the hole into it.

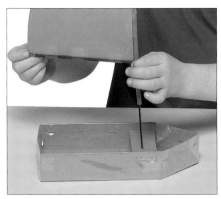

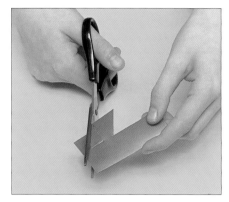

4 Cut a sail from coloured paper with a base of about 20cm. Attach the straw along the side and a garden cane along the bottom with sticky tape. Slip the straw over the mast.

5 Cut an L-shape (about 8cm long, 4cm wide at the base and 2cm wide at the top) from the small plastic bottle. Cut the base of the L in half to make two slanted tabs, as shown.

6 Fold back the two tabs of the L-shaped plastic in opposite directions, as shown, and staple them to the stern (back) of the boat. This is the boat's rudder.

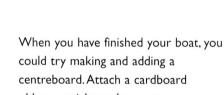

7 Cut a piece of string about 20cm long. Tape one end to the back of the boom (the cane) and feed the other end through a paper clip attached to the back of the boat.

8 To test out how your sail boat works, make a breeze by waving a large sheet of paper near to the boat. Adjust the string to move the sail into the right position.

When you have finished your boat, you could try making and adding a centreboard. Attach a cardboard oblong at right angles to the bottom of the boat. It will stop your boat drifting sideways in the wind.

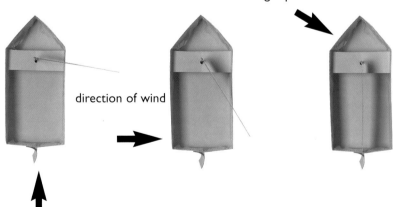

direction of wind

When you test your boat, set the sail in these different positions. Alter the position of the sail by using the string taped to the boom (cane). Follow the arrows shown here to see which way the wind should be blowing from in each case. Try blowing from other directions to see if this makes a difference to your boat.

How ships float

The simplest boats, such as rafts, float because the material they are made of is less dense (lighter) than water. Heavy ships can float because the water they are floating in pushes upwards against them. This pushing force is called upthrust. The first experiment shows that an object will float if the upthrust of the water is great enough to overcome the downwards push of the object's weight. The size of the upthrust depends on how much water the object pushes out of the way. When you put an object in water and let it go, it settles into the water, pushing liquid out of the way. The farther it goes in, the more water it pushes away and the more upthrust acts on it. When the upthrust becomes the same as the object's weight, the object floats.

The second project shows you a hollow hull. If you push a light, hollow ball under water, it will spring back up. Upthrust from the water makes a hollow hull float in the same way. The higher the density of water, the greater the upthrust. This means that ships float slightly higher in salt water as it is more dense than fresh water.

salt water

fresh water

▲ **Measuring density**
The density of water is measured with a hydrometer. You can make one by putting a lump of modelling material on the end of a straw. Put it in a glass of water and mark the water level with tape. Now put the straw in an equal amount of salty water. What happens?

Testing upthrust

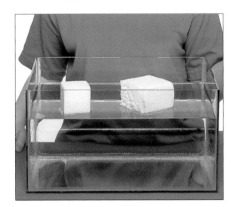

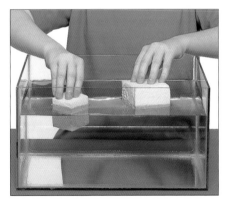

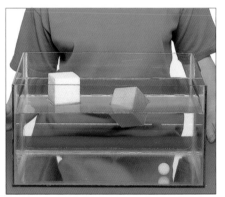

1 Put the two polystyrene blocks into a tank of water. They will float well, because their material, polystyrene, is so light. Only a small amount of upthrust is needed.

2 Try pushing the blocks under the water. Now you are pushing lots of water aside. Can you feel upthrust pushing back? The bigger block will experience more upthrust.

3 A wooden block floats deeper in the water, because wood is more dense (heavier) than polystyrene. A marble sinks, because the upthrust on it is not as great as its weight.

Hollow hulls

1 Put a piece of foil about 20cm by 15cm into a tank of water. With just the slightest push, it will sink. This is because it does not displace much water so there is very little upthrust.

2 Lift the sheet of foil out of the water and dry it carefully with some kitchen paper. Now mould it into a simple boat shape with your fingers. Take care not to tear the foil.

3 Put your foil boat into the water. It should now float. It will not sink so easily. Its shape pushes aside much more water than it did when it was flat, so the upthrust is greater.

Try filling your foil boat with small objects such as marbles, for cargo. As you put more marbles in it will float lower and lower. How many marbles can your boat hold before it sinks?

This simple foil boat works like a real ship's hull. Even though it is made of metal, it is filled with air. This gives the hull shape a much lower overall density.

What's in a hull?

Whenever an object such as a ship moves through the water, the water slows it down. The push made by the water is called water resistance, or drag. The faster the object moves, the greater the water resistance becomes.

If you look around a busy harbour, you will see dozens of different hull designs. Sleek, narrow hulls with sharp bows cause less resistance than wide hulls with square bows, so they can move through the water faster.

You can test how the shape of a bow affects the speed of a ship in this experiment. The deeper a hull sits in the water, the more resistance there is. Some hulls are designed to sit just on top of the water. For example, a small speedboat has a flaring, shallow V-shaped hull designed to skim across the surface. A cargo ship has a square hull that sits lower in the water. Speed is not as important for the cargo ship as it is for the speedboat. Instead, the cargo ship is designed for stability and to carry as much as possible.

Testing hull shapes

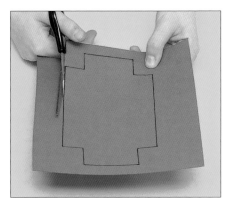

1 Use a ruler to draw the three templates shown left on sheets of stiff card. Make sure the corners are square and the edges straight. Carefully cut out the shapes.

3 cm

15 cm

15 cm

3 cm

3 cm

15 cm

10 cm

15 cm

10 cm

3 cm

3 cm

▲ **Templates**
Use these three templates to help you cut out and make the three boat shapes in this project.

2 Using scissors, score along the lines inside the base of the square boat (shown as dotted lines left). Bend up the sides and use sticky tape to fix the corners together.

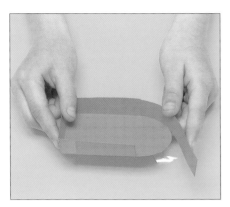

3 Make the round-ended and pointed boats in the same way as the first boat. Use a separate piece of card to make the round bow and tape to the base in several places.

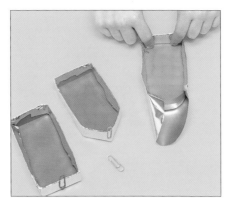

4 Now cover the outside of each shape with foil, neatly folding the foil over the sides. This will make the shapes more waterproof. Fix a paper clip to the bow (front) of each boat.

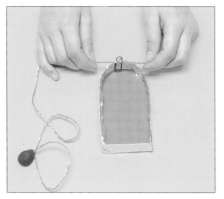

5 Roll out three balls of modelling material about the size of a walnut. Weigh the balls to make sure they are the same weight. Attach a ball to the bow of each boat with string.

6 Put a large plastic bowl or a long trough on to a table or a strong box. Use a watering can to fill the trough with water to about 1cm from the top of the bowl.

7 Line up the boats at one end of the bowl. Hang the strings and modelling material balls down over the other end. Put a small wooden brick inside each boat.

Release the boats all at the same time. The weighted strings will pull them along down the length of the bowl. Which one wins the race to the other end of the bowl? Try timing the boats with a stopwatch to work out the difference between the fastest and slowest.

Ship stability

Many ships look as though they are top heavy, so how do they manage to stay upright and not capsize? These projects will help you understand why. When a ship tips over, the hull on that side sinks into the water. On the other side it rises up out of the water. The water creates more upthrust on the side that sinks in, pushing the ship upright again. The more one side of the hull sinks in, the greater the resistance, and the harder it is for the hull to tip over further. A catamaran like the one in the project is extra-stable because it has double hulls against which the water can push.

The position of the cargo in the hull of the ship is important. Heavy cargo high up on deck makes the ship top-heavy and more likely to tip over. Heavy cargo low down in the hull gives the ship stability. Cargo that can move is dangerous, because it could slip to one side of the ship, causing it to tip suddenly. You will be able to test the effects of different weights in square and rounded hulls in the second experiment.

YOU WILL NEED

Make a catamaran: small plastic bottle, scissors, garden cane, elastic bands, tank or bowl of water, cargo.
Loading cargo: plastic bottle and square tub of similar size, scissors, tank or bowl of water, wooden bricks, non-hardening modelling material.

Make a catamaran

I Remove the top from a small plastic bottle and carefully cut the bottle in half lengthways. This will leave you with two identical shapes to form the catamaran hulls.

Put your completed catamaran into a tank or bowl of water. Load the hulls with cargo such as wooden bricks. Can you make your boat capsize?

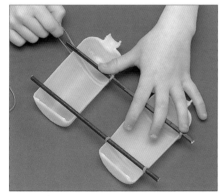

2 Place the two halves of the bottle side by side. Lay two medium-length pieces of garden cane on top. Securely fasten the canes to the bottle halves using elastic bands.

Loading cargo

I For this project you need one container with a round hull shape and another about the same size with a square hull shape. Cut a strip from the round container to make a hold.

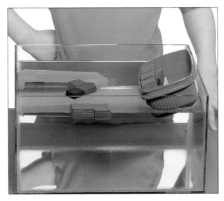

2 Put both containers in a tank or bowl of water. Gradually load one side of each hull with wooden bricks. Which hull capsizes first? Which hull is more stable?

3 Now load the square hull evenly with wooden bricks. You should be able to get a lot more in. Press down on one side of the hull. Can you feel the hull trying to right itself?

4 To stabilize the round hull, press some lumps of modelling material into the bottom of the hull. This adds weight known as ballast to the bottom of the hull.

Reload the round hull with wooden bricks. Can you see how the modelling material ballast low down in the hull has made the craft more stable?

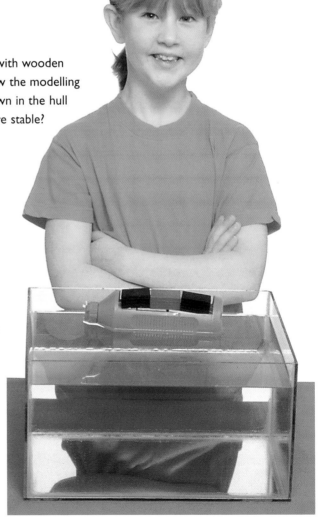

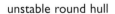
unstable round hull

stable square hull

When a round hull tips to one side, there is little change to the amount of hull underwater. This makes the shape unstable. When a square hull tips to one side, there is a great change in the amount of hull underwater on that side. This makes it stable.

Power and steering afloat

The model boat in this project is fitted with two basic devices for controlling water craft. Both operate underwater. The propeller is driven by the engine of a motor- or steam-powered boat. It rotates very fast and pushes the craft through the water. In the project the engine power comes from the energy stored in a wound-up elastic band. As in real life propellers, the blades are set at different angles, and push the water backwards, so thrusting the vessel forwards, as it spins. You could try making different propeller designs – with more blades set at different angles, for example – and testing them to see which works best.

A rudder is used to steer both sail- and motor-powered boats. It is controlled by a handle called a tiller, or a wheel, on the boat. As in your model boat, the rudder can be moved to different positions to make the boat turn left or right, but will only work when the boat is actually moving. In addition to making the boat turn left and right, the rudder also keeps the boat going in a straight line when it is set straight.

▲ **Making a connection**

In a large cruise yacht, the rudder is moved by wires linked to the wheel in the cockpit. The wheel drives the sprocket, which moves a chain. Wires attached to the chain move the rudder via pulleys. The yacht is also equipped with a diesel engine that is connected to a single propeller via a driveshaft.

YOU WILL NEED

cork, bradawl, scissors, small plastic bottle, large plastic bottle, large paper clip, pliers (optional), ruler, bead, long elastic bands, small pencil, paddling pool, thin garden cane.

Make a powered boat

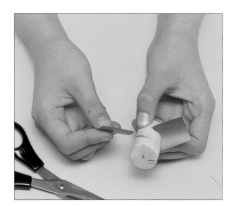

1 Make a hole through the middle of the cork using a bradawl. Cut a diagonal slot in either side of the cork. Push two strips of plastic cut from a small bottle into the slots.

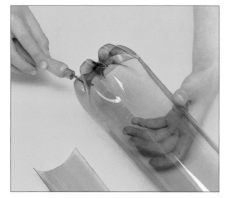

2 Cut an oblong strip from one side of the large plastic bottle. This slot is the top of your boat. With the bradawl, make a small hole at the back of your bottle in the bottom.

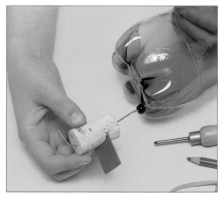

3 Straighten a large paper clip (you may need pliers). Bend the last 1.5cm of wire at right angles. Push the wire through the cork and thread it through the bead and small hole.

4 Bend over the end of the wire inside the bottle. Hook an elastic band over the wire and stretch it up through the neck of the bottle. Secure it in place with a pencil.

5 To wind up the band, turn the pencil as you hold on to the propeller. Keep holding the propeller until you put the boat into the water and release it. What happens?

6 Now make a rudder for your boat. Cut a piece of plastic about 4cm x 4cm and pierce two holes near one edge. Push a length of thin cane through the two holes.

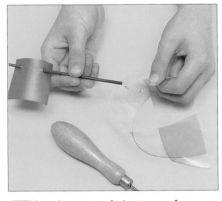

7 Use the strip of plastic cut from the large bottle to support your rudder. Pierce two holes about 2cm apart in the centre of the strip and push the cane through them.

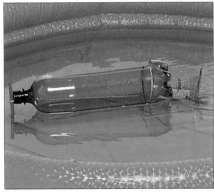

8 Fix the rudder support to the bottle with an elastic band so that the rudder is clear of the propeller. Wind up the pencil and put your boat back in the water.

Like a real boat-builder, you will want to test the controls of your boat. To do this, start with the rudder centred to make the boat go straight. Next, try turning the rudder from side to side. What happens? How tight a circle can you make your boat turn in?

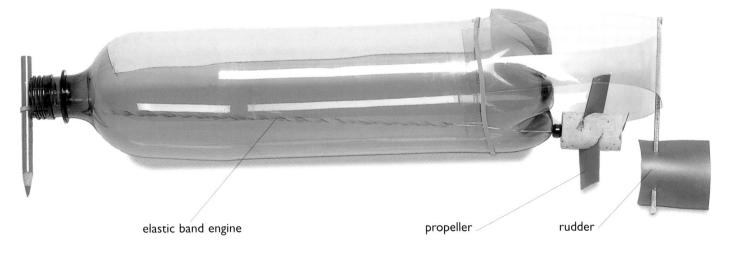

elastic band engine   propeller   rudder

Safety measures at sea

There are various ways in which ships can be designed to keep afloat. All ships have bilge pumps that pump out water that has collected in the bottom of the hull and expel it into the sea or river. Many sailboats and canoes are fitted with bags of air or blocks of polystyrene inside to keep them buoyant (afloat). Most lifeboats are self-righting, which means that they bob back upright if they capsize, like the model in the first project. Self-righting lifeboats are completely watertight – even the air inlets in inflatable lifeboats have seals to keep out water. Heavy engines are set low down, while the hull and high cabins are full of air. This arrangement ensures the lifeboat flips upright automatically.

The second and third projects show how hydrofoils and hovercrafts work. These are fast boats, designed for short sea crossings. A hydrofoil is the fastest type of ferry. Under the hull there are wing-like foils. Water flows faster over the foil's curved upper surface than it does over the flat lower surface, creating lift. When travelling at high speed, the foils lift the hull clear of the water.

Try the third project to see how hovercrafts skim across the water supported on cushions of air. Buoyancy tanks stop the hovercraft from sinking if the air cushion fails.

YOU WILL NEED

pencil, ruler, polystyrene tile, scissors, non-hardening modelling material, elastic bands, tank or bowl of water, small plastic tub.

Self-righting boat

1 Cut a boat shape about 15cm x 10cm from polystyrene. Attach a golf-ball sized lump of modelling material to one side of your boat shape with an elastic band.

2 Put your boat into a tank or bowl of water. Have the modelling material, which represents the crew and equipment, on top. If you capsize the boat it will stay capsized.

3 Add another lump of modelling material underneath the boat to represent heavy engines or ballast. Add an upturned plastic tub on top to represent a watertight cabin.

4 Now try to capsize it again and it will flip back upright. This is because the air, trapped underwater by the tub and a heavy weight on top, forces the boat upright again.

How a hydrofoil works

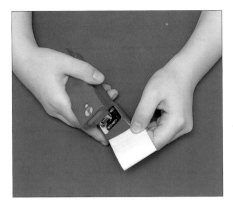

I Cut a rectangle of plastic, about 5cm x 10cm, from the lid of the margarine container. Fold it in half. Staple the ends together 1cm in from the back edge.

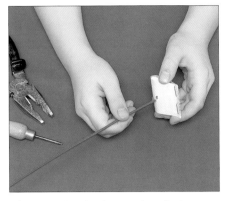

2 Use a bradawl to make a hole in the front of the hydrofoil 1cm away from the folded edge. Use pliers to bend 1.5cm of one end of the wire. Slide the hydrofoil on to the wire.

3 Make sure the hydrofoil moves freely on the wire. Move your hydrofoil in air – it will not lift up because air is far less dense than water. Pull it through water and it will rise up the wire.

How a hovercraft works

YOU WILL NEED

How a hydrofoil works:

margarine tub lid, ruler, scissors, stapler, bradawl, pliers, coat hanger wire (ask an adult to cut it), tank or bowl of water.

How a hovercraft works: ruler, polystyrene tray, pencil, balloon, balloon pump, button.

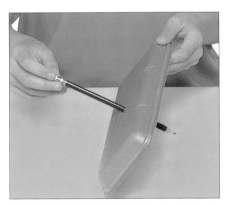

I Use a ruler to find the middle of the polystyrene tray. Poke a hole through the middle with the pointed end of a pencil. The hole should be about 1cm across.

2 Blow up the balloon with the pump and carefully push its neck through the hole. Keep pinching the neck of the balloon to stop the air from escaping.

3 Keep pinching the neck of the balloon with one hand, using the other hand to slip the button into the neck. The button will control how fast the air escapes.

4 Place the tray on a table. Air escapes steadily from under the tray's edges, lifting it up a few millimetres. Give the tray a gentle push and it will skate over the surface.

Submarine action

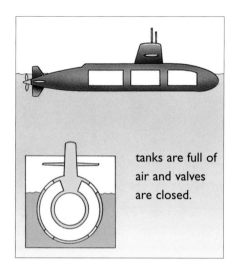

tanks are full of air and valves are closed.

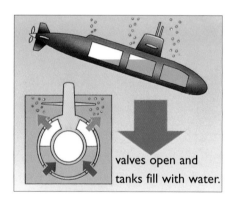

valves open and tanks fill with water.

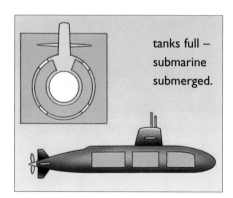

tanks full – submarine submerged.

air is forced in, so water is forced out

A submarine dives by making itself heavier so that it sinks. It surfaces again by making itself lighter. Submarines use large tanks called buoyancy tanks. When the submarine is on the surface, these tanks are full of air. To make the submarine dive, the tanks are flooded with seawater, making the submarine heavy enough to sink. To make the submarine surface again, compressed air is pumped into the tanks, forcing the water out. This makes the submarine lighter and it floats to the surface. When submarines are underwater, they move up and down using tiny wings called hydroplanes. These work like rudders to control the submarine's direction. Submarines need very strong hulls to prevent them from being crushed by the huge pressure under the water. As submarines dive, the weight of the water pressing down on them becomes greater and greater. You can see how this works by making this model.

YOU WILL NEED

large plastic bottle, sand, plastic funnel, tank of water, two small plastic bottles, bradawl, scissors, ruler, two plastic drinking straws, elastic bands, non-hardening modelling material, two bulldog clips.

Make a submarine

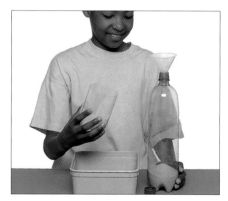

1 Fill the large plastic bottle with sand using a funnel. Fill it until it just sinks in a tank of water. Test out the bottle (cap firmly screwed on) to find the right amount of sand.

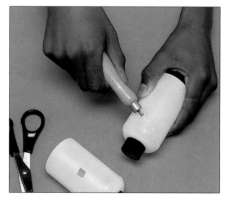

2 Make a large hole (about 1cm across) in one side of two small plastic bottles. On the other side make a small hole, big enough for a plastic straw to fit into.

3 Attach the two small bottles to either side of the large bottle using elastic bands. Twist the small bottles so that the small hole on each one points upwards.

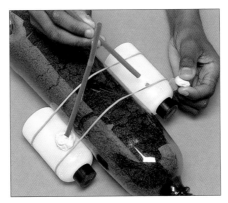

4 Push a plastic drinking straw into each small hole so that a bit pokes through. Seal around the base of the straws with modelling material to make a watertight join.

5 Put a small bulldog clip about halfway down each straw. The clips need to be strong enough to squash the straw and stop air being forced out by the water.

6 Put your model submarine in a tank of water. With the clips on, it should float. Remove the clips and water will flood the buoyancy tanks. The submarine will sink.

7 To make the submarine surface again, blow slowly into both straws at once. The air will force the water out of the buoyancy tanks and the submarine will rise to the surface.

This is the finished model submarine. You might find that your model sinks bow (front) first, or stern (back) first. If this is the case, level it by shaking the sand evenly inside the bottle.

8 When your model submarine has resurfaced, keep blowing slowly into the tanks. Replace each bulldog clip and your model submarine will remain floating on the surface.

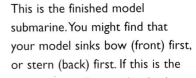

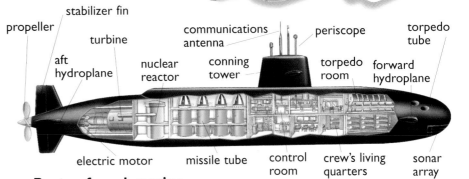

propeller · stabilizer fin · turbine · aft hydroplane · nuclear reactor · communications antenna · conning tower · periscope · torpedo room · torpedo tube · forward hydroplane

electric motor · missile tube · control room · crew's living quarters · sonar array

▲ Parts of a submarine

A modern submarine, such as this nuclear ballistic missile submarine, is nearly as long as a football pitch — around 91m. It has an engine and propeller at the stern, and is operated by a crew of 140. Steam drives the turbines that turn the propeller. A submarine's hull is strong but few submarines can go below 500m.

Making rails

A fully laden freight or passenger train is heavy, so the track it runs on has to be tough. Nowadays, rails are made from steel, which is a much stronger material than the cast iron used for the first railways. The shape of the rail also helps to make it strong. If you sliced through a rail from top to bottom you would see it has an 'I'-shaped cross section. The broad, flat bottom narrows into the 'waist' of the I and widens again into a curved head. Most countries use a rail shaped like this.

Tracks are made up of lengths of rail, which are laid on wooden or concrete crossbeams called sleepers. Train wheels are a set distance apart, so rails must be a set distance apart, too. The distance between rails is called the gauge. This project will show you how to make sets of railway tracks for the models on the following pages. Make at least two sets of tracks – the more tracks you make the further your train can travel.

<table>
<tr><td>YOU WILL NEED</td></tr>
<tr><td>two sheets of stiff card measuring 26 x 11cm, pencil, ruler, scissors, PVA glue and glue brush, silver and brown paint, paintbrush, water pot, one sheet of foam board measuring 13 x 20cm, one sheet of A4 paper, masking tape, one sheet of thin card measuring 10 x 5cm.</td></tr>
</table>

direction of train

guard rails guide wheels and avoid derailment

rodding leads from points signal box

points

points are moved by an electric motor

◀ Points system

Trains are switched from one track to another using points. Part of the track (the blade) moves to guide the wheels smoothly from one route on to another. A signaller moves the blades by pulling a lever in the signal box. The blade and the lever are connected by metal rods. The lever cannot be pulled unless the signal is clear.

Making tracks

1 Place one 26 x 11cm piece of card lengthways. Draw a line 1cm in from each of the outside edges. Draw two more lines, each 3.5cm in from the outside edges. This is side A.

2 Turn the card over (side B) and place it lengthways. Measure and draw lines 4cm and 4.75cm in from each edge. Repeat steps 1 and 2 with the second piece of 26 x 11cm card.

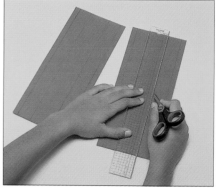

3 Hold the ruler firmly against one of the lines you have drawn. Use the tip of a pair of scissors to score along the line. Repeat for all lines on both sides of both pieces of card.

4 Place the cards A side up. For each piece in turn, fold firmly along the two lines. Fold up from the scored side. Turn the card over. Repeat for the lines on side B.

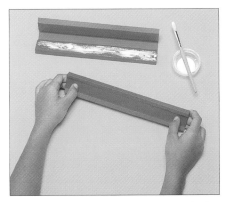

5 With the A side up, press the folds into the I-shape of the rail. Open out again. Glue the B side of the 2cm-wide middle section as shown. Repeat for the second rail.

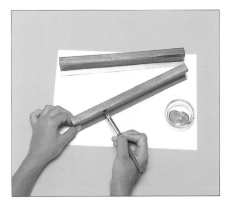

6 Give your two rails a metallic look by painting the upper (A) sides silver. Leave the paint to dry, and then apply a second coat. Leave the second coat to dry.

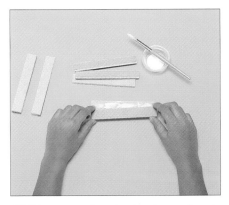

7 Use a pencil and ruler to mark out ten 13 x 2cm strips on the foam board. Cut them out. Glue two strips together to make five thick railway sleepers. Leave them to dry.

8 Paint the sleepers brown on their tops and sides to make them look like wood. Leave them to dry, then apply a second coat of paint. Leave the second coat to dry, too.

9 Lay the sleepers on the piece of A4 paper, 3cm apart. Make sure that they are exactly parallel to each other. Run a strip of masking tape down the middle to hold them in place.

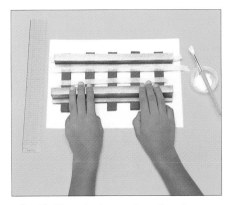

10 Glue the base of a rail and press into place with the outside edge of the rail 1.5cm in from the edge of the sleeper. Repeat with the other track. Secure with masking tape until dry.

Make several sets of rails. To join the rails together, roll up the thin card. Insert one end into the top of the I-shape. Push the second rail on to the other end.

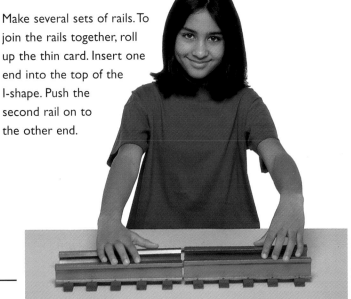

Rolling stock

The vehicle and machinery that is carried by a modern locomotive's underframe and wheels may weigh up to 100 tonnes. As bigger and more powerful locomotives were built, more wheels were added to carry the extra weight. Early steam locomotives had only two pairs of wheels. Later steam locomotives had two, three or four pairs of driving wheels, one pair of which was directly driven from the cylinders. The cylinders house the pistons, whose movement pushes the driving wheels around via a connecting rod.

The other wheels are connected to the driving wheel by a coupling rod, so that they turn at the same time. The small wheels in front of the driving wheels are called leading wheels. The ones behind are the trailing wheels. Locomotives are defined by the total number of wheels they have. For example, a 4-4-0 type locomotive has four leading, four driving and no trailing wheels. This project shows you how to make an underframe for a 4-4-0 type locomotive, which will run on the tracks described on the previous page. The following page shows how to make a locomotive to sit on the underframe.

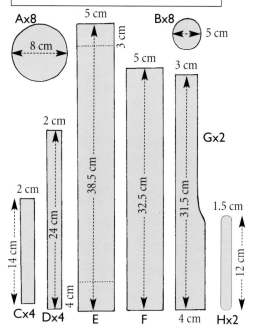

▲ **Templates**
Draw and cut out the templates from the stiff card. Use a pair of compasses to draw the wheel templates A and B.

Make an underframe

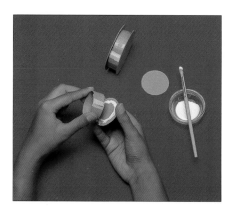

1 Roll the rim templates C and D into rings. Glue and tape to hold. Glue each small wheel circle on to either side of a small ring as shown. Repeat for big wheels. Leave to dry.

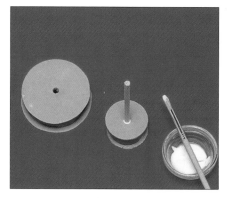

2 Use a pencil to enlarge the compass hole on one side of each wheel. Glue one end of each piece of dowel. Push them into the holes of two big and two small wheels.

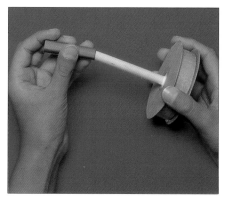

3 Roll the 5 x 5cm card into sleeves to fit loosely over each piece of dowel. Tape to hold. Make wheel pairs by fixing the remaining wheels on to the dowel as described in step 2.

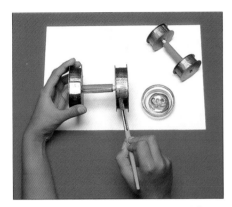

4 When the glue is dry, paint all four pairs of wheels silver. You do not need to paint the dowel axles. Paint two coats, letting the first dry before you apply the second.

5 Use a ruler and pencil to mark eight equal segments on the outside of each wheel. Paint a small circle over the compass hole, and the centre of each segment black.

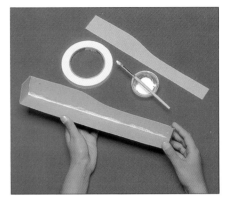

6 Fold along the dotted lines on E. Glue all three straight edges of template G and stick to template E. Repeat this for the other side. Secure all joins with masking tape.

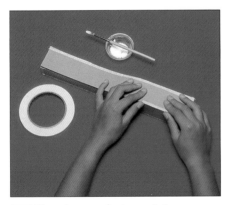

7 Glue the open edges of the underframe. Fit template F on top and hold until firm. Tape over the joins. Give the underframe two coats of black paint. Leave to dry.

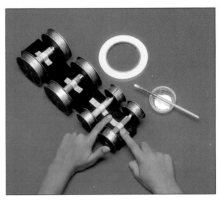

8 Glue the card sleeves on to the base of the underframe. Small wheel axles go 3cm and 7cm from the front, big wheels 3.5cm and 13cm from the back. Tape to secure.

9 Paint the coupling rods (H) with a coat of silver paint. Allow the paint to dry thoroughly. Then give the coupling rods a second coat of paint and leave them to dry.

10 Press a map pin through each end of the coupling rods, about 0.5cm from edge. Carefully press the pin into each big wheel about 1.5cm beneath the centre.

The wheels of the underframe will fit on the model tracks just like those of a real train. In real trains, however, the wheels are mounted in swivelling units called 'bogies'.

Locomotive

Toy trains started to go on sale during the mid-1800s. Early models were made of brightly painted wood, and often had a wooden track to run along. Soon, metal trains went on sale, many of them made from tinplate (thin sheets of iron or steel coated with tin). Some of these metal toy trains had wind-up clockwork motors. Clockwork toy trains were first sold in the USA during the 1880s. The most sophisticated model trains were steam-powered, with tiny engines fired by methylated-spirit burners. Later models were powered by electric motors.

Railway companies often devised special colour schemes, called liveries, for their locomotives and carriages. Steam locomotives had brass and copper decoration, and some also carried the company's special logo or badge. Many toy trains are also painted in the livery of a real railway company. The shape of the locomotive you can make in this project has an engine house typical of the real locomotives made in the 1930s. The driver and fireman would have shared the cabin of the locomotive. The driver controlled the speed of the train while the fireman ensured a good supply of steam.

YOU WILL NEED
26 x 26cm card, ruler, masking tape, scissors, 10 x 10cm card, pencil, PVA glue and glue brush, stiff card for templates, paints, paintbrush, water pot, underframe from previous project, two drawing pins, 11 x 1cm red card, split pin.

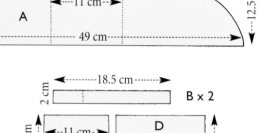

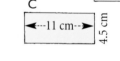

▲ Templates
Draw and cut out the templates from the stiff card.

Make a toy train

1 Roll the 26 x 26cm card into an 8cm-diameter tube. Secure it with masking tape. Using the scissors, carefully cut a 6cm slit, 21cm from one end of the tube.

2 Hold the tube upright on the 10 x 10cm piece of card. Draw around it. Cut this circle out. Glue the circle to the tube end farthest away from the slit. Tape to secure.

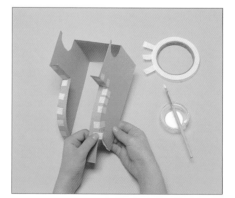

3 Copy and cut out the templates. Fold template A along the dotted lines. Fold templates B upwards along the dotted line. Glue both strips to the cabin as shown and secure with tape.

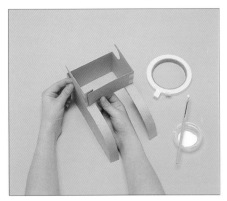

4 When the glue is dry, gently peel off the masking tape. Now glue on template C as shown above. Hold it in place with masking tape until the glue dries and then remove the tape.

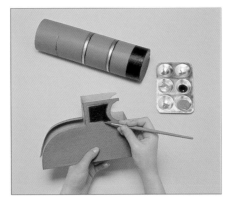

5 Apply two coats of green paint to the outside of the locomotive. Let the first coat dry before applying the second. Then paint the black parts. Add the red and gold last.

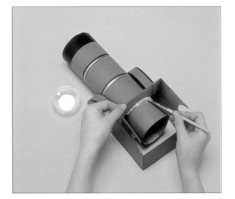

6 Glue around the bottom edge of the cabin front C. Put a little glue over the slit in the tube. Fit the front of the cabin into the slit. Leave the locomotive to one side to dry.

7 Give roof template D two coats of black paint. Let the paint dry between coats. Glue the top edges of the cabin, and place the black roof on top. Leave until dry and firm.

8 Glue the bottom of the cylindrical part of the train to the underframe you made in the *Underframe* project. Press drawing pins into the back of cabin and underframe.

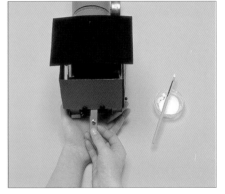

9 Glue both sides of one end of the red strip. Slot this between the underframe and the cabin, between the drawing pins. When firm, fold the strip and insert the split pin.

10 Paint one side of template E black. When dry, roll it into a tube and secure with masking tape. Glue the wavy edge and secure it to the front of the locomotive as shown.

Just like a real locomotive, the basic colour of your model train has been enhanced with red, black and gold decoration. The locomotive is now ready to run on the railway line you made in the *Making tracks* project on p206.

Brake van

Few early steam locomotives had brakes. If the driver needed to stop quickly, he had to throw the engine into reverse. By the early 1860s, braking systems for steam locomotives had been invented. Some passenger carriages also had their own handbrakes that were operated by the carriage guards. A brake van was added to the back of trains, too, but its brakes were operated by a guard riding inside. Old-style brake vans, like the one in this project, sat at the end of the train so that the guard could make sure that all the carriages stayed coupled.

The problem was that the train driver had no control over the rest of the train. When he wanted to stop, he had to blow the engine whistle to warn each of the carriage guards to apply their brakes. The brakes on a locomotive and its carriages or wagons needed to be linked. This was made possible by the invention of an air-braking system in 1869. When the driver applies the brakes, compressed air travels along pipes linking all the train, and presses brake shoes. Air brakes are now used on nearly all the world's railways.

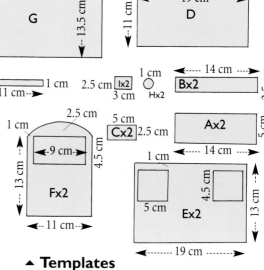

▲ **Templates**

Make a brake van

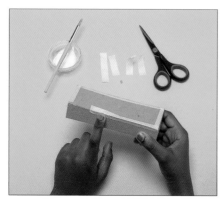

1 Copy the templates on to card and cut them out. Glue templates A, B and C together to make the underframe as shown. Tape over the joins to secure them.

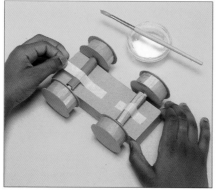

2 Make and paint two pairs of small wheels (diameter 5cm) following steps 1 through 3 in the *Underframe* project on p208. Glue and tape the wheel pairs to the underframe.

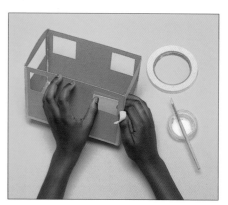

3 Glue the bottom edges of the van sides (E) to the van base (D). Then glue on the van ends (F). Secure the joins with masking tape until the glue is dry.

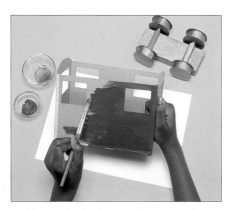

4 Paint the brake van brown with black details and the wheels and underframe black and silver. Apply two coats of paint, letting each one dry between coats.

5 Paint one side of template G black. Let the paint dry before applying a second coat. Glue the top edges of the van. Bend the roof to fit on the top of the van as shown.

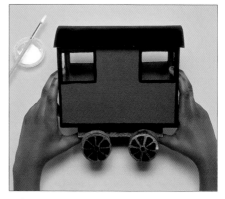

6 Apply glue to the top surface of the underframe. Stick the brake van centrally on top. Press together until the glue holds firm. Leave the model to dry completely.

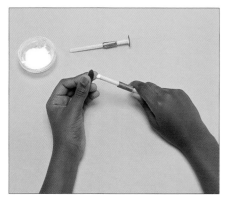

7 Roll up templates I into two 2cm tubes to fit loosely over the 3cm lengths of dowelling. Tape to hold. Paint them silver. Paint the buffer templates H black and stick on each dowelling.

8 Use compasses to pierce two holes 2.5cm from each side of the van and 1.5cm up. Enlarge with a pencil. Glue the end of each dowelling buffer. Slot it into the hole. Leave to dry.

9 Cut a 2cm slot between the buffers. Fold red card template J in half. Glue each open end of the loop and push them through the slot. Press down to hold firm.

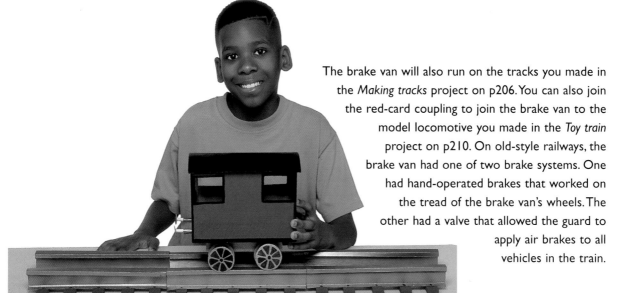

The brake van will also run on the tracks you made in the *Making tracks* project on p206. You can also join the red-card coupling to join the brake van to the model locomotive you made in the *Toy train* project on p210. On old-style railways, the brake van had one of two brake systems. One had hand-operated brakes that worked on the tread of the brake van's wheels. The other had a valve that allowed the guard to apply air brakes to all vehicles in the train.

Monorail

The first trains to run on a single rail rather than a twin track date back to the 1820s. As with early trains, these early monorails were pulled by horses and carried heavy materials such as building bricks, rather than passengers. About 60 years later, engineers designed steam locomotives that hauled carriages along an A-shaped rail. However, neither the trains nor the carriages were very stable. Loads had to be carefully balanced on either side of the A-frame to stop them tipping off.

Today's monorails are completely stable, with several sets of rubber wheels to give a smooth ride. They are powered by electricity, and many are driverless. Driverless monorail trains are controlled by computers that tell them when to stop, start, speed up or slow down. This project shows you how to make a train that runs on the 'straddle' system monorail. The body of the train straddles over the rail.

Monorails are not widely used today because they are more expensive to run than two-track railways. The special track costs more to build than twin rails and the cars cannot be switched from one track to another.

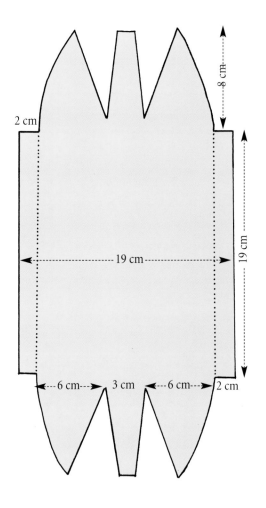

▲ **Template**
Draw and cut out the template from the stiff card.

Make a monorail

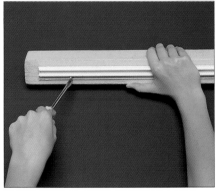

YOU WILL NEED

protective paper, 72cm length of wood (4 x 4cm), acrylic paints, paintbrush, water pot, 67cm length of plastic curtain rail (with screws, end fittings and four plastic runners), saw, screwdriver, sheet of stiff red card, pencil, ruler, scissors, double-sided sticky tape, 18cm length of 2.5cm-thick foam board, PVA glue and glue brush, black felt-tipped pen.

1 Cover the work surface with paper to protect it. Then paint the block of wood yellow. Let the first coat dry thoroughly before applying a second coat of paint.

2 Ask an adult to saw the curtain rail to size if necessary. Place the track centrally on the wood and screw it into place. Screw in the end fittings at one end of the rail.

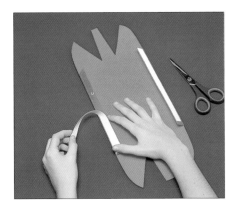

3 Copy the template on to the red card and cut it out. Score along the dotted lines and fold inwards. Stick double-sided tape along the outside of each folded section.

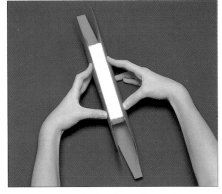

4 Remove the backing from the tape. Stick one side of the foam on to it. Fold the card over and press the other piece of double-sided tape to the opposite side of the foam.

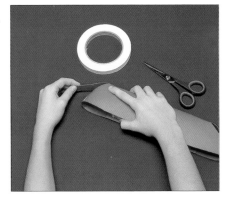

5 Overlap the pointed ends at the back and front of the train and glue. Then glue the inside end of the top flaps, back and front. Fold them over and press firmly to secure.

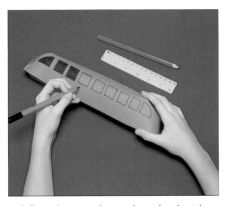

6 Pencil in windows along both sides of the train. Fill them in with a black felt-tipped pen. Paint decorative yellow and black stripes along the bottom of the windows.

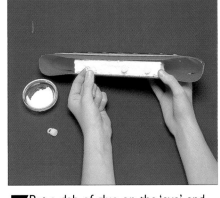
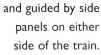

7 Put a dab of glue on the 'eye' end of each plastic runner. Hold the train, foam bottom towards you. Push each runner in turn into the foam at roughly equal intervals.

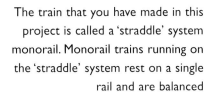

The train that you have made in this project is called a 'straddle' system monorail. Monorail trains running on the 'straddle' system rest on a single rail and are balanced and guided by side panels on either side of the train.

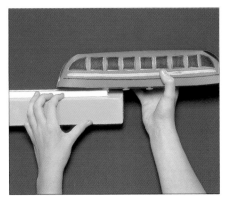

8 Stand the track on a flat surface. At the end of the track without an end stop, feed each plastic runner into the track. Run the train back and forth along the track.

Making car wheels turn

cylinder head

spark plug

cylinder

piston

con
(connecting) rod

crankshaft

▲ Working together

Most car engines have four cylinders arranged like this. You can see the pistons and cylinders. Four rods, one from each piston, turn metal joints attached to the crankshaft. As the rods turn the joints, the crankshaft moves round and round. This movement is transmitted to the wheels, via the gearbox, which controls how fast the wheels turn relative to the engine.

This experiment shows how one kind of movement – that goes round and round – can be converted into an up-and-down movement. This idea is applied to cars to make the wheels go round, but it happens the other way around. The up-and-down movement of the pistons is changed into the circular motion of the crankshaft and wheels.

When a car engine is switched on, fuel ignites and hot gases are produced in the cylinders. The gases force close-fitting pistons down the cylinders in which they are housed. The pistons are connected to the crankshaft (a rod that connects eventually to the wheels) so that as they move up and down, the crankshaft rotates. This, in turn, makes the wheels go round. One up-and-down movement of a piston results in one turn of the crankshaft. The wheels rotate once for about every three to six turns of the crankshaft.

YOU WILL NEED

shoebox, thin metal rod about 2mm diameter, pliers, jam jar lid, sticky tape, scissors, thick plastic straw, ruler, pencil, stiff paper, at least four colour felt-tipped pens, thin plastic straw.

Changing motion

1 Place the shoebox narrow-side-down on a flat surface. With one hand push the metal rod through the centre, making sure that your other hand will not get jabbed by the rod.

2 Using the pliers, bend the rod at right angles where it comes out of the box. Attach the jam jar lid to it with sticky tape. Push the lid until it rests against the side of the box.

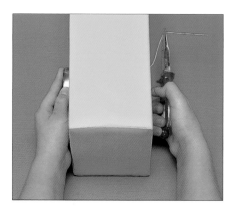

3 Carefully use the pliers to bend the piece of rod sticking out of the other side of the box. This will make a handle for the piston so that you will be able to turn it easily.

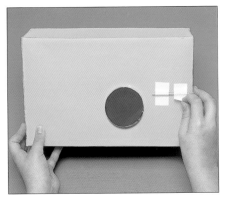

4 Cut a piece of thick plastic straw about 5cm long and tape it to the side of the box close to the jam jar lid. Make sure that it just sticks up beyond the edge of the box.

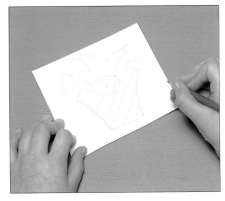

5 Draw a design in pencil on a piece of stiff paper. Copy the jester shown in this project or draw a simple clown. Choose something that looks good when it moves.

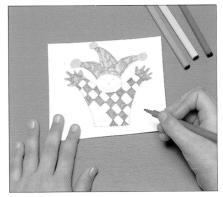

6 Using the felt-tipped pens, colour the design until it looks the way you want it to. The more colourful the figure is, the nicer it will look on the top of the piston.

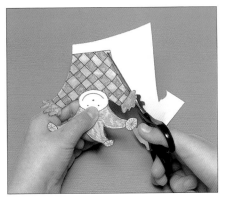

7 Carefully cut the finished drawing out of the paper. Make sure that you have a clean-edged design. Try not to smudge the felt-tipped colour with your fingers.

8 Turn the drawing over. Use the sticky tape to attach the thin plastic straw to the bottom of the drawing. About 2cm of straw should be attached.

Place the box on end so the jester is at the top. Turn the handle on the front. As you turn the handle, the jam jar lid revolves and pushes the jester up and down, like a piston.

9 Slide the straw attached to the drawing into the straw taped to the box. It will come out of the other end. Push down so that the straw touches the edge of the jam jar lid.

Changing gear

Gears in a car help transfer movement in the most efficient way. They do this by transmitting movement from the crankshaft (which links engine and wheels) to another shaft called the propeller shaft. The propeller shaft rotates more slowly than the crankshaft and adapts the movement so that the car can cope better with different speeds and efforts such as starting or going uphill. The change in speed of rotation between the two shafts is controlled from the car's gearbox. As a driver changes gear, toothed wheels connected to the crankshaft engage with other toothed wheels joined to the propeller shaft. The difference in the number of teeth on each wheel determines the number of times the wheels turn, as the first project demonstrates. The second project shows how gear wheels work in a car. The larger corrugated card wheel has more teeth than the two smaller wheels.

crankshaft

propeller shaft

high gear

low gear

▲ Wheels within wheels

The car's engine turns the crankshaft with different sized gears (toothed wheels) on it. High gears are used for more speed because the big wheel turns the small wheel faster. The gear system is called the transmission — it transmits (moves) the engine's power to the car's wheels. Most cars have five gears. The biggest is needed for slow speeds and the smallest for high speeds.

YOU WILL NEED

pair of compasses, ruler, pencil, A4 sheet of white paper, black pen, scissors, A4 sheet of thin card, two strips of corrugated card, sticky tape, three coloured felt-tipped pens.

Drawing the gears

1 Using the pair of compasses, trace a 14cm-diameter circle on the paper. Draw over it with the pen and cut it out. On the card, trace, draw and cut out an 11cm-diameter circle.

2 Tape corrugated card around the circles. Make a hole in the small circle wide enough for the tip of a felt-tipped pen. Turn the small wheel inside the larger. Trace the path in felt-tipped pen.

3 Make a second hole in the small wheel. Turn the small gear inside the larger using another felt-tipped pen. Make a third hole in the small wheel and use a third colour pen.

Three-gear machine

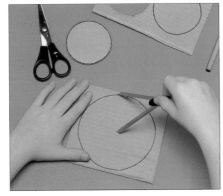

1 Use the compasses to trace one 14cm-diameter and two 11cm-diameter circles on the card. Draw around the circle edges with the pen and cut the circles out.

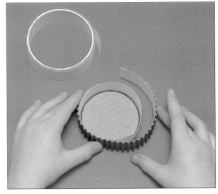

2 Carefully wrap the strips of corrugated card around the circles, using one strip per circle, corrugated side out. Tape each strip to the bottom of the circles.

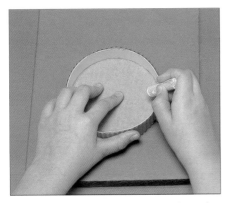

3 Place the largest gear wheel on the piece of fibreboard. Hold the gear down and glue the dowelling on to the side of the gear base at the edge of the wheel. Leave it until it is dry.

4 Position all three gears on the fibreboard, edges just touching each other. Pin each of them firmly to the fibreboard with a map pin but allow them to turn.

As you turn the gears, notice how they move in opposite directions to each other. Now you have a three-gear machine where the energy from each gear is being transferred to the others, just like the gears in a car.

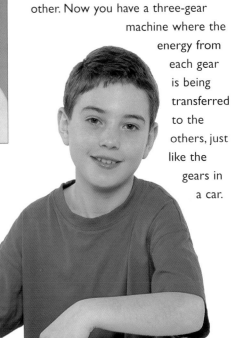

5 Gently turn the dowelling on the largest gear. As that gear turns, the two others that are linked together by the corrugated card will turn against it.

Car control

Cars have two kinds of brakes. Parking brakes lock the rear wheels when the car is standing still. Disc brakes slow down the car when it is moving, in the same way that the sandpaper slows the model wheel in the first experiment.

The second project shows how a device called the camshaft controls the flow of fuel into the cylinders. The camshaft is designed so as to have a regular action that opens one valve and closes another at the same time. Inlet valves let fuel and air into the engine, while burned waste gases are removed via the outlet valves. The camshaft controls make the engine run smoothly.

YOU WILL NEED

Disc brakes: scissors, 40cm length of fabric, circular card box with lid, sticky tape, pencil, 20cm length of 12mm-diameter wood dowelling, PVA glue, glue brush, 7 x 11cm medium sandpaper, 6 x 10cm wooden block, two plastic cups, insulation tape.

How valves work: scissors, 12cm square of stiff card, masking tape, cardboard tube with plastic lid, pencil.

Stopping ▶

When a driver presses the brake pedal, a piston presses together two pads, one on either side of the disc to which the wheel is attached. This strong grip stops the disc from turning, and as the disc slows, so do the wheels.

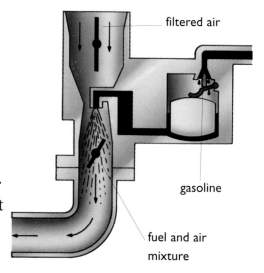

filtered air

gasoline

fuel and air mixture

▲ The carburettor

Fuel and air enter the carburettor in just the right quantities for the car to run smoothly. The mixture is then fed into the cylinders. Pressing the accelerator pedal in a car allows more air and fuel into the engine to make it run faster, so speeding up the car.

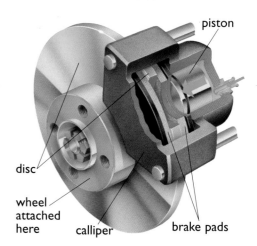

piston

disc

wheel attached here

calliper

brake pads

Disc brakes

1 Use the scissors to cut a narrow 40cm strip from the fabric. You may have to use special fabric cutting scissors if your ordinary scissors are not sharp enough.

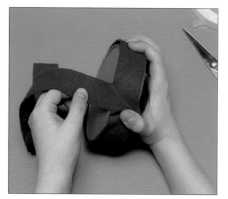

2 Take the strip of fabric you have cut out and wrap it around the rim of the circular cardboard box. Secure it firmly in place with small pieces of sticky tape.

3 Make a hole in the centre of the box's lid with a pencil. Twist the pencil until it comes through the base of the box. Now gently push the wood dowelling through both holes.

4 Spread lots of glue on to the sandpaper's smooth side. Wrap the sandpaper carefully over the top of the wood block. Pressing firmly, stick it together. Leave it to dry.

5 Stand two plastic cups upside down. Rest either end of the dowelling on each cup. Cut two small pieces of insulation tape. Use them to fix each end of the dowelling to the cup bases.

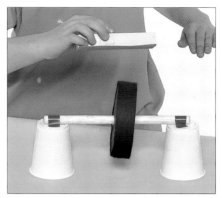

6 Spin the lid fast on the dowelling. As it spins, bring the sandpaper into contact with the edge of the lid. Test your brake disc to see how quickly you can stop the lid.

How valves work

1 Use scissors to cut a 1 x 12cm strip from the stiff card. Double it over in the centre. Hold it with your fingertips. Bend the two ends of the card away from one another.

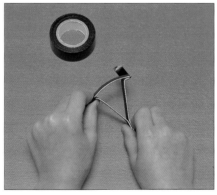

2 Cut a 1 x 4cm strip from the original piece of card. Use masking tape to fix the card strip to the bent bottom ends of the first piece. This makes a triangle shape.

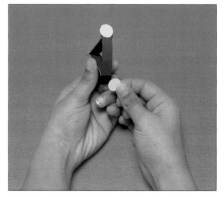

3 Use the scissors to cut out two small circle shapes from the original piece of card. Use masking tape to secure them to the bottom piece of the triangle you have made.

4 Put the stiff card triangle on top of the cardboard tube. The circles should touch the plastic lid. With a pencil, mark the position where the circles sit on the lid.

5 Using the scissors, carefully cut around the pencil marks you have made in the plastic lid of the tube. These form an inlet and an outlet. As one valve opens, the other will close.

6 Now you can rock the triangle back and forth to cover and uncover the two holes. This is just how a camshaft opens and shuts the inlet and outlet valves in a car's cylinder.

Keeping cool

The explosion of fuel and air that fires a car's engine generates a great deal of heat. Friction (rubbing together of two surfaces), as the engine parts move together at speed, also creates heat. If the heat level is not kept down, the engine stops working. Metal parts expand, seize up and stop. To cool the engine, water from the car's radiator is pumped around the hottest parts of the engine – the combustion chambers where the fuel ignites, and the cylinders.

▲ Mass production

All the separate parts of a car are mass-produced and then assembled (put together) on a production line to make the finished vehicle. Almost all cars are assembled on production lines today. Robots do much of the work.

The moving water carries heat away from the hottest parts of the engine. The radiator cools the hot water from the engine by using a fan. The fan is driven by a belt connected to the engine. This project shows how a belt transfers turning movement from one shaft to another. This is how a car's engine turns the fan belt.

YOU WILL NEED

ruler, 16cm square of thin cloth, scissors, five cotton reels, glue stick, A4 wooden board, pencil, five flat-headed nails 4cm in length, hammer, 1m x 2.5cm velvet ribbon, sticky tape, pair of compasses, five pieces of 10cm-square coloured card, five wooden skewers.

Fan belt

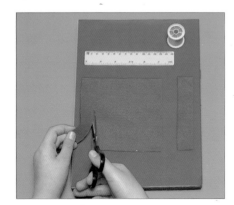

1 Using the ruler, measure five 2.5cm-wide strips on the thin cloth. The height of the cotton reels should be more than 2.5cm. Use the scissors to cut out each strip.

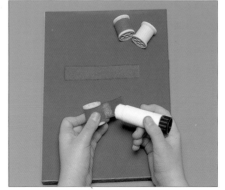

2 Wrap one of the fabric strips around each of the five cotton reels. Glue each strip at the end so that it sits firmly around the reel and will not come loose.

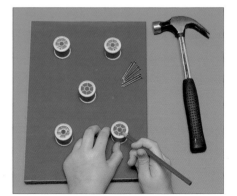

3 Place the reels on the wooden board as shown above. Trace the outlines with a pencil. Put the nails through the centre of the reels and carefully hammer them into the board.

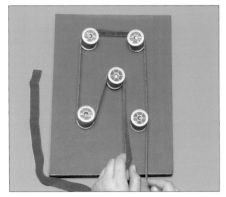

4 Wind the ribbon around the reels with the velvet side against four of the reels. Cut the ribbon at the point where you can join both ends round the fifth reel.

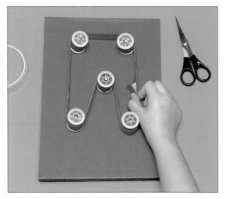

5 Tape the two ends of the ribbon together firmly. Make sure that the ribbon wraps firmly around all of the five reels, but not so tightly that it can't move.

6 Use the pair of compasses to draw circles about 7cm in diameter on to the five pieces of coloured card. Then draw freehand spiral shapes inside each circle.

7 Use the scissors to cut each spiral out of each of the pieces of coloured card. Start from the outside edge and gradually work your way in along the lines of the spiral.

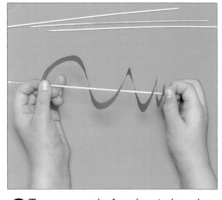

8 Tape one end of each spiral to the end of a skewer. Wind the other end of the spiral around the skewer stick a few times. Tape it close to the opposite end of the skewer.

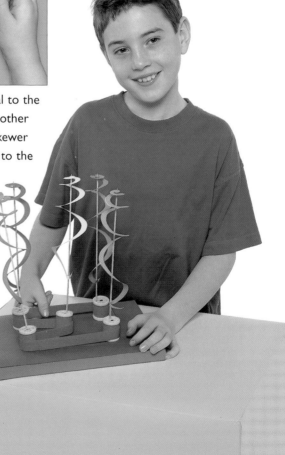

Now you are ready to turn the belt. Like a fan belt in a car, it turns the fans around. This is a five-fan machine. You can add more fans if you like.

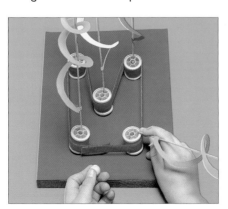

9 Put a small amount of sticky tape on to the end of each skewer. Then place each skewer into one of the empty holes in the top of each cotton reel.

Prototype car

When you make your model car, choose the colours carefully. Do you want bright colours that will be noticed easily, or cool, fashionable colours? Car manufacturers call in teams of people to help them decide what a car should look like. Stylists, design and production engineers join forces with the sales team to develop cars they hope people will buy. They think about the colours, how much people are prepared to pay, and what features they want, from air-conditioning to special car seats.

Before a new car is launched to the public, detailed models are made and tested to investigate the car's aerodynamics (how air flows over its shape). Finally, a prototype (early version) of the car is built and tested for road handling, engine quality and comfort.

Wire basket ▶
Car designers today make use of CAD (computer-aided design) software to help them create a three-dimensional image of a new car design. Wire-frame (see-through) computer images show the car from any angle. They also show how all the parts of the car fit together.

Model car

1 Draw and cut out four 2.5cm and eight 6cm diameter card circles. Glue the 6cm circles together to make four wheels. Glue a 2.5cm circle to the centre of each wheel.

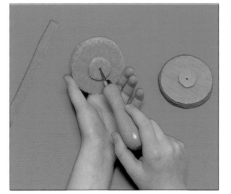

2 Use the bradawl to make a hole in the centre of each wheel. Cut four 4mm strips of coloured card. Wrap one each around the wheel rims. Glue the overlapping ends.

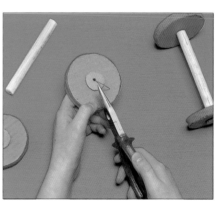

3 Push straightened paper clips into the holes and bend the outer ends with pliers. Fix the wheels to the two pieces of dowelling by pushing the paper clips into the ends.

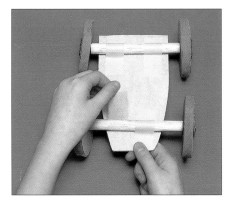

4 Cut a piece of card to 8 x 15cm. Trim one end to make it 6cm wide. Tape the two axles to the card, one at each end. Ensure they are long enough for the wheels to rotate freely.

5 Cut a piece of card 8 x 35cm. Double it over and bend it into a cab shape. Tape the two loose ends together. Stick the base of the cab shape to the car base.

6 Cut two cardboard shapes 15cm long x 10cm high. Trim them with the scissors to the same shape as the side of your car cab. Attach the sides to the cab with sticky tape.

Decorate your car

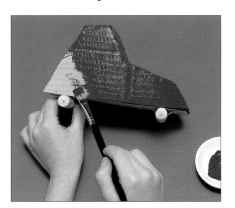

1 Remove the wheels from your car. Paint the sides and top of the cab with one of the two colours of paint. Leave it to dry. Then paint it with the same colour again and leave it to dry.

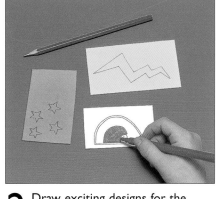

2 Draw exciting designs for the sides of the car and a driver to go behind the windscreen. Draw some headlamps and some exhaust fumes. Add colour with the felt-tipped pens.

Replace the wheels when they are dry. Now your car looks just like a real street machine. Cut photographs of cars from magazines for ideas for new designs.

3 Let the paint dry for a couple of hours. Cut the designs out of the card. Glue them to the sides and back of the car. Paint the wheels with the colour of paint not yet used.

Parachutes and balloons

Parachutes fall slowly because air is trapped beneath them. They are deliberately designed to have very high drag. Drag is the force that works against the direction of anything flying through the air. The amount of drag depends on the shape. A fat, lumpy shape, like the parachute in the first project, has lots of drag and falls slowly.

Hot air balloons rise into the air because the hot air inside them is lighter than the air outside. Real balloons use gas burners, but the project here uses a hair dryer to make the balloon rise.

Mini parachute jump

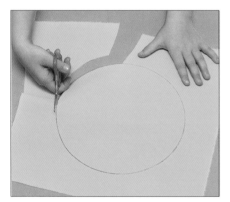

1 Use the felt-tipped pen to draw around the plate on the fabric. Using the scissors, carefully cut out the circle to make what will be the parachute's canopy.

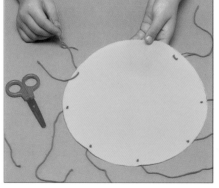

2 Make about eight equally spaced marks around the edge of the circle. Use a needle to sew on one 30cm long piece of cotton thread to each point you have marked.

3 Use sticky tape to secure the free end of each thread to a reel. Use a plastic reel, since a wooden one will be too heavy for your parachute.

4 Hold the parachute so that the canopy is open and the cotton reel dangles down. Stand by an upstairs window or use a step-ladder to get as high as you can – but be very careful!

Let your parachute go from as high up as possible. As it falls, the canopy will open and fill with air. The larger the canopy, the slower the parachute will fall.

Ballooning around

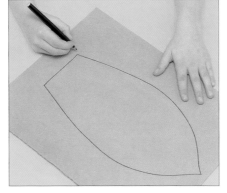

1 To make a template, draw a petal shape on card and carefully cut it out. The shape should be 30cm long and 12cm across with a flat bottom edge.

2 Draw around your template on seven pieces of coloured tissue paper. Be very careful not to rip the tissue paper with the tip of your pencil.

3 Use the pair of scissors to carefully cut out the shapes you have drawn. You should now have seven petals that are all the same size and shape.

4 Glue along one edge of a petal. Lay another petal on top and press it down. Open it out and stick on another petal in the same way. Keep going until the balloon is complete.

To fly your balloon, hold its neck open and fill the inside with hot air from a hair dryer. After ten seconds, switch off the hair dryer and let go of your balloon to launch it into the air.

Streamlined design

Think of a sleek canoe moving through water. Its streamlined shape hardly makes any ripples as it passes. Streamlined shapes also move easily through air. They have low drag (air resistance). Angular shapes have more drag than rounded ones. The shape of a fast-moving fish has to be very streamlined. A fish such as a tuna has a blunt front end, is broadest about a third of the way along, then tapers towards the tail. This creates less drag as it moves through water than a shape with a pointed front end that broadens at the back. Water flows along each side of the tuna to rejoin without creating turbulence. The *Shape race* gives you a chance to design and test your own streamlined shapes.

Just as things that are moving in the air experience drag, so do stationary objects in the wind. Kites, such as the one here, are held up in the air by drag from the wind. For more than 3,000 years, people have been making and flying kites. The essential but simple secret is that it must be as light as possible for its size, so that it catches as much wind as possible. The kite design shown in this project has been used for many hundreds of years. Try flying it first of all in a steady wind and experiment with the position of the bridle and the length of the tail.

YOU WILL NEED

pen, ruler, two bamboo canes (one about two-thirds as long as the other), string, scissors, sticky tape, sheet of thin fabric or plastic, fabric glue, coloured paper.

▲ **How air flows work**
Air flows in gentle curves around the streamlined shape (*top*). Angles or sharp curves break up the flow and increase drag (*bottom*).

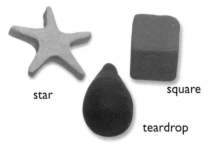

star

teardrop

square

▲ **Shape race**
Make different shapes (*as shown above*) from balls of modelling material that are exactly the same size. Race your shapes in water – the most streamlined shape should reach the bottom first.

Make a kite

1 To make the frame, mark the centre of the short cane and mark one-third of the way up the long cane. Tie the canes together crosswise at the marks with string.

2 Tape string around the ends of the canes and secure it at the top. This will stop the canes from moving, and it will also support the edges of your finished kite.

3 Lay the frame on top of the sheet of fabric or plastic. Cut around it, 2cm away from the kite's edge. This will give you enough to fold over the string outline.

4 Fold each edge of the material over the frame and stick the edges down firmly with fabric glue (or sticky tape if you are making the kite from plastic). Let the glue dry.

5 Tie a piece of string to the long cane, as shown – this is called the bridle. Tie the end of the ball of string to the middle of the bridle to make the tether.

6 Fold sheets of paper in zigzags. Tie them at about 25cm intervals along a piece of string that is about twice as long as the kite. Glue or tie the tail to the bottom tip of the kite.

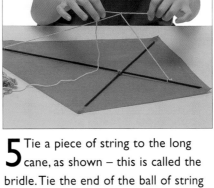

bridle

tail

tassel

tether

Now your kite is ready to fly! With the wind blowing on your back, reel out about 10m of tether. Ask an adult to gently launch the kite into the air. If it is not very windy, run into the breeze, pulling the kite to get it airborne. Now that you have built this kite, try experimenting with other materials and shapes to find which work well.

Curve and lift

Birds, gliders and aeroplanes all have wings. Their wings can be all sorts of different shapes and sizes, but they all have the same aerofoil design. This means that the top side of the wing is more curved than the underside. The aerofoil shape provides lift when air moves over it. Air flows faster over the curved upper surface than over the flatter lower surface. This reduces the air pressure above the wing and lets the higher air pressure underneath lift it up.

You can make and test a model aerofoil by following the instructions in these projects. In the frisbee project, the shape of the frisbee enables the air to move smoothly over and under it. The frisbee spins as it flies. The spinning motion helps to steady it. The second project shows you how moving air, in this case from an electric fan or hair dryer, can lift the wings with an aerofoil shape upwards.

Fly your frisbee outside, away from people. Hold it at the front and spin it away from you and up. It should glide through the air smoothly as the air pressure above it is reduced. Play toss-and-catch games with your friends. You could even have your own championship match! Commercial frisbees were introduced into the USA in the 1950s.

YOU WILL NEED

Fly a frisbee: large plate, thick card, pencil, scissors, ruler, sticky tape.
Aerofoil antics: paper, pencil, ruler, scissors, sticky tape, glue stick, plastic drinking straw, thick cotton thread, fan or hair dryer.

Fly a frisbee

1 Place the plate face down on the card and draw around it with a pencil. Cut out the circle of card. Draw slots 1.5cm deep around the edge and cut these, as shown.

2 The cut slots around the edge will make tabs. Bend the tabs down slightly. Overlap them a little and stick them together with small pieces of sticky tape.

Aerofoil antics

1 Use a ruler to measure a rectangle of coloured paper about 15cm wide and 20cm long. Use scissors to carefully cut out the shape. This will be your wing.

2 Fold the paper over, approximately in half. Use sticky tape to fix the top edge 1cm away from the bottom edge. Take care not to crease the paper as you do this.

3 Cut out and stick on a small paper fin near the rear edge of your wing, as shown. This will keep the wing facing into the airflow when you test it.

4 With a sharp pencil, carefully poke a hole through the top and bottom of your wing, near the front edge. Push a straw through the holes and glue it in place in the middle.

5 Cut a 1m long piece of thick cotton thread and thread it through the straw. Make sure the cotton can slide easily through the straw and does not catch.

Hold the cotton tight and ask a friend to blow air from a fan or hair dryer over the wing. Watch it take off! This happens because the shape decreases the air pressure above the wing.

Jet propulsion

A jet engine produces thrust from a roaring jet of super-hot gas. Its construction looks complicated, but the way it works is very simple. A powerful jet of gas moving in one direction produces thrust in the other direction. Imagine you are standing on a skateboard and squirting a powerful hose forwards. Jet propulsion will push you backwards. This reaction has been known for nearly 2,000 years, but it was not until the 1930s that it was applied to an engine.

In the first experiment, you can make a jet zoom along a string. The jet engine is like a balloon that produces thrust from escaping air. The second project demonstrates how a turbine works. Hot air produced by the gas jet turns the blades of the turbine. The turbine drives the fan at the front of the jet engine. These projects may seem simple, but they use the same scientific principles that propel all jet aeroplanes through the air.

Balloon jet

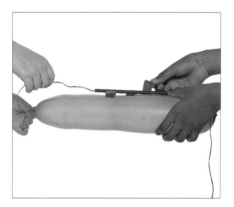

I Blow up the balloon and, while a friend holds the neck, tape the straw to its top. Thread the string through the straw and, holding it level, tie it to something to keep it in place.

▲ **Practical plane**
This passenger plane has four engines, two on each wing. Jet engines have revolutionized international travel. Passenger planes carry millions of travellers around the world every year.

2 Let go of the neck of the balloon. A stream of air jets backwards and produces thrust. This propels the balloon forwards along the string at high speed.

Turbine lights

1 Cut out the bottom of a large aluminium pie dish as evenly as possible. Make a small hole in the centre with the point of a pair of compasses.

2 Mark a smaller circle in the centre. Use a protractor to mark 16 equal sections of 22.5 degrees and cut along each one to the inner circle. Use one scissor cut along each line, if possible.

3 Angle the blades by holding the inner tip and twisting the outer edges 20 to 30 degrees. The centre of the inner tip should be flat, in line with the centre of the disc.

◀ Jet engine
The huge blades at the front of a jet engine suck in air and compress it. Fuel burns in the air to produce jets of hot air that blast from the rear of the engine, producing thrust.

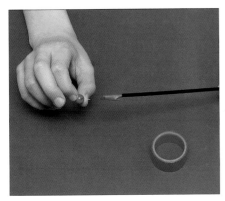

4 Tape the blunt end of the dressmaking pin to one end of the dowelling. Place the bead on the pin. This will allow the finished turbine to spin freely.

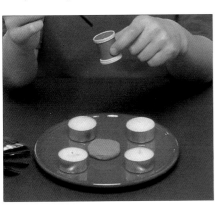

5 Put the dowelling in the reel and press the reel into the modelling material in the centre of the plate. Place the four night lights on the plate around the reel.

Place the hole in the centre of the turbine over the pin. Ask an adult to light the night lights. Hot air will spin the blades.

Propeller flight

Propellers work in two different ways. When a propeller spins, it makes air move past it. Propeller-driven aircraft use this effect to produce thrust. Moving air also causes the propeller to spin. The projects here look at propellers working in these two ways. In the first you can make a simple paper propeller called a spinner. As the spinner falls, moving air rushes past the blades, making it revolve. This acts just like the fruits and seeds of maple and sycamore trees, which have twin propeller blades. As they drop from the tree, they spin and catch the wind, and are carried far away.

In the second project, you can make a spinning propeller fly upwards through the air. The propeller-like blades are set at an angle, like the blades of a fan. They whirl around and make air move. The moving air produces thrust and lifts the propeller upward. Children first flew propellers like these 600 years ago in China.

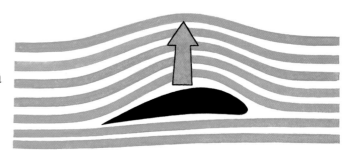

▲ Lift off

An aerofoil's curved shape causes the air to flow faster over its upper surface than its lower surface. This reduces pressure from above and causes lift.

In a spin

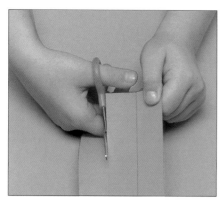

1 Take a piece of paper, 15 x 9cm, and draw a T-shape on it, as shown in the picture above. With a pair of scissors, cut along the two long lines of the T.

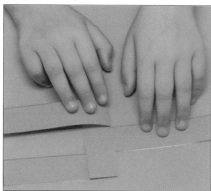

2 Fold one side strip forwards and one backwards, as shown above, making two blades and a stalk. Attach a paper clip to the bottom. Open the blades flat.

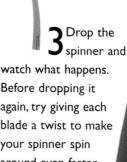

3 Drop the spinner and watch what happens. Before dropping it again, try giving each blade a twist to make your spinner spin around even faster.

Let's twist

YOU WILL NEED

In a spin: thin paper, ruler, pencil, scissors, paper clip.

Let's twist: thick card, ruler, pair of compasses, protractor, pen, scissors, 1cm slice of cork, bradawl, 7.5cm length of 3mm-diameter dowelling, model glue, string, cotton reel.

1 With the compasses, draw a circle 10cm across on the card. Draw a circle 4cm across in the centre. With the protractor, draw lines across the circle, dividing it into 16 equal sections.

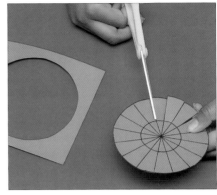

2 Carefully cut out the circle and along the lines to the smaller circle. Twist the blades sideways a little. Try to give each blade the same amount of twist, about 20 or 30 degrees.

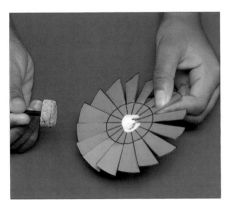

3 Make a hole in the centre of the cork slice with a bradawl. Put glue on the end of the dowelling and push it into the hole. Glue the cork to the middle of the propeller.

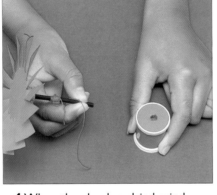

4 When the glue has dried, wind a long piece of string around the dowelling. Drop the dowelling into the cotton reel launcher. You are now ready for a test flight.

Pull steadily on the string to whirl the propeller around. As the end of the string comes away, the blades produce enough thrust to lift the spinning propeller out of the launcher and into the air.

Model planes

Although a model is much smaller than a real full-size aircraft, it flies in exactly the same way. The control surfaces on the wings and the tail of a model plane or real aircraft work by changing the way in which air flows over the aircraft. This allows the pilot to steer the aircraft in different directions. Working together, the rudder and movable flaps called ailerons on the rear edge of each wing make the plane turn to the left or right. Moving flaps called elevators on the tail make the nose of the plane go up or down.

The scientific rules of flying are the same for any aircraft, from an airliner weighing 350 tonnes to this model made from paper, tape and a drinking straw. Making this model plane allows you to see how control surfaces such as the aileron, rudder and elevators work. The flight of any plane is very sensitive to the angle of the controls. They need to be only a slight angle from their flat position to make the plane turn. Too big an angle will make the model unstable.

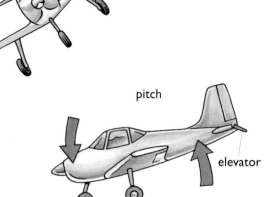

ailerons

roll

pitch

elevator

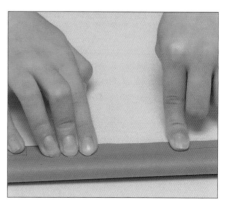

rudder

yaw

▲ How to fly a plane

To turn the aircraft (yaw), the pilot turns the rudder to one side. To make the aircraft descend or climb (pitch) the pilot adjusts the elevators on the tailplane. To roll (tilt or bank) the aircraft to the left or right, the ailerons are raised on one wing and lowered on the other.

Glide along

YOU WILL NEED

pencil, set square, ruler, paper, scissors, glue stick, sticky tape, drinking straw, paper clips or non-hardening modelling material.

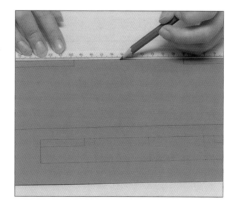

1 Draw two paper rectangles, 22 x 10cm and 20 x 3.5cm. Mark ailerons 6 x 1cm on two corners of the larger one. Mark two elevators 3.5 x 1cm on the other. Cut them out.

2 To make the wings, wrap the larger rectangle over a pencil and glue along the edges. Remove the pencil and make cuts along the 1cm lines to allow the ailerons to move.

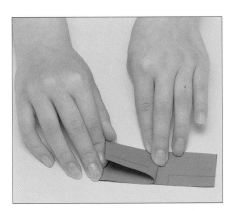

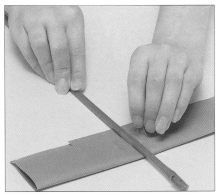

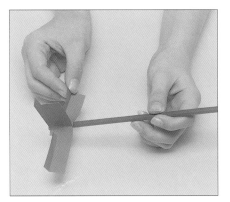

3 To make the tail, fold the smaller rectangle in half twice to form a W. Glue its centre to make the fin. Cut along the two 1cm lines. Make a 1cm cut on the fin to make a rudder.

4 Use sticky tape to fix the wings and tail to the drinking straw (the plane's fuselage, or body). Position the wings about one quarter of the way along the straw.

5 Try adjusting the control surfaces. Bend the elevators on the tail slightly up. This will make the plane climb as it flies. Bend the elevators down to make it dive.

6 Bend the left-hand aileron up and the right-hand aileron down the same amount. Bend the rudder to the left. This will make the plane turn to the left as it flies.

Launch your plane by throwing it steadily straight ahead. To make it fly even farther, use paper clips or modelling material to weight the nose.

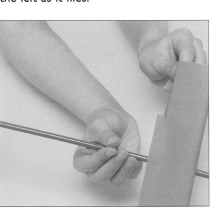

7 Bend the right-hand aileron up and the left-hand aileron down. Bend the rudder slightly to the right and the plane will turn to the right. Can you make it fly in a circle?

Escaping from Earth

The function of a space rocket is to carry a satellite or astronauts into Space. To do this, it has to overcome gravity (the force that pulls everything down to Earth). If a rocket's engines are not powerful enough, gravity will win and pull the rocket back to Earth. With more powerful engines, the rocket's attempt to fly into Space is exactly equalled by the pull of gravity. With these two forces in perfect balance, a spacecraft will continue to circle the Earth. If the rocket is even more powerful, it can fly fast enough to escape from Earth's gravity altogether and head towards the Moon or the planets. The speed that it needs to reach to do this is called escape velocity. You can see this in action by trying out an experiment using a magnet and ball-bearings. You can also try launching your own cork model rocket from a plastic bottle.

Launch a rocket

I Place a teaspoon (5ml) of baking soda directly in the middle of a 10 x 20cm piece of paper towel. Roll up the towel and twist the ends to keep the baking soda fuel inside.

2 Pour half a cup of water and the same amount of vinegar into the bottle. Fix paper streamers or a ribbon to the the cork with a drawing pin. Drop the paper towel inside the bottle.

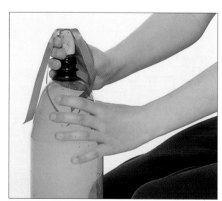

3 Push the cork in immediately so that it is a snug fit, but not too tight. Quickly take the bottle outside. Then move at least 3m away from it and watch what happens.

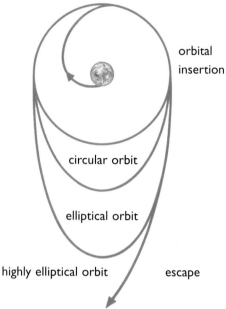

orbital insertion

circular orbit

elliptical orbit

highly elliptical orbit   escape

▲ Escape velocity

To go into orbit around the Earth, a spacecraft must reach a velocity of at least 28,500km/h. Depending on how fast it is travelling, the spacecraft may go into a circular, elliptical, or highly elliptical orbit. If it reaches a velocity of 40,200km/h, the spacecraft escapes from the Earth's gravity altogether.

A chemical reaction between the vinegar (representing liquid oxygen) and baking soda (representing fuel) produces carbon dioxide gas. The gas pressure inside the bottle pushes against the cork. The cork is blasted into the air like a rocket lifting off. However, in a real rocket, the gas is jetted out of the actual spacecraft, propelling it forward.

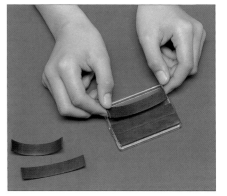

YOU WILL NEED

Launch a rocket: baking soda, paper towel, water, vinegar, 2-litre plastic bottle, paper streamers or ribbon, cork, drawing pin.

Escaping from gravity: thin card, ruler, pencil, scissors, magnetic strip, PVA glue, glue brush, 10 x 5cm piece of plastic, baking tray, non-hardening modelling material, sticky tape, ball-bearings.

Escaping from gravity

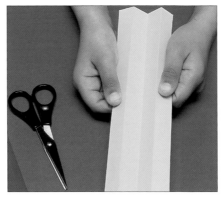

1 Measure out a 30 x 10cm strip of thin card using a ruler. Cut it out with the scissors. Fold it lengthways into four sections to form an M-shaped trough.

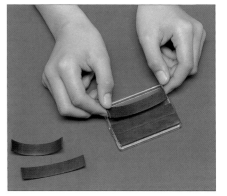

2 Cut the magnetic strip into five short pieces. Glue these short strips to the plastic base so that they form a large, square bar magnet, as shown above.

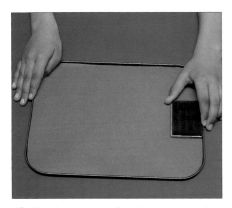

3 Fix the magnet firmly to one end of the tray with some of the modelling material. Position it roughly in the middle. The magnet simulates the pull of the Earth's gravity.

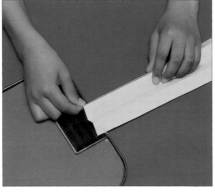

4 Position one end of the trough over the edge of the magnet. Attach it to the magnet with sticky tape. The trough represents the path of a rocket as it ascends into orbit.

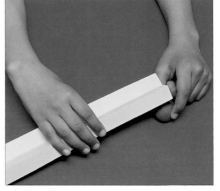

5 Roll the remaining modelling material into a round ball. Position the ball underneath the other end of the M-shaped trough. This raises the trough at a slight angle.

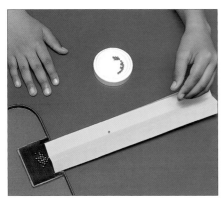

6 At the end of the trough place a ball-bearing and let it roll down. It sticks to the magnet. The ball-bearing's velocity along the trough isn't fast enough to escape the magnet's pull.

Raise the trough and roll another ball-bearing along it. The steeper angle increases the ball-bearing's velocity. Keep raising the trough and rolling ball-bearings until one shoots past the magnet. It has then achieved escape velocity!

Rocket launch

Space rockets rely on jet propulsion to fly. When the rocket burns its fuel, a stream of hot gases roars out from the tail end and the rocket surges forward. Jets flying lower than 25,000m can burn their fuel using oxygen from the air. Space rockets need to carry oxygen with them because above 25,000m, the air thins out and there is not enough oxygen.

Deep in the sea, octopuses also rely on jet propulsion to escape from their enemies. They squirt out a jet of water and shoot off in the opposite direction.

This experiment shows you how to make and fly a rocket that uses jet propulsion. The thrust of a rocket depends on the mass of propellant it shoots out every second. Water is a much better propellant than hot gas because it is so much heavier.

Follow these instructions carefully and your rocket could fly to over 25m above the ground. You may need adult help to make some parts of this rocket and to launch it. When you are ready for a test flight, set your rocket up in an open space, well away from trees and buildings. This rocket is very powerful – you must not stand over it while it is being launched. Wear clothes that you do not mind getting very wet!

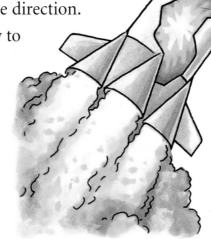

oxygen

hydrogen

combustion chamber

▲ **Inside a rocket**
This is a liquid-fuelled rocket. It carries liquid oxygen to burn its fuel (liquid hydrogen). The hydrogen and oxygen are pumped into the combustion chamber. The hydrogen burns furiously in the oxygen. The exhaust produces immense thrust.

Make a rocket

> ### YOU WILL NEED
> plain card, pen, ruler, coloured card, scissors, plastic bottle, strong sticky tape, funnel, jug of water, cork, bradawl, air valve, plastic tubing, bicycle pump.

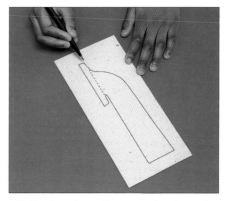

1 Rockets have fins to make them fly straight. Draw out this fin template (it is about 20cm long) on to plain card and use it to cut out four fins from coloured card.

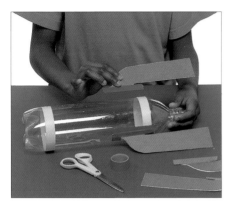

2 Decorate your bottle to look like a rocket. Fold over the tab at the top of each fin. Use long pieces of strong sticky tape to firmly attach the fins to the bottle.

3 Use the funnel to half-fill the bottle with water. (The water is the propellant. Compressed air above the water will provide the energy that makes the thrust.)

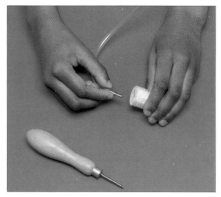

4 Use the bradawl to carefully drill a hole through the cork. Push the wide end of the air valve into the plastic tubing. Push the valve through the hole in the cork.

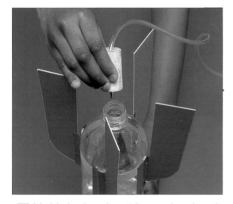

5 Hold the bottle with one hand and push the cork and the valve into the neck of the bottle using the other hand. Push it in firmly so that the cork does not slide out too easily.

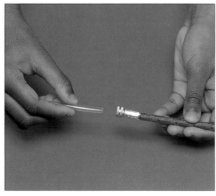

6 Attach the other end of the plastic tubing to the bicycle pump. Turn your rocket the right way up – you are now ready to launch your rocket out of doors.

Look for a launch site well away from trees and buildings. Stand the rocket on its tail fins and tell everyone to stand well back. Start pumping. Bubbles of air will rise up through the water. When the pressure in the bottle gets high enough, the cork and water will be forced out and the rocket will fly upwards. Be careful not to stand over the bottle!

Going to the Moon

Plotting a course through Space is more complicated than travelling over land. Pilots follow natural features, such as hills, valleys and rivers, or at high altitudes use radio beacons on the ground or satellite signals. The problem with travelling from the Earth to the Moon is that both are moving, as the first project illustrates. The second project shows how a heavy craft gets to the Moon. Staged rockets release their sections as they progress into Space, so reducing the weight of the rocket.

If a spacecraft was aimed straight at the Moon when it set off from Earth, the Moon would have moved on around its orbit by the time the craft arrived. If the spacecraft corrected its direction to follow the Moon's orbit it would use too much fuel. Spacecraft are therefore aimed at the position the Moon will be in by the time the craft arrives. They navigate by the stars.

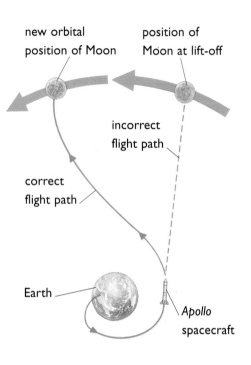

▲ **Moving targets**
This diagram shows two possible flight paths for an *Apollo* spacecraft. Aiming directly at the Moon does not allow for its movement as it orbits the Earth. The correct, efficient route compensates for the Moon's orbital movements by aiming ahead of its position at lift-off.

YOU WILL NEED

Moving target: string, ruler, scissors, masking tape, metal washer, book, small balls of paper.

Two-stage rocket: two paper or plastic cups, scissors, long balloon and pump, sticky tape, round balloon.

Moving target

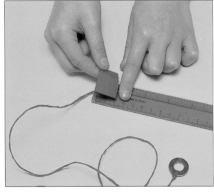

1 Measure out 60cm of string with the ruler. Cut it off with scissors. Tape one end of the string to one end of the ruler. Tie a washer to the other end of the string.

2 Place the ruler on a table or box with the string hanging over the edge. Weigh it down with a heavy book. Try hitting the washer by throwing small balls of paper at it.

3 Start the washer swinging and try to hit it again with the paper balls. See how much more difficult it is to hit a moving target, like a spacecraft aiming at the moving Moon.

242

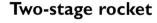

third stage powers
command/service module
(CSM) towards the Moon

Two-stage rocket

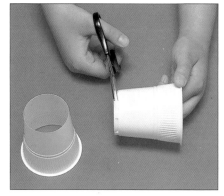

second
stage fires

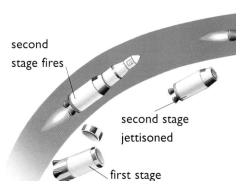

third
stage fires

second stage
jettisoned

first stage
jettisoned

▲ Rocket staging

The *Saturn 5* rocket had three stages.
The first two powered the spacecraft up
through the atmosphere. The third
stage propelled it into orbit and then
gave an extra push to send the craft
on its way to the Moon.

I Using scissors, carefully cut the
bottoms out of the paper or plastic
cups. These will serve as the linking
collar between the two stages of the
balloon rocket.

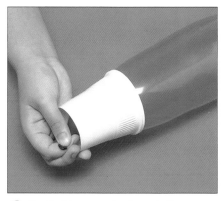

2 Partly blow up the long balloon
with the pump. Pull the neck of
the balloon through the paper or
plastic cups. This balloon will be your
two-stage rocket's second stage.

3 Fold the neck of the long balloon
over the side of the cups. Tape
the end of the neck of the balloon
to the cups to stop the air from
escaping, as shown.

4 Carefully push the round balloon
into the open end of the paper or
plastic cups, as shown. This balloon will
form the first stage of your two-stage
balloon rocket.

5 Blow up the round balloon so that
it wedges the neck of the long
balloon in place inside the cups. Hold
the neck of the round balloon to
keep the air inside it.

Peel the tape off the
neck of the long balloon.
Hold the rocket as shown.
Let go of the round
balloon's neck. Air rushes
out, launching the first stage
of the rocket. It then falls
away, launching the second-
stage balloon.

Artificial gravity

Space travellers in orbit or far away from Earth do not feel the pull of gravity. They feel weightless, as if they are forever falling. In a state of weightlessness there is no up or down, because up and down are created by the force known as gravity. Even experienced pilots and astronauts sometimes feel uncomfortable or ill until they get used to being weightless. Weightlessness also has damaging effects on the human body. Future space stations and spacecraft designed for very long spaceflights may create artificial gravity to protect their occupants from the effects of weightlessness.

In this project you can explore a theoretical method of creating artificial gravity that uses rotation by making a centrifuge. Moving objects tend to travel in straight lines. When you whirl around a ball attached to the end of a piece of string, it tries to fly off in a straight line, stopped only by the string. Inside a rotating spacecraft, the solid outer walls would stop astronauts flying off in straight lines. This would feel like the astronauts were being pushed down to the ground, just like the effect of gravity on Earth.

Make a centrifuge

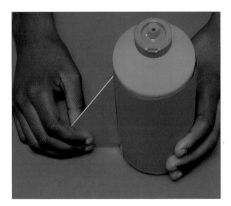

1 Take the four card triangles and tape them to the sides of the bottle, as shown. These will provide the washing-up-bottle centrifuge with a broad, stable base to stand on.

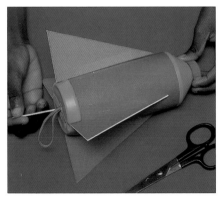

2 Using the bradawl, make a hole in the bottom of the washing-up bottle. Push one end of the elastic band nearly all the way into the hole using a wooden skewer.

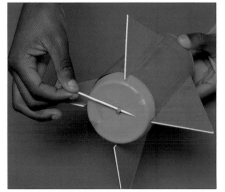

3 Pass the wooden skewer right through the small loop of elastic band projecting from the hole, as shown. Leave an equal amount of skewer on either side of the bottle.

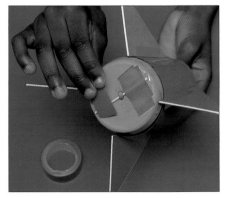

4 Take the masking tape and firmly secure the wooden skewer to the base of the washing-up-liquid bottle. Make sure that the skewer is fixed so tightly that it cannot move.

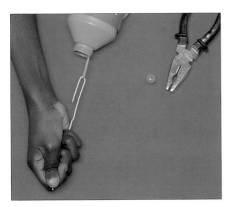

5 Straighten out one end of a paper clip with pliers. Dip the hooked end of the clip into the neck of the bottle. Catch the elastic band with the hook and pull it out.

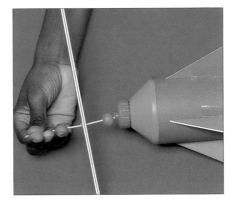

6 Using the bradawl, make a hole in the middle of the 50 x 5cm card strip. Thread the end of the hooked paper clip through the bead. Then thread it through the hole in the card.

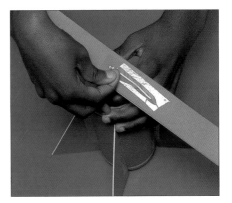

7 Carefully bend the end of the paper clip down on to the card strip. Using sticky tape, fix the end of the clip securely into place, as shown above.

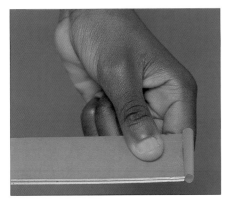

8 Use the scissors to cut two short pieces of drinking straw. Each piece should measure 5cm in length. Fix one piece to each end of the card strip with sticky tape.

9 Take one of the small plastic cups. Carefully make a hole with the scissors on either side of the cup near the top. Now make holes in the second cup in the same way.

Stick the centrifuge to a flat surface with modelling material. Fill the cups one-quarter full with water. Add food colouring to make the water show up clearly. Then turn the card strip until the elastic band is wound up. Let the strip go and watch the cups as they spin around rapidly. The cups fly outwards, but the water is held in place by bases of the cups.

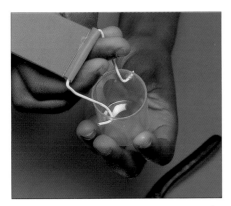

10 Straighten two paper clips with pliers. Thread a clip through each straw. Bend the ends of the clips into hooks using pliers. Thread the ends of the clips through the holes in the cups.

Working in Space

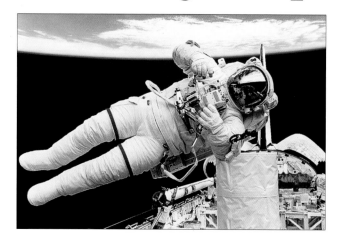

▲ Working in a spacesuit
Bulky spacesuits make working in space difficult. Spacesuit designers are always trying to improve them. The more flexible a suit is, the less tiring it is to work in. This means that an astronaut can work outside for longer periods, a great help when they are carrying out repairs.

There is no gravity outside the pressurized crew compartment of a shuttle in Space. This makes work more difficult than on Earth. On Earth, gravity pulls us down on to the ground. We can then use friction against the ground in order to move about. If a weightless astronaut pushes a handle in zero gravity, he or she would fly away in the opposite direction! This means that astronauts have to be anchored to something solid before doing any work. A spacesuit makes it even more difficult to move. The astronaut has to push against the suit to close a hand or bend an arm or leg.

Spacesuit gloves have thin rubber fingerpacks so that astronauts can feel things through them, but their sense of touch is still very limited. The first project simulates the experience of working in a spacesuit by using rubber gloves, a bowl of water and some nuts and bolts. Then make a robot arm like the shuttle's remote manipulator system (RMS), which is used to launch and retrieve satellites.

Working in Space

1 Take the nuts and bolts and place them on a table. Now try picking them up and screwing them together. You should find this a very easy task to achieve!

2 Now try screwing the nuts and bolts together with the gloves on. This is more difficult, like trying to carry out a delicate task on Earth wearing bulky spacesuit gloves.

3 Fill the bowl with water. Add the nuts and bolts. Try screwing them together with the gloves on. This is very difficult, like working in a spacesuit outside a spacecraft.

Make a robot arm

1 Use the ruler to measure out three 28 x 5cm card strips. Cut them out. Use a bradawl to make a hole 2.5cm from the ends of each strip. Join the strips with split pins.

2 Take the hook and screw it into the end of the dowelling. The dowelling will be used to remotely control the robot arm, just as shuttle astronauts remotely operate the RMS.

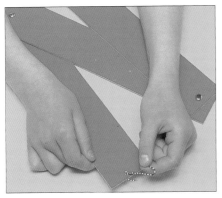

3 Now carefully bend one of the paper clips into the shape of the letter S. To attach the paper clip, pass it through the hole in the end of the cardboard arm, as shown.

Pass the hook on the dowelling through the hole in the end of the cardboard arm. Move the dowelling to remotely operate the robot arm. Try to pick up the ball using the S-shaped paper clip.

4 Take the modelling material and roll it into a ball about the size of a walnut. Then take the second paper clip and push it firmly into the ball, as shown.

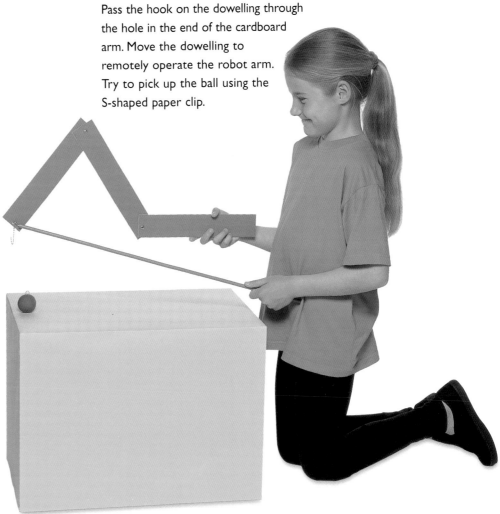

Glossary

A

aerodynamics The way in which objects move through the air.

aerofoil An object, shaped like a wing, that creates lift in the air.

aileron A moving flap on the trailing (rear) edge of an aircraft wing.

air pressure The force with which air presses on things. Changes in air pressure makes air move and causes different weather conditions.

alloy A material, usually metal such as bronze or brass, that is made from a mixture of other materials.

aperture A hole behind the lens of a camera, which can be adjusted to let more or less light on to the film.

APS (Advanced Photographic System) A camera that allows you to change the format for individual shots.

artificial Describes something that is not created as part of a natural process or with naturally occuring materials.

atmosphere The layer of air that surrounds a planet and is held to it by the planet's gravity.

atom The smallest part of an element that can exist. It is made up of many other smaller particles including electrons, neutrons and protons.

autofocus A feature on a camera that automatically adjusts the lens position to ensure that a scene is in focus.

B

bacteria A simple living organism, usually consisting of a single cell. Many bacteria are parasites and cause disease.

battery A container of chemicals holding a charge of electricity.

binary code The digital code computers use, made up of two numbers, '0' and '1'.

bow The front end of a ship.

brake A pad or disc that slows a moving surface down by pressing it.

brake van A carriage at the back of trains used in the mid-1800s. A guard riding in the brake van applied the brakes on instructions from the driver in the locomotive.

C

CAD Computer-aided design.

camouflage The adoption of colours, patterns or texture in order to merge with the environment and so be hidden or disguised.

camshaft A device that creates a regular, rocking movement, such as the opening and shutting of a valve on a car cylinder head.

carbon dioxide A colourless, odourless gas containing the elements carbon and oxygen, which is a part of air.

cargo Goods carried in a ship or other vehicle.

caterpillar The larva of a butterfly or moth.

CD-ROM (compact disc read-only memory) A portable computer disk, similar to an audio CD, that stores information.

chemical A substance used by scientists, in industry or at home.

chemical reaction The process by which one or more substances react together and change into one or more different chemicals.

chlorophyll The green pigment of plants that absorbs light energy from the Sun.

climate The typical weather pattern of an area.

cocoon A silky, protective envelope, such as that secreted by silkworms and other insect larvae to protect the developing pupa.

compass An instrument containing a magnetized strip of metal, used for finding direction.

compressed air Air that has been squashed into a smaller volume than usual.

condensation The process by which water vapour becomes a liquid.

conductor A material through which heat or electricity can travel.

continental drift The generally accepted theory that continents move slowly around the world.

continental shelf The zone of shallow water in the oceans around the edge of continents.

convection The rising of hot air or fluid, caused by the fact that it is lighter than its surroundings.

counterweight A weight that balances another weight.

coupling A connecting device that joins a locomotive to a carriage to make a train.

coupling rod A link that connects the driving wheels on both sides of a locomotive.

crankshaft An axle that has parts of it bent at right angles so that up-and-down motion can be turned into circular motion.

crystal A mineral or other substance that forms in a regular, 3-dimensional shape.

cylinder A hollow or solid tube shape.

D

data Pieces of information.

database An organized store of information.

deciduous Describes trees and shrubs that shed their leaves at the end of each growing season.

density A measure of how tightly the matter in a substance is packed together.

deposition The laying down of material, particularly of material eroded from the Earth's crust and carried by rivers, sea and ice.

depth of field In photography, the

distance in focus between the nearest and farthest parts of a scene.

digital camera A camera that takes electronic images that are downloaded on to a computer to be viewed.

dish antenna A large, dish-shaped aerial used to receive signals in radar, radio telescopes and satellite broadcasting.

disk drive The device that holds, reads and writes on to a disk.

drag A force that acts in the opposite direction to motion and creates resistance.

driving wheel The wheel of a locomotive that turns in response to power from the steam engine.

E

Earth's crust The outermost, solid rock layer of the planet Earth.

ecosystem A community of living things that interact with each other and their surroundings.

effort The force applied to a lever or other simple machine to move a load.

electricity A form of energy caused by the movement of electrons (charged particles) in atoms.

element A substance that cannot be split by chemical processes into simpler parts.

elevator In aircraft, a movable flap on the tailplane or rear wing that causes the nose to rise or fall.

engine A device that uses energy in fuel to make movement.

environment The external conditions in which people, animals and plants live on Earth.

epicentre The region on the Earth's surface that lies directly above the focus of an earthquake.

Equator The imaginary circle around the middle of the Earth between the Northern and Southern Hemispheres,

where day and night are equal in length, and the climate is constantly hot and wet.

erosion The gradual wearing away of the land by agents of erosion such as ice, rain, wind and waves.

escape velocity The minimum speed that a body must have to escape from the gravitational force of a planet.

evaporation The process by which something turns from liquid to vapour.

evergreen Describes plants that bear leaves all the year round.

exoskeleton Outer skeleton – the hard case that protects an insect's soft body parts.

exposure time The time it takes for a camera to take a picture.

exposures Photographs on a film.

F

fault A break in the Earth's crust that causes one block of rock to slip against an adjacent one.

fax machine A machine that photocopies and electronically sends and receives written words and pictures over a telephone line.

fertilization The act or process of the male part of a plant or a male animal that enables a female's egg or eggs to produce young.

focal plane The area at the back of a camera where the exposed film is held flat.

force A push or a pull.

fossil The remains, found preserved in rock, of a creature that lived in the past.

freight Goods transported by rail, road, sea or air.

friction The force caused by the two surfaces rubbing together. This results in the slowing down of movement and heat being produced.

fumarole An opening in the ground in volcanic regions, where steam and gases can escape.

G

gauge The width between the inside running edges of the rails of a train track. In Britain, the USA and most of Europe, the gauge is 1, 435mm.

gear A toothed wheel designed to interact with other toothed wheels to transfer motion in a controlled way.

generate To produce energy such as electricity.

geology The scientific study of the origins and structure of a planet and its rocks.

geothermal energy The energy created by the heat of the rocks underground.

germination The point at which a plant seed or an egg in an animal is fertilized and begins to grow.

geyser A fountain of steam and water that spurts out of a vent in the ground in volcanic regions.

gravity The pulling force that exists between large masses.

H

hard disk A computer's main storage disk, which holds the operating system and application files.

hardware All the equipment that makes up a computer – disk drives, monitor, keyboard, mouse etc.

hemispheres The top and bottom halves of the Earth, divided by the Equator and known as the Northern and Southern Hemispheres.

hibernation A period when many animals save energy by remaining inactive in order to survive the winter.

hot spot A place where plumes of molten rock in the Earth's mantle burn through the Earth's crust to create isolated areas of volcanic activity.

hot springs Water that has been heated underground and bubbles to the surface in volcanic regions.

hull The frame or body of a ship or aircraft.

humidity The amount of water, or moisture, in the air.

hydraulics The use of water or other liquids to move devices such as pistons.

hydrometer An instrument for measuring the density of liquids.

hygrometer An instrument for measuring humidity.

I

igneous rock A rock that forms when magma (hot, molten rock) cools and becomes solid. One of three main types of rock, created as hot molten rock from the Earth's interior, cools and solidifies.

infrared Electromagnetic radiation with a wavelength between the red end of the visible spectrum and microwaves and radio waves.

insulate To cover or protect something to reduce the amount of heat or electricity entering and/or leaving it.

J

jet engine a type of engine that propels a vehicle, such as a car or a plane, by the the forceful expulsion of hot gases.

jet propulsion Reactive movement to a jet of fluid or gas.

K

keystone The central stone in the arch of a bridge or curved part of a building.

L

larva The immature stage in the life of many insects, amphibians and fish.

lava Hot, molten rock emerging through volcanoes, known as magma when underground.

leading wheel The wheel at the front of a locomotive.

lens A transparent object, such as glass, that is curved on one or both sides. A lens bends and directs beams of light to form or alter the view of an image.

lever A long bar that moves around a pivot to help move a heavy object.

lift The force generated by an aerofoil that counters the force of gravity and keeps a flying object in the air.

light spectrum The colours that light can be split into.

lithosphere The rigid outer shell of the Earth, including the crust and the rigid upper part of the mantle.

load The weight moved by a lever or other machine.

locomotive An engine powered by steam, diesel or electricity and used to pull the carriages of a train.

M

magma Hot, molten rock in the Earth's interior, known as lava when it emerges on the surface.

magnetism An invisible force found in some elements but especially in iron, which causes other pieces of iron to be either pushed apart or drawn together.

mantle The very deep layer of rock that lies underneath the Earth's crust.

mass The amount of matter there is in a substance or object. Mass is measured in kilograms, tonnes etc.

metamorphic rock Rock that has been chemically changed by heat or pressure to form a different rock.

metamorphosis Change, as in the life cycles of some animals, that involve a complete change of form, appearance and other characteristics.

meteorologist A person who studies the science and patterns of weather and climate.

mineral A naturally occurring substance found in rocks.

molten Something solid that has been melted, such as lava, which is molten rock.

monochrome Shades of black and white, with no other colours.

monorail A train that runs on a single rail.

mould A kind of fungus in the form of a woolly growth that is often found on stale or rotten food.

mummy An embalmed or preserved body.

N

navigation The skill of plotting a route for a ship, aircraft or other vehicle.

negative In photography, the image on the developed film from which photographic prints are made. The colours in a negative are reversed, so that dark areas appear to be light and light areas appear to be dark.

O

orbit In astronomy, the curved path followed by a planet or other body around another planet or body.

order A major grouping of animals, larger than a family.

organism Any living thing, such as a plant or animal, that is capable of growth and reproducing itself.

osmosis The movement of a solvent, such as water, from a more dilute solution to a more concentrated one.

P

palaeontology The study of fossils.

photosynthesis The process by which plants make food using energy from sunlight.

piston A cylindrical device that moves up and down a cylinder in response to the application and release of pressure from liquid or gas.

pivot A central point around which something revolves, balances or sways.

plastic A durable, synthetic material that is easily moulded or shaped by heat.

plumb line A string with a weight at one end that is used to check whether a building is vertical.

points Rails on the track that guide the wheels of a locomotive on to a different section of track.

precipitation Any form of water (rain, hail, sleet or snow) that comes out of the air and falls to the ground.

primary colours Red, blue and green, or magenta, cyan (blue) and yellow. These colours are the basis for all other shades and colours.

prism Specially shaped glass used to split white light into the spectrum, or to refract light rays away from their normal path.

propellant The fuel or force that causes something to go forward, such as the fuel in a rocket.

propeller A device, with blades, that rotate to provide thrust for a vehicle such as a ship or plane.

prototype The first working model of a machine from a specific design.

pupa Inactive stage in the life cycle of many insects such as butterflies and moths.

R

RAM (random access memory) Computer memory that holds data temporarily until the computer is switched off.

reflecting telescope A telescope that uses mirrors.

refracting telescope A telescope that uses lenses.

refraction The bending of light rays.

rolling stock The locomotives, carriages, wagons and any other vehicles that operate on a railway.

ROM (read-only memory) Computer memory that holds information permanently.

rudder A device for controlling the direction of a ship or plane.

S

satellite A celestial or artificial body orbiting around a planet or star.

savanna Tropical grassland.

sediment Solid particles of rock or other material.

sedimentary rock A rock made up of mineral particles that have been carried by wind or running water to accumulate in layers elsewhere, most commonly on the beds of lakes or in the seas and oceans.

seismology The study of earthquakes.

shutter Camera mechanism that controls the amount of time light is allowed to fall on to the lens.

software Applications that enable computers to carry out specific tasks.

Solar system The family of planets, moons and other bodies that orbit around the Sun.

solution A mixture of something solid and the liquid into which it has been completely dissolved.

sound wave Energy that transmits sound.

space probe A spacecraft that works in deep space.

space shuttle A vehicle designed to be used for at least 100 space flights.

space station A large, artificial satellite in which astronauts live and work.

species A group of animals that share similar characteristics and can breed successfully together.

steam traction Pulling movement achieved through the conversion of water to steam.

streamlined A shape that moves through air or water in the most efficient manner, with the least resistance from drag or friction.

T

tectonic plates The 20 or so giant slabs of rock that make up the Earth's surface.

tectonics The study of the structures that make up the Earth's surface.

thermometer An instrument for measuring temperature.

thorax The part of an insect's body between the head and the abdomen, which bears the wings and legs.

thrust The force that pushes something such as an aircraft forwards.

tidal wave A huge ocean wave.

transpiration The process in the water cycle by which plants release water vapour into the air.

tropical A climate that is very hot and humid.

tropics Part of the Earth's surface that is between the Tropic of Cancer and the Tropic of Capricorn.

turbine A propeller-like device driven by fast-moving gas currents, wind, or water.

turbulence Air or water movement that consists of eddies in random directions, with no smooth flow.

U

upthrust The force that makes a ship float or an aircraft take off.

V

valve A device that controls the flow of a liquid.

W

waterwheel A simple, water-driven turbine used to drive machinery.

weather The condition of the atmosphere at any particular time and place.

weathering The breakdown of rock and other materials when exposed to the weather.

weightlessness In space, a state in which an object has no actual weight because it is not affected by gravitational attraction.

wind Air moving in relation to the Earth's surface.

windmill A machine for grinding or pumping, driven by vanes or sails that are moved by the wind.

Index

Acknowledgements

This edition published by Hermes House
an imprint of
Anness Publishing Limited
Hermes House
88-89 Blackfriars Road
London SE1 8HA

A CIP catalogue record for this book is available from the British Library

Publisher Joanna Lorenz
Managing Editor, Children's Books Gilly Cameron Cooper
Project Editor and Picture Researcher Rasha Elsaeed
Consultant Chris Oxlade
Contributing Authors Stephen Bennington, John Farndon, Ian Graham, Jen Green, Peter Harrison, Robin Kerrod, Peter Mellett, Al Morrison, Chris Oxlade, Steve Parker, John Roston, Rodney Walshaw
Contributing Editors Gilly Cameron Cooper, Rebecca Clunes, Louisa Somerville, Joy Wotton
Editorial Readers Diane Ashmore, Jonathan Marshall, Richard McGinlay
Designer Sandra Marques/Axis Design Editions Ltd
Jacket Design Sarah Williams
Photographers Paul Bricknell, John Freeman, Don Last, Tim Ridley
Nature Photographer Robert Pickett
Illustrators Cy Baker/Wildlife Art, Stephen Bennington, Peter Bull Art Studio, Stuart Carter, Simon Gurr, Richard Hawke, Nick Hawken, Michael Lamb, Alan Male/Linden Artists, Guy Smith, Clive Spong, Stephen Sweet/Simon Girling and Associates, Alisa Tingley, John Whetton
Stylists Ken Campbell, Jane Coney, Marion Elliot, Tim Grabham, Thomasina Smith, Isolde Sommerfeldt, Melanie Williams

10 9 8 7 6 5 4 3 2 1

The publishers would like to thank all the children modelling in this book.

Picture Credits
b=bottom, t=top, c=centre, l=left, r=right
Bruce Coleman Ltd: 87cl. Frank Lane Picture Agency: 87bl, 96bl, 96bc, 96br. Nature Photographers Ltd: 76bc